REFERENDUMS AS REPRESENTATIVE DEMOCRACY

In referendums on fundamental constitutional issues, do the people come together to make decisions instead of representatives? This book argues no. It offers an alternative theory of referendums whereby they are one of many ordinary ways that voters give direction to their representatives. In this way, the book argues that referendums are better understood as exercises in representative democracy.

The book challenges the current treatment of referendums in processes of constitutional change both in the United Kingdom and around the world. It argues that referendums have been used under the banner of popular sovereignty, in a way that undermines representative institutions. This book makes the case for the use of referendums stronger by showing how they can support, rather than undermine, institutions of representative democracy.

Understanding referendums as exercises in representative democracy has broader implications for constitutional democracy as well. Rather than see the power to constitute constitutions as something that happens occasionally in exceptional moments through referendums, this book argues instead that voters constantly have the power to constitute and reconstitute their constitutions.

Referendums as Representative Democracy

Leah Trueblood

·HART·
OXFORD · LONDON · NEW YORK · NEW DELHI · SYDNEY

HART PUBLISHING

Bloomsbury Publishing Plc

Kemp House, Chawley Park, Cumnor Hill, Oxford, OX2 9PH, UK

1385 Broadway, New York, NY 10018, USA

29 Earlsfort Terrace, Dublin 2, Ireland

HART PUBLISHING, the Hart/Stag logo, BLOOMSBURY and the Diana logo are trademarks of Bloomsbury Publishing Plc

First published in Great Britain 2024

A catalogue record for this book is available from the British Library.

A catalogue record for this book is available from the Library of Congress.

Library of Congress Control Number: 2024931043

ISBN: HB: 978-1-50994-080-6
ePDF: 978-1-50994-082-0
ePub: 978-1-50994-081-3

Typeset by Compuscript Ltd, Shannon

For the Women's Centre at the John Radcliffe Hospital, Oxford

ACKNOWLEDGEMENTS

This book grew out of my DPhil thesis, which was awarded by the Faculty of Law at the University of Oxford in 2019. Les Green agreed to supervise the project, guided it through its many vicissitudes, and gave me the opportunity to work with one of the world's great legal philosophers. It was a privilege to undertake this thesis under his supervision. I came to Oxford thanks to the generous support of my tutors at the London School of Economics, particularly Alex Green, Susan Marks, Jo Murkens, Kristen Rundle, Emmanuel Voyiakis, Stephen Watterson, Charlie Webb, and Grégoire Webber. I am fortunate that my thesis was examined at different stages by Kimberley Brownlee, James Edwards, Aileen Kavanagh, John Gardner, and Stephen Tierney. They were all insightful, generous, and constructive in their assessment of the work. While John Gardner tragically passed away in 2019, I continue to reflect on the questions he asked of my DPhil. I will always be grateful for the kindness he showed me as a student.

As my research moved on from the thesis, Nick Barber, Timothy Endicott, Jillian Stirk, Grégoire Webber, and Alison Young provided patient, indispensable mentorship throughout the revision process. Revisions were undertaken with the encouragement of wonderful colleagues at Worcester College, Oxford. Tsilly Dagan, James Edwards, Hilary Hogan, Aiden Lerch, Donal Nolan, and Joshua Pike are all brilliant people in every sense of the word. I could not have finished the book without their support. I am grateful as well for the opportunity to teach the extraordinary students at Worcester College, who are a constant source of inspiration and joy.

Throughout the DPhil and revision journeys, it was discussions with generous friends and colleagues that made this research worthwhile. I continue to wrestle with challenges from everyone mentioned above, as well as Annalise Acorn, Tom Adams, Shreya Atrey, Raquel Barradas de Freitas, Joanna Bell, Udit Bhatia, Achas Burin, Oliver Butler, Li-Kung Chen, Rachel Clement, Hasan Dindjer, Andrea Dolcetti, Nick Freidman, Dev Gangjee, Jodi Gardner, Arushi Garg, Caitlin Goss, Kate Greasley, Michaela Hailbronner, Hayley J Hooper, Jeff King, Hafsteinn Kristjánsson, Sam Kukathas, Joanna Langille, Ron Levy, Ryan Liss, Miles Jackson, James Manwaring, Richard Martin, Rob Mullins, Peter Niesen, Markus Patberg, Adam Perry, Matt Qvortrup, Lea Raible, Sylvia Rich, Lucia Rubinelli, Jake Rowbottom, Alice Schneider, Silvia Suteu, Jonathan Turner, Léticia Villeneuve, and Emily Kidd White. I am so grateful that my research benefits from the insights of this incredible group of people.

Thank you to Oxford University Press for the permission to republish parts of my article 'Are Referendums Directly Democratic?' (2020) 40 *Oxford Journal of Legal Studies* 425 throughout this book. I am grateful to University College Oxford, the Pierre Elliott Trudeau Foundation, the John Fell Fund, the Leverhulme Trust, and the British Academy for the funding that made this research possible. I am grateful to Kate Whetter, Verity Stuart, Ceri Warner, and the anonymous reviewers at Hart Publishing for their generous, patient help turning it into a book. I am fortunate to hold an academic affiliation with the Bonavero Institute of Human Rights which improved this book's equality enormously. Thank you to Zoe Davis-Heaney, Tarun Khaitan, Liora Lazarus, Sarah Norman, and Kate O'Regan for making that opportunity possible.

In my personal life, my wonderful parents Brian and Arla, brothers Robert and Kev, and extended family supported every step of the book's journey. I will never be able to thank them all enough for everything they have done for me. Additionally, Don Carmichael, Nicholas Dehod, Zachary Fentiman, Rory Tighe and Anne Gordon, Lauren Bokenfohr and Paul Finlay, Michael Gaultois and Katherine Fairhurst, Amanda Henry and Roy Coulthard, Celine Zeng and Viral Gandhi, as well as Carl and Ellen Amrhein provided the comradery and good humour to see this project through. All their fingerprints are on this book, and it is much better for it.

This book is dedicated to the Women's Centre at the John Radcliffe Hospital, Oxford. Throughout four operations while I was writing this book, the Women's Centre took actions which saved my life. I am so grateful to have received this treatment, and every person on the planet deserves such care. Throughout that period, I would not have been able to keep working without the wise counsel of my brilliant friend Michelle Chan. Michelle stayed with me on the worst days, and that will always stay with me.

In 2013, I learned the lesson from Peter Hatfield which allowed me to both start and finish this book. He taught me that the most important thing about learning is having fun. Our son Teddy has already mastered this lesson, and I am so grateful to him and Peter for reminding me of its importance every day. Irrespective of whether you agree with a word of this book, I am grateful to you for picking it up. Most of the time I had fun writing this book, and I hope you have some fun reading it as well.

Worcester College
Oxford
September 2023

CONTENTS

1

Introduction

I. A Guide to this Book

In many[1] democracies, significant constitutional questions – for instance, those about secession, devolution, or joining supranational bodies like the European Union – must be put to a referendum. One reason referendums are used for significant constitutional questions is that democratic constitutions tend to distinguish between those decisions which may be made by politicians, and those which must be made by the people.[2] This distinction between fundamental constitutional decisions, which must be made by the people, and ordinary decisions, which may be made by their representatives (in most cases, elected politicians), is so influential that Tuck argues it is the 'basic fact of modern politics'.[3] The aims of this book are threefold. First, to demonstrate that Tuck is right. This division of labour between people and politicians is the basic fact of modern constitutional law and politics. Second, to provide support for those challenging the helpfulness of this basic fact. Third, to offer an alternative role for referendums in answering fundamental constitutional questions. Referendums are not ways for voters rather than their representatives to make higher-order decisions. They are better understood as exercises in representative democracy.

While most terms will be defined below, one clarification is required up front: what amounts to a 'significant' or 'fundamental' constitutional question? This category is contested and will be explained and interrogated in section IV, but the idea is that some fundamental constitutional questions are 'constitutive' of constitutions. Galligan, for instance, says constitutive constitutional questions 'expres[s] democratic sovereignty'.[4] Similarly, Tierney says constitutive constitutional questions

[1] Although, as discussed in section II, not all democracies. Referendums are not part of the amending formulas in, among other places, Belgium, Canada (at the federal level), Indonesia, Malaysia, and the United States of America (at the federal level). Even in these jurisdictions, though, this book will show that referendums have still played influential roles in processes of constitutional change.

[2] This idea can be traced even prior to Roman times. The Romans adapted it from Germanic tribes, and it has persisted even today. M Qvortrup (ed), *Referendums Around the World: The Continued Growth of Direct Democracy* (Palgrave 2014) 3–4.

[3] R Tuck, 'Democratic Sovereignty and Democratic Government' in R Bourke and Q Skinner (eds), *Popular Sovereignty in Historical Perspective* (Cambridge University Press 2016) 141.

[4] B Galligan, 'Amending Constitutions through the Referendum Device' in M Mendelsohn and A Parkin (eds), *Referendum Democracy: Citizens, Elites, and Deliberation in Referendum Campaigns* (Palgrave 2001) 109.

are those which 'amend sovereign relations'.[5] These constitutive questions are considered then different because they concern the people's capacity to create constitutions in the first place. Decisions concern the allocation of authority in a democracy, so, the argument goes, those decisions cannot be made by representatives. The claim is that representatives cannot decide, for instance, to secede from a state or join the European Union. That would be *ultra vires* because representatives never had that power in the first place. Bogdanor explains the ultra vires argument by saying: 'The electorate, it might be said, entrust their MPs as agents with legislative power; but they give them no authority to transfer this power. Such authority, it is natural to suggest, can be obtained only through a specific mandate, that is, a referendum.'[6] This book challenges this argument and does not accept the existence of a category of 'constitutive' constitutional question and uses the terms 'significant' and 'fundamental' interchangeably instead.

To be clear: this book is not arguing for or against the use of referendums. It is only arguing against one reason for holding a referendum on a fundamental constitutional question. The claim that some decisions *must* be made by voters because they cannot be made by representatives is the wrong kind of reason to hold a referendum. There are all kinds of good reasons to hold referendums on important constitutional questions. When decisions are being deeply entrenched, for instance, democracies should do everything they can to get them right. The idea that some decisions *must* be made by the people through referendums, however, is not the right kind of reason to hold a referendum. This book offers an alternative account of the role for referendums in constitutional democracy. On this alternative view, even on the most fundamental questions, the purpose of referendums is to help provide direction to representatives.

This introduction is a reader's guide to this book. Section II demonstrates that the distinction between decisions that may be made by politicians, and those that must be made by the people, is the 'basic fact' of contemporary constitutional law and politics. Section III explains the challenge this book offers to this basic fact. It does so by (i) offering a broad overview of the book; (ii) providing a chapter-by-chapter breakdown of the book's arguments; and (iii) clarifying the book's contribution to the literature. Section IV confronts the tricky question of how to define a referendum, and section V explains the book's scope and methodology. Section V clarifies the terms and conditions of this book: what the book is, and is not, arguing. Finally, section VI situates this research in a global context. It explains the difference this argument makes in constitutional law and practice around the world, and how changing the reasons why referendums are used will improve their use.

[5] S Tierney, 'Constitutional Referendums: A Theoretical Enquiry' (2009) 72 MLR 360, 361.
[6] V Bogdanor, *The People and the Party System* (Cambridge University Press 1981) 76–77.

II. The 'Basic Fact' of Modern Politics

This book is a response to the claim that there are some decisions in democracies which must be made by voters. If voters are the ultimate source of authority in a democracy, so the argument goes, it is conceptually necessary that there are some kinds of decisions they *must* make, instead of these decisions being made by their representatives. This distinction between 'normal' politics and 'constitutional politics',[7] which distinguishes 'the Will of We the People from the act of We the Politician[s]',[8] was not always the central feature of constitutions,[9] but became the dominant approach after the American and French revolutions.[10] The distinction between decisions that legislators can make and decisions that the people must make has been carved up in a range of ways,[11] including[12] by Lawson,[13] Schmitt,[14] and most famously by Locke and Sieyès.

For Locke, the idea motivating this distinction is the idea that the people's ultimate authority is a 'trust that cannot be delegated'.[15] Locke says that '[t]he

[7] 'Constitutional moments differ from ordinary politics both in terms of their significance but also in the way they change how ordinary politics is thereafter conducted.' Tierney (n 5), citing B Ackerman, *We the People, Volume 1: Foundations* (Belknap Press 1993).

[8] '… We need to distinguish constitutional politics from normal politics: "the will of We the People from the act of We the Politician." The two are quite different.' Galligan (n 4) 111.

[9] 'The language of *pouvoir constituant* demands that we distinguish between an older meaning of constitution, as the sum total of political circumstances and the new, revolutionary meaning of constitution as a written text that lays out the competences of government organs and can be changed at will … distinguishing norm-setting competences from norm-exciting or judicative competences, and extraordinary powers from normal government authorisations.' P Niesen, 'Extinguishing the Burning Embers: Rubinelli on Sieyès' *Verfassungsblog* (19 December 2020), verfassungsblog.de/extinguishing-the-burning-embers-rubinelli-on-sieyes, accessed 20 January 2021.

[10] 'Constituent power is a modern concept. Its source can certainly be traced to debates in medieval political thought, but it emerges in a distinct form only with the establishment of modern institutions of the state. The concept is a product of the secularizing and rationalizing movement of late eighteenth century European thought known as the Enlightenment and it comes to occupy a central place in constitutional thought only after the late eighteenth century American and French Revolutions.' M Loughlin, 'On Constituent Power' in M Dowdle and M Wilkinson (eds), *Constitutionalism Beyond Liberalism* (Cambridge University Press 2017) 151.

[11] Another version of this distinction is the difference between the exercise of sovereignty and the exercise of government. Tuck (n 3) 115. Note too that some scholars such as Rubinelli are sometimes concerned about the conflation of sovereignty and constituent power, but Rubinelli is clear that the version of the distinction drawn by Tuck here does broadly correspond to Sieyès's distinction between constitutive and constituted power. 'The distinction between [constituted and constitutive powers and sovereignty and government] thus enshrines the distinction between political acts establishing the foundations of the state and ordinary legislation.' L Rubinelli, *Constituent Power: A History* (Cambridge University Press 2020) 227.

[12] There is deep disagreement in the literature about how broadly this distinction can be attributed. Lee, for instance, also explores the significance of this kind of distinction to the work of Montesquieu, Madison, and Rousseau. D Lee, *Popular Sovereignty in Early Modern Constitutional Thought* (Oxford University Press 2016) 1.

[13] G Lawson, *Politica Sacra et Civilis* [1660] (ed C Condren, Cambridge University Press 1992) 47.

[14] A democratic constitution, Schmitt says, is the result of the exercise of constituent power by a politically united people. C Schmitt, *Constitutional Theory* [1928] (J Seitzer trs, Duke University Press 2008) 75–85.

[15] J Lenowitz, '"A Trust That Cannot Be Delegated": The Invention of Ratification Referenda' (2015) 109 *American Political Science Review* 803, 806.

legislative cannot transfer the power of making laws to any other hands: for it being but a delegated power from the people, they who have it cannot pass it over to others'.[16] It would therefore be *ultra vires* for representatives to make decisions about the ultimate allocation of authority in a democracy. Representatives never had this power in the first place. Similarly,[17] Sieyès distinguishes between *pouvoir constituant* and *pouvoir constitute*; constitutive and constituted powers, which operate on two levels. The first level is the level of constitutive power, and this first level exists prior to everything and is above the law. On the second level of constituted power, legislatures can act only within the limits laid down by constitutive powers through the constitution.[18] So influential is the approach taken by Sieyès, Tuck argues, that it has become the 'default constitution' and 'basic fact' of modern politics.[19] Tuck says that in contemporary constitutions: 'Fundamental laws are prescribed through plebiscites or referendums rather than through representative bodies, and … the distinction between a sovereign democratic legislator and a representative government is a basic fact of modern politics.'[20]

As a matter of constitutional law, Tuck's view that the distinction between sovereign democratic legislator and representative bodies is the 'default constitution' or 'basic fact' of modern politics overstates the point a little. There are some jurisdictions which do not structure their constitutions this way. Referendums are also not required for constitutional change in Belgium[21] or Indonesia,[22] and are not part of the text of any of Canada's Constitutional amending formulas,[23] but provinces have nevertheless said they would use them in playing their role in changing the constitution.[24] In Canada, referendums have clearly been influential

[16] J Locke, *The Second Treatise of Government* [1689] (Hackett 1980) 141 (emphasis in original).

[17] 'No type of delegated power can modify the conditions of its delegation.' E Sieyès, *Political Writings: Including the Debate between Sieyès and Tom Paine in 1791* (M Sonenscher ed, Hackett 2003) 136.

[18] 'Sieyès's idea of constituent power not only refers to a specific way of conceiving popular power but also underpins a precisely defined political project – one in which popular authority is restrictively defined as an authorising power, exercised in two moments. The first is the moment of foundation. It enshrines the authority of the people to create the political order and express itself in the ex ante authorisation of a constitutional text written by extra-ordinary elected representatives. The second corresponds to moments of ordinary politics and reduces popular power to the elections of ordinary representatives authority to act within the limits set by the constitution.' Rubinelli (n 11) 73.

[19] Tuck (n 3).

[20] ibid.

[21] 'In Belgium, there is no constitutional or even legislative basis for a referendum and a decision-making (legally binding) referendum is considered unconstitutional. A consultative referendum – the constitutionality of which has been strongly disputed – was organised in 1950 further to a specific decision of parliament.' Venice Commission, 'Referendums in Europe – An Analysis of the Legal Rules in European States' (2005) 287/2004, 15, www.venice.coe.int/webforms/documents/default.aspx?pdffile=CDL-AD(2005)034-e, accessed 5 August 2023.

[22] Provisions for national referendums were repealed in Indonesia in 1999. Electoral Knowledge Network, 'Indonesia', aceproject.org/regions-en/countries-and-territories/ID/default?set_language=en, accessed 26 October 2023.

[23] 'The Constitution Act 1982 instituted a new amending formula. It was complex, with five sub-formulae applicable to different matters.' J Webber, *The Constitution of Canada: A Contextual Analysis* (Hart 2021) 43.

[24] 'Some provinces adopted statutes requiring referenda prior to their ratification of any constitutional amendments.' ibid 49.

in the way Tuck outlines: they have become associated with higher-order decisions by the people about fundamental constitutional questions.[25] While the idea that some decisions must be made by representatives is of enormous constitutional importance in the United States, referendums are not required as part of the federal amending formula,[26] although they are employed by more than half of American states.[27] The idea that the 'we the people' are the foundation of the Constitution, however, is enormously influential in the United States,[28] and is incredibly influential throughout the world.[29] This claim that some decisions must be made by voters is thought to follow inexorably from the idea that the people are the ultimate source of authority in a democracy.[30] While Griffiths himself dismissed the helpfulness of the distinction, he argued that this 'nonsense' was clear in the constitutions 'as varied as [those of] China, the Soviet Union and the United States'.[31] Finally, and at a macro-level, the distinction between constitutive and constituted powers has been essential in establishing the general principle of self-determination in international law.[32] It has been used as the standard of success in the context of the European Union law, in trying to find a stronger democratic footing for the supranational body.[33]

This distinction between decisions which may be taken by voters, and those which may be taken by politicians, tracks the distinction between constitutional and ordinary politics. This distinction between constitutional and ordinary

[25] 'In the Charlottetown [constitutional amendment] process … the federal government agreed to submit the proposal to referenda across the country. These referenda would have no formal role; amendments would still have to be passed by the legislatures, as the constitutional amending formula required. But the principle that the public had to be involved was widely accepted.' ibid.

[26] The American Constitution outlines two methods of amendment. Amendments may be proposed either by the Congress, through a joint resolution passed by a two-thirds vote, or by a convention called by Congress after applications from two-thirds of the state legislatures. Constitution of the United States of America, Article V (1787).

[27] National Conference of State Legislatures, 'Initiative and Referendum Processes' (2022), www.ncsl.org/elections-and-campaigns/initiative-and-referendum-processes, accessed 22 August 2023.

[28] 'We the People of the United States, in Order to form a more perfect Union, establish Justice, insure domestic Tranquility, provide for the common defense, promote the general Welfare, and secure the Blessings of Liberty to ourselves and our Posterity, do ordain and establish this Constitution for the United States of America.' Constitution of the United States of America (n 26).

[29] L Orgad, 'The Preamble in Constitutional Interpretation' (2010) 8 *International Journal of Constitutional Law* 714, 714.

[30] As Loughlin argues in Loughlin (n 10) 151, and is both explained and interrogated in ch 2 of this book.

[31] 'In [the United Kingdom] we have stayed clear of one bit of nonsense which is commonly advanced in countries as diverse as the Chinese People's Republic, the Soviet Union, and the United States of America. I mean the view that sovereignty resides in the people who delegate it to their politicians who hold it in trust for them. I suppose John Locke is to blame for offering this particular cover-up for authoritarianism.' JAG Griffith, 'The Political Constitution*' (1979) 42 *Modern Law Review* 1, 3.

[32] R Miller, 'Self-Determination in International Law and the Demise of Democracy' (2003) 41 *Columbia Journal of Transnational Law* 601, 605.

[33] 'Citizens [in the European Union] are mostly relegated to the role of passive observers. To capture the legitimacy gap that opens up here, I have proposed an understanding of constituent power as political autonomy at the level of constitutional politics.' M Patberg, *Constituent Power in the European Union* (Oxford University Press 2020) 215 and discussed at S Verdugo, 'Is it Time to Abandon the Theory of Constituent Power?' (2003) 21 *International Journal of Constitutional Law* 14, 15.

politics itself tracks the deeper distinction between direct and representative democracy.[34] Those who argue that some decisions must be made by the people argue that those kinds of referendums are instances of direct democracy.[35] They must be direct because some kinds of decisions cannot be made by representatives. The idea behind referendums as representative democracy that that no decisions, no matter how fundamental, can ever be made by voters *directly*, *instead* of by representatives.

This is all to say: the distinction between decisions which must be made by voters, and those which must be made by politicians, comes in different forms, but it is enormously influential both in theory and in law all over the world. This distinction between decisions made by the people and decisions made by politicians tracks other distinctions between constitutional and ordinary politics, and direct and representative democracy. This book argues, however, that it can *both* be the case that the people are the ultimate source of authority in a democracy and that there is no clear division of labour between decisions the people must make, and decisions representatives may make. The book supports accounts of democracy on which the decision-making processes of voters and representatives are inseparable, even on fundamental constitutional questions.

III. An Alternative: Referendums as Representative Democracy

This book puts forward an alternative conception of referendums. This section introduces this alternative conception of referendums, and its normative rationale, in three steps. First, it offers an overview of the arguments made in this book and anticipates some concerns with the approach the book takes. Second, it outlines a chapter by-chapter breakdown of how the book is developed. Third, it clarifies the contribution this book is making to the literature.

A. Referendums as Representative Democracy: An Overview

This book has two parts. The first part of the book makes negative arguments. It argues that the way that referendums are currently understood in contemporary constitutional law, as exercises in direct democracy, is misleading. The second,

[34] 'At the first-order level of ordinary legislation, politicians and political institutions represent the people functionally in terms of will-formation and expression. And at the constitutional level … the institutions of the constitution come to represent the people in acts of will-formation and expression when the constitution is amended by institutions in place of and in the name of the people.' Tierney (n 5) 367.

[35] 'This supplanting of representative constitutionalism is a very different function from that performed by ordinary referendums.' ibid 361.

positive part of the book puts forward an alternative conception of referendums as exercises in representative democracy. The book concludes by demonstrating how the arguments made in this book matter, and why they can make a difference to the use of referendums around the world.

Two broad concerns might be raised with the thrust of this book. First, that it takes the status quo too literally. The claim that decisions are made by voters rather than by representatives, it might be argued, is a figurative claim, not a literal one. It is a useful, or perhaps rhetorical, fiction which is used to justify democracies.[36] While it is certainly true that the claim might be mythical or normative, the aim of this book is to argue that the myth that decisions are made by voters rather than by representatives is misleading as well. The claim that democracy has two tracks – one for voters on higher-order decisions and one for politicians on quotidian questions – is not a helpful idea around which to orient constitutions. Constitutions are weaker for adopting this approach. This response connects to the second possible worry regarding the thrust of this book: what does it mean to make a constitution stronger? Crucially, this book is not arguing that constitutions are stronger when voters are less involved. The point of this book is not to argue against referendums, or public participation in constitution-making. The point of the book is also emphatically not to constrain the disruptive power voters may have when they participate in constitution-making. Rather, the point of this book is that while it may appear superficially emancipatory to say fundamental constitutional decisions must be made by voters through referendums, this appearance is misleading. The 'basic fact' or 'default approach' to constitutions instead constricts voters, limiting the influence over constitutions to exceptional constitutional moments. The point of advocating referendums as representative democracy is to demonstrate the many ways voters shape their constitutions.

B. Chapter Summaries

Chapter two explains why distinguishing between decisions which must be made by voters, and those which may be made by politicians, is an unnecessary and unhelpful false choice for democracies to make. It labels this approach 'two-track democracy' and argues that this unhelpful approach follows from three deeper misunderstandings about democratic constitutionalism. First, two-track democracy treats constitutions as principally textual, suggesting that authority can be clearly delineated in democracies. Second, the division of labour between people and politicians rests on a view of legitimate authority grounded in the social contract, where voters delegate some powers to representatives on a limited basis but reserve others. Third and finally, two-track democracy rests on an agential

[36] Verdugo (n 33) 15.

approach to constitutional authorship, and the chapter puts forward the counter-argument that the idea of constitutional authorship is itself unhelpful.

Chapter three then shifts the book's focus away from democracy in general to referendums. The chapter shows why, even if democracy did require decisions to be made by voters instead of representatives, referendums could not play such a role. It breaks down the claim that in democracies voters must make decisions instead of representatives into parts: *the people* in a democracy, *come together* to *make decisions*, *instead of representatives* and challenges each part of the claim in turn. It argues that the people are not the right kind of group, and voting not the right kind of practice, where voters, rather than representatives, can make decisions. The chapter focuses particularly on the relationship between decisions and choices, showing that voting is at most a choice that voters make, but decisions require actions taken by representatives. In this way, actions to create, amend, and transform constitutions are multi-stage processes which necessarily engage both voters and their representatives.

Chapter four kicks off the second, positive part of the book. It offers a positive alternative view of referendums as representative democracy. It explains the claims and commitments of the idea that referendums are instances of representative democracy. The most controversial of these claims are that (i) referendums are not distinct from elections, (ii) they are not overriding and are instead (iii) processes of negotiation with representatives. The chapter also demonstrates the benefits of understanding referendums as representative democracy, both normatively and practically, and how these normative and practical differences make an impact on the law.

Since the purpose of this book is to argue against elections being held for the wrong kinds of reasons, chapter four explains what are the right kind of reasons to hold referendums. It argues that the reasons to hold referendums are issue and jurisdiction-dependent but identifies three broad reasons why referendums might be held: (i) outcomes are being entrenched; (ii) the divisiveness of questions; and (iii) issues arising between elections. Chapter four also clarifies further wrong reasons to hold referendums. It argues that voter ignorance, or the claim that political choices cannot be binary, are unhelpful reasons to hold referendums. Indeed, when referendums are understood to be exercises in representative democracy it is possible to respond to a range of arguments against their use, and to integrate both their liberal and their populist tendencies.

Chapter five begins to put the ideas advocated here into practice. It outlines what the principles are for the use of referendums in practice. It emphasises the importance of, *inter alia*, supermajority requirements, referendums as approving rather than initiating constitutional change, and engaging voters in referendums beyond the voting stage(s). The aim of these principles is to understand referendums as ongoing stages of contestation and negotiation with representatives of all kinds, both elected and in citizens' assemblies. These principles will have different applications in different contexts, and they are illustrative rather than exhaustive, but they do establish a general framework for what it means to use referendums successfully in a constitutional context. Chapter five also argues for two, minimal success conditions for referendums. First, referendums must help to address disagreement. Second, they should provide those who do not support the substance of the outcome a reason to nevertheless accept it. Chapter six argues for the value of the principles outlined in chapter five through three case studies: the referendum in the United Kingdom on whether to leave the European Union (Brexit), the referendum in Northern Ireland on whether to support the Belfast/Good Friday Agreement, and the referendum in Chile on the constitutional process of reform. These case studies demonstrate how the principles outlined in chapter six improve the use of referendums in practice.

The final chapter, chapter seven, situates the arguments made here in contemporary and global context, particularly debates about liberalism and populism. It argues that referendums are not going away, and neither is representative democracy, and so it is necessary to find a way to reconcile the use of referendums with other principles of representative democracy. Crucially, democracy requires heeding both counter-majoritarian and majoritarian considerations. The alternative view of referendums put forward here is about integrating both the counter-majoritarian and majoritarian parts of democracy into their use. This integration both strengthens the normative case for the use of referendums and improves their use in practice.

C. Contribution to the Literature

To clarify this book's contribution to the literature is, this section will first clarify what the book's contribution to the literature is not. This is not the first book to argue that referendums are not directly democratic. This argument was made, for instance, by Schmitt who argued that the agenda-setting power of elites was inescapable.[37] Normatively, Dicey argued that referendums are used to best effect when understood as 'the people's veto' and so he did not suggest a role for referendums as bypassing representatives.[38] In addition to these influential texts, there is also a growing contemporary literature challenging the plausibility of the term 'direct' democracy,[39] and Altman has long argued persuasively that the distinction

[37] 'The question [in a referendum] can only be posed from above; the answer only comes from below.' C Schmitt, *Legality and Legitimacy* [1932] (J Seitzer trs, Duke University Press 2004) 90.

[38] Dicey argued that the United Kingdom should introduce the referendum to prevent the government from instructing a majority in Parliament to push through changes that '[did] not command the sanction of electors'. AV Dicey, *Introduction to the Study of the Law of the Constitution* [1915] (RE Michener ed, 8th rev edn, Liberty Fund 1982) cix.

[39] R Van Crombrugge, 'Are Referendums Necessarily Populist? Countering the Populist Interpretation of Referendums through Institutional Design' (2020) 56 *Representation* 109 and A el-Wakil and S McKay, 'Disentangling Referendums and Direct Democracy: A Defence of the Systemic Approach to Popular Vote Processes' (2020) 56 *Representation* 449.

between representative and direct democracy is oversimplistic.[40] This book is also not novel in arguing that democracy is inherently representative. This book builds on work by Urbinati,[41] Plotke,[42] and Young[43] who all (to different degrees) make this kind of claim. All this literature is significant, and the book draws on it extensively.

While this book draws on a familiar dissatisfaction with the term 'direct democracy', it nevertheless makes a distinct contribution to literature. The contribution here is distinct in two ways. First, the focus here is on referendums on fundamental constitutional issues. These referendums, which are argued to be held because certain decisions cannot be made by representatives, present distinct questions about direct democracy. These claims have existential implications for democratic constitutions. Second, the focus of this book is normative rather than descriptive. The aim is to argue why, as a normative matter, it is better to understand referendums on constitutional issues as exercises in representative democracy, and to understand the implications of this shift for constitutional democracy. The idea that some decisions must be made by the people instead of representatives is fundamental to contemporary democracy, and letting it go has significant implications for constitutional law and theory.

This book is also not alone in challenging the conceptual necessity for referendums in processes of constitutional change. Lenowitz rightly argues that ratification is not required for constitutional change although, as seen in chapter four, both his reasoning and conclusions are very different from those in this book.[44] This book is also not the only work to challenge the helpfulness of distinguishing between constitutive and constituted powers. While his focus is on constituent power itself, Verdugo effectively and persuasively challenges the idea of constituent power[45] and offers a useful survey of many other challenges to the concept as well.[46] Finally, there is a general liberal challenge to the helpfulness of referendums on the basis that they undermine representative democracy.[47] This book draws on some of this reasoning but does not accept the conclusion that referendums are undemocratic or illiberal. It also does not accept that all the populist tendencies of referendums

[40] This is the argument across D Altman, *Direct Democracy Worldwide* (Cambridge University Press 2011) and D Altman, *Citizenship and Contemporary Direct Democracy* (Cambridge University Press 2018).

[41] 'My intention is not to put into question the normative value of direct participation but to argue for the relevance of representation.' N Urbinati, 'Representation as Advocacy: A Study of Democratic Deliberation' (2000) 28 *Political Theory* 758, 759.

[42] 'Democratic politics is *constituted* partly through representation.' D Plotke, 'Representation Is Democracy' (1997) 4 *Constellations* 31 (emphasis in original).

[43] 'Political representation is both necessary and desirable.' IM Young, 'Deferring Group Representation' (1997) 39 *Nomos* 349–76.

[44] J Lenowitz, *Constitutional Ratification Without Reason* (Oxford University Press 2022).

[45] Verdugo (n 33) 20.

[46] Citing Kelsen, Arendt, Dyzenhaus, Jackson, Vinx, Comella, Landau, Hasebe, and Duke. ibid 18.

[47] J Haskell, *Direct Democracy or Representative Government? Dispelling the Populist Myth* (Perseus 2000).

are unwelcome. The book aims to offer a theory of referendums that even liberals who are sceptical of their use can accept, by arguing that the purpose of referendums can never be to get representatives out of the way.

IV. What is a Referendum?

This section defines the term 'referendum' for purposes of this argument. A referendum is defined by Setälä as 'a vote by the public on a matter of policy'.[48] This is a broad and popular approach, but it is not universally accepted, and is not consistently used in the literature.[49] Popular votes on matters of policy vary so enormously that it is not always clear what counts as a referendum and what does not. There is, as Suksi rightly says, no universal referendum terminology.[50] It is not clear in the law or literature, for instance, how referendums should be distinguished from plebiscites, which may be undemocratic or have a narrower focus,[51] or from initiatives. Setälä and Qvortrup both take initiatives to be 'popular votes on laws proposed by citizens',[52] as opposed to referendums that are proposed by legislatures.[53] Indeed, so inconsistent is the use of the term referendum that Gallagher and Uleri argue it is used to refer to a wide variety of phenomena which bear very little if no resemblance to each other.[54] Similarly, Smith worries that referendums are such a varied phenomenon and that nothing can really be said about referendums in general, and so that no general definition is possible.[55]

To respond to the wide range of ways in which referendums can be used, most books about referendums begin with taxonomies. These taxonomies try to pin down some of these differences between popular votes to bring order to the chaos. Some theorists distinguish, for instance, between law initiating and law controlling

[48] M Setälä, *Referendums and Democratic Government* (Macmillan 1999) 4.

[49] As Altman argues, the confusion is profound. The terms referendums, initiatives, and plebiscites have been used synonymously even within the same piece of legislation. Altman, *Citizenship and Contemporary Direct Democracy* (n 40) 6.

[50] M Suksi, *Bringing in the People: A Comparison of Constitutional Forms and Practices of the Referendum* (Cambridge University Press 1993) 10.

[51] Setälä (n 48) 3–4; And sometimes the term plebiscite is used to refer to votes just about territorial boundaries: 'The term plebiscite … is probably the oldest of the three terms … general agreement on the distinction between plebiscite and referendum is lacking … the term plebiscite has been used, – particularly after World War I – to denote popular votes held to solve sovereignty conflicts over territories and boundaries … However in some countries, the term still has a negative connotation: it generally means something that is not democratic.' M Gallagher and P Uleri (eds), *The Referendum Experience in Europe* (Macmillan 1996) 3.

[52] Setälä (n 48) 3–4; Qvortrup (n 2) 1.

[53] Qvortrup (n 2) 2.

[54] 'Referendums "fail to fit any clear universal pattern': Gallagher and Uleri (n 51) 2, citing A Lijphart, *Patterns of Democracy: Government Forms and Performance in Thirty-six Countries* (Yale University Press 1984) 206.

[55] G Smith, 'The Functional Properties of the Referendum' (1976) 4 *European Journal of Political Research* 1.

referendums[56] and (or) constitutional and ordinary referendums.[57] Theorists also distinguish different constitutional roles for referendums: Hollander's recent taxonomy, for example, distinguishes five different ways that referendums are triggered.[58] These distinctions and taxonomies are important and make a difference for evaluating referendums both conceptually and practically. Taxonomies draw attention to differences in the relationships (especially the textual constitutional relationships) between referendums and other democratic processes and institutions. The focus on taxonomies is strength of the literature on referendums and is helpful for identifying and comparing the salient differences between the use of referendums in different jurisdictions.

This book adopts Setälä's definition of a referendum, while taking seriously the limitations flagged by the literature. It treats a referendum as a popular vote on a matter of policy without regard for its subject matter, democratic credentials, or how it is triggered. Setälä's broad approach is taken because, while these distinctions between types of popular votes matter for all kinds of reasons in specific jurisdictions, this book is concerned with the broad justification for holding these kinds of votes. The book will argue that there are features of the relationship between votes and representatives that hold in general, namely that votes cannot be held without mediating processes of representation, and so general claims can be made about referendums as well. This does not mean these taxonomies are irrelevant or unimportant, only that they do not bear on the feature of referendums at issue here. The book also embraces the complexity this sceptical literature emphasises about referendums. This book is not arguing that a general, exhaustive theory of referendums is possible, even for referendums on fundamental constitutional questions. Indeed, the argument here is that the reasons to hold referendum on fundamental constitutional questions cannot be stipulated in general terms. The reasons to hold referendums on fundamental constitutional questions will depend on the context.

One final clarification about the meaning of referendums is required. This book is concerned with one reason to hold one kind of referendum: a referendum on a fundamental constitutional issue. This kind of referendum is conventionally called a 'constitutional' referendum, as opposed to an ordinary referendum. This book does not adopt the terminology of 'constitutional referendum' because the purpose of this book to challenge this concept. The book uses the term 'referendum' interchangeably with 'constitutional referendum' because it argues that there can be no clear category of constitutional referendums distinct from ordinary

[56] Gallagher and Uleri (n 51) 11.

[57] Tierney (n 5) 360; Galligan (n 4) 109.

[58] 'This book distinguishes five types of referendums based on who triggers the vote, since this ultimately determines *who controls the referendum process*: (1) legislative majority referendums … (2) presidential referendums, (3) legislative minority referendums (4) citizen-initiated referendums … and (5) mandatory referendums (triggered by the constitution).' S Hollander, *The Politics of Referendum Use in European Democracies* (Palgrave Macmillan 2019) 8 (emphasis in original).

referendums. Similarly, this book does not adopt the language of constitutive constitutional questions, or constitutive constitutional referendums, because the whole point of the book is to challenge the existence of this category. It instead uses the terms 'fundamental', 'significant', or 'important' when referring to constitutional matters, precisely because these terms are vague. The objective of chapter two is to demonstrate that it is neither helpful nor possible to carve out a category of decision as 'constitutive' decisions that democracy conceptually requires must be made by representatives.

V. Scope and Methodology

This section outlines the book's terms and conditions, explaining what it is and is not arguing. It clarifies the tools that will be used to answer questions in this book, and what kinds of questions it seeks to answer in the first place. The primary message of this section is that this is a book in constitutional theory. This is because the book makes normative claims about constitutions. Its focus is on the reasons to hold referendums on fundamental constitutional questions, and the impacts of these reasons on constitutions.

A. Methodology

While this book seeks to make a constitution to constitutional theory, it draws on many other bodies of literature to do so. Chapters two, three, four, and five invoke ideas from legal and political theory about the nature of democracy, authority, representation, and legal systems. Further, chapters six and seven draw on comparative constitutional law to put forward an account for how referendums should work in practice. In describing how referendums work, chapters two, four, five, and six draw on literature from politics and political science. In chapter three, the book also invokes social choice theory when discussing the nature of voting. Across the book, however, the purpose of invoking this literature is to make a theoretical claim about what kinds of reasons can justify the use of referendums.

B. Scope

In some ways, the aim of this book is incredibly broad. It makes claims about all referendums on constitutional questions in all jurisdictions, irrespective of constitutional history or what the law says about referendums. It takes this approach even though, plainly, constitutional history and what the law says about referendums make an enormous difference to how referendums are used in different jurisdictions. This book emphasises that while context makes a huge difference in the reasons to hold referendum, this book argues the idea that some decisions must be made by the people rather than representatives is *always* the wrong kind of reason to hold a referendum. In this way, the arguments made in this book are incredibly narrow. The core thesis is just about one kind of reason to hold one kind of referendum and why that reason conceptually fails and in practice is misleading. Irrespective of jurisdiction, referendums are not exceptional, overriding ways of making decisions. When used that way, they will undermine representative democracy. There is another path forward, where voters constantly control their constitutions, and referendums are part of the picture. That picture plays out differently across jurisdictions, as the case studies in chapter six demonstrate. This book explains the context-dependency of reasons to hold referendums, but also argues in chapters four and five that there are motifs and themes that emerge around the world as well.

C. A Note about Citizens' Assemblies

In thinking about ways for voters to make decisions instead of representatives doing so, the other clear candidate apart from a referendum is a citizens' assembly.[59] This book is not about citizens' assemblies because, while they are on the rise,[60] they have not become as deeply enshrined in constitutional law and thought as referendums. Many of the arguments made here about how referendums rely on, and cannot be separated from, a broader environment of elected representatives apply to citizens' assemblies as well, but unpacking this is beyond the scope of this book. Some theorists, Sieyès[61] in a classical context and King in a contemporary context,[62] do think that voters' ultimate authority in a democracy can be exercised through constituent assemblies. This book does not attempt to weigh in on that question. It only seeks to show that (i) it is neither possible nor helpful to distinguish between decisions which must be made by voters and those which may be made by representatives; and (ii) that a referendum cannot be a way for voters to make decisions instead of representatives doing so.

[59] Indeed, for Sieyès, this is the appropriate method for the expression of constituent power. Crucially, such a body is not composed of ordinary elected representatives. Rubinelli (n 11).

[60] OECD, 'Innovative Citizen Participation and New Democratic Institutions: Catching the Deliberative Wave' (2021), www.oecd.org/gov/open-government/oecd-deliberative-wave-database-update.pdf, accessed 25 August 2023.

[61] For Sieyès, 'the people, as holders of constituent power, do not create the constitution themselves but delegate the writing process to extraordinary elected representatives'. Rubinelli (n 11) 57.

[62] 'A constituent assembly is a body – a type of constitutional convention – convened for the particular purpose of drafting or revising a constitution, and which, crucially, has its own legislative authority. Constituent assemblies are there to constitute, not only to deliberate and report.' J King, 'The Democratic Case for a Written Constitution' (2019) 72 *Current Legal Problems* 1, 27.

VI. Referendums in a Global Context

Referendums are essential legal and political processes. They have been central to three of the most significant legal and political endeavours across the world in the last century: the project of self-determination;[63] the collapse of the Soviet Union;[64] and European integration.[65] Referendums have also been used to ask an enormous range of important questions including questions about conscription,[66] electoral reform,[67] the acceptability of economic bailouts,[68] migration,[69] pension reform,[70] abortion,[71] term limits,[72] annexation of territory,[73] the use of nuclear power,[74] and extradition.[75] Referendums have been used to approve new constitutions, both successfully[76] and unsuccessfully.[77] They have permanently changed voters' expectations about participation in the approval of new or revised constitutions.[78]

Despite this ubiquity, this book argues that referendums have been fundamentally misunderstood in constitutional theory and law. They have been treated as exercises in direct democracy – in other words, ways of taking decisions away from representatives – rather than as ways of supporting decision-making by representatives. The consequences for democracies are significant, and referendums have come to be attached to the worst impulses of populism because of this misunderstanding[79] – homogenising 'the people' to get representatives out of the way.[80] A different way forward is possible where referendums are part of representative

[63] Miller (n 32).

[64] S White and RJ Hill, 'Russia, the Former Soviet Union and Eastern Europe: The Referendum as a Flexible Political Instrument' in M Gallagher and P Uleri (eds), *The Referendum Experience in Europe* (Palgrave 1996).

[65] Hollander (n 58).

[66] Australia 1916 and 1917, Canada 1942.

[67] United Kingdom 2022.

[68] Greece 2015.

[69] Hungary 2016.

[70] Russia 2000.

[71] Ireland 2018.

[72] Central African Republic 2023.

[73] Crimea 2014.

[74] Sweden 1980.

[75] Ecuador 2023.

[76] Kenya 2010.

[77] Chile 2022.

[78] 'Public participation in constitution-making is now both an established international norm and a widespread practice.' H Landemore, 'When Public Participation Matters: The 2010–2013 Icelandic Constitutional Process' (2020) 18 *International Journal of Constitutional Law* 179, 179.

[79] 'While populists often call for referenda, such exercises are … not about democratic will formation among citizens. Populists simply wish to be confirmed in what they have already determined the will of the real people to be. Populism is not a path to more participation in politics.' JW Müller, *What Is Populism?* (University of Pennsylvania Press 2016) 102.

[80] Mehmet Ucum, judicial consultant to President Erdogan, said that the aim of these constitutional amendments was to 'strengthen the ordinary citizen's relationship with the state' and for President Erdogan, as with many dictators, he is the state. Ucum has also said that 'any attempt to form an institutional control over the people's will is against democracy'. B Bora, 'Turkey's Constitutional Reform'

democracy; where referendums improve both decision-making and offer voters meaningful opportunities for participation. What this looks like will vary from jurisdiction to jurisdiction, but it never looks – literally or metaphorically – like replacing representatives.

Further, by thinking about referendums differently, a stronger version of democratic constitutionalism is possible. A vision of democratic constitutionalism where voters do not merely weigh in occasionally through exceptional constitutional moments, but rather see themselves as constantly in charge of their democracies. Constitutions cannot be controlled or created – still less through referendums. Constitutions, however, can and do change. Voters have the ultimate authority to create, change, and challenge their constitutions, not limited to occasionally in exceptional constitutional moments where referendums replace representatives.

VII. Conclusion

The idea that democracy has two tracks, and that fundamental decisions must be made by representatives, is inextricably connected to the claim that people are born free and equal.[81] The commitment to the freedom and equality of people is an enormous and enormously significant historical development. It is a triumph of enlightenment thinking. This book will argue, however, that it does not follow from the truth that all people are born free and equal that they must author the texts of their constitutions through processes such as referendums.[82] Further, the idea that constitutions can and must be authored by the people through constitutions undermines the emancipatory ideas of freedom and equality.

The idea of exceptional constitutional authorship through referendums is limiting because constitutions cannot be directly controlled, still less through referendums. Constitutions are in a constant state of flux, shaped by protests and public opinion, and significant constitutional changes may happen gradually and by accident. The picture of voters controlling constitutions through referendums appears to prioritise their role, but instead limits it by holding that they can only change constitutions occasionally through exceptional constitutional moments where they create or amend texts. Constitutions are not just constituted in moments, and they are not just constituted in texts. They are ongoing processes of constitution and re-constitution; they are continually in flux. Referendums are more useful when they are seen as part of this ongoing process of negotiation, rather than as one-off moments on a higher democratic plane. It is tempting

Aljazeera (17 January 2017), www.aljazeera.com/indepth/features/2017/01/turkey-constitutional-reform-170114085009105.html, accessed 28 February 2017.

[81] As discussed in greater detail in ch 7, section I.

[82] Or indeed citizens' assemblies although, as stated in section V, that is beyond the scope of this book.

in constitutional law, as it is in all parts of life, to think we are in control of our circumstances, and that there is a clear, direct connection between our actions and the results of those actions. This idea of control has the greatest appeal where it is the least helpful: on fundamental constitutional questions. Constitutions cannot and should not be authored in a singular or static way, still less by referendums. Democracy will work better if this reality is confronted directly, and referendums – even on fundamental constitutional questions – are understood as exercises in representative democracy.

2

The People *or* Politicians? A False Choice

I. Introduction

This book challenges an argument that goes like this: there are two decision-making paths in democracies, one for 'we the people' and one for politicians. Call this idea 'two-track democracy'.[1] A simple and powerful idea drives two-track democracy: some fundamental constitutional decisions cannot be made by representatives and so must be made by the people instead. The appeal of two-track democracy particularly in mass, pluralist democracies is clear. There must be a way for voters to remain in control of their democracy without making all the decisions, so they can get on with their lives. This chapter challenges the idea that there can or must be two decision-making paths in a democracy. Two-track democracy takes a needlessly narrow view of (i) constitutions, (ii) democratic authority, and (iii) constitutional authorship. This chapter begins with an account of two-track democracy, raises three challenges to it, and concludes by confronting the key advantage of two-track democracy: it appears emancipatory.

Two-track democracy appears emancipatory because it offers voters an exceptional decision-making path. This exceptional decision-making path appears to give voters control over their constitutions. This appearance is misleading. This book argues that constitutions can never be controlled or authored, still less that this could be done through referendums. Indeed, two-track democracy limits voters' control over constitutions rather than enabling it. It is through protests, public opinion, and their perceptions of legitimacy that voters exercise their authority, and constantly challenge and change their constitutions. This does not mean this book is arguing against the use of referendums. The point of this book

[1] Although Ackerman calls this idea 'dualism' the term 'two track-democracy' is chosen here to avoid confusion with ideas of monism and dualism in international law. Ackerman says: 'Above all else, a dualist Constitution seeks to distinguish between two different decisions that may be made in a democracy. The first is a decision by the American people; the second, by their government. Decisions by the People occur rarely, and under special constitutional conditions … [in] *constitutional politics*, from the Founding onward, called upon their fellow Americans to engage in acts of citizenship that, when successful culminates in the proclamation of higher law in the name of We the People.' B Ackerman, *We the People, Volume 1: Foundations* (Belknap Press 1993) 6–7 (emphasis in original).

is just to say this: the claim that some decisions cannot be made by representatives is the wrong kind of reason to hold a referendum. Two-track democracy sets up a false choice by claiming that some decisions are made by the people and others by politicians. This book argues that it is not descriptively possible, or normatively helpful, to separate the actions of the people and politicians in processes of democratic decision-making.

II. Two-track Democracy

Modern democracies are built on the idea that the people are the ultimate source of authority.[2] From this claim, it is thought to necessarily follow that there are some kinds of decisions about democracy that only the people can make.[3] The moves in this argument are straightforward. For a political community to count as a democracy, voters need to have meta-control of how power is allocated. Therefore, democracy requires two different kinds of power: the power to constitute an authority and the power to exercise that authority on the people's behalf. This distinction is famously articulated in Sieyès's distinction between *pouvoir constituant* and *pouvoir constitute*, ie the distinction between constitutive and constituted powers.[4] The idea motivating this distinction[5] is that people's ultimate authority is a 'trust that cannot be delegated'.[6] As Kalyvas argues, democracy is inseparable from the concept of constituent power.[7] The people are the only possible source of legitimacy, and therefore they must determine the ultimate allocation of authority in a democracy.[8]

[2] 'The modern state is built upon the principle that political power belongs to the people.' L Rubinelli, *Constituent Power: A History* (Cambridge University Press 2020) 1.

[3] 'The people as democratic reality rather than as represented constitutional symbol is *the only* legitimate source of democratic authority. It is a short step to argue for a constitutional referendum on the basis that when an issue that goes to the heart of the constitutional settlement is implicated, then the people should be directly engaged in the decision-making process.' S Tierney, 'Constitutional Referendums: A Theoretical Enquiry' (2009) 72 *Modern Law Review* 360, 372 (emphasis in original).

[4] 'As Sieyes modestly argued to the Assembly: 'A sound and useful idea was invited in 1789; the separation of the constituent power from constituted powers. It will go down in history as a discovery that advances sciences, for which the French can be thanked.' Rubinelli (n 2) 49.

[5] 'No type of delegated power can modify the conditions of its delegation.' E Sieyès, *Political Writings: Including the Debate between Sieyès and Tom Paine in 1791* (M Sonenscher ed, Hackett 2003) 136.

[6] 'Only the people have the unique moral capability to make and unmake the set of fundamental laws that undergird their state.' J Lenowitz, '"A Trust That Cannot Be Delegated": The Invention of Ratification Referenda' (2015) 109 *American Political Science Review* 803, 810.

[7] 'The constituent power answers the need for democratic legitimacy and allows for a rethinking of the problem of legitimation deficit that unavoidably plagues the normal politics of all modern, constitutional representative democracy. "Democratic theory," Schmitt powerfully argued "knows as a legitimate constitution only the one that rests on the constituent power of the people."' A Kalyvas, 'Popular Sovereignty, Democracy, and the Constituent Power' (2005) 12 *Constellations* 223, 237, citing C Schmitt, *Verfassungslehre* (Duncker and Humblot 1928) 94–95.

[8] Kalyvas (n 7).

Which decisions concern the allocation of authority in a democracy and are so fundamental that they must be made by the people? Tierney says they are those which 'amend sovereign relations between people and their government',[9] and helpfully provides four examples. Decisions cannot be taken by representatives if they 'found new states … create or radically change constitutions … establish complex new models of sub-state autonomy; and … transfer sovereign powers from the state to international institutions'.[10] Galligan makes a similar claim, arguing that constitutional referendums are 'expressions of democratic sovereignty'[11] and must be used for matters that are constitutive of their authority. Bogdanor makes the same point but uses Locke's language of transferring powers to representatives to convey the idea. Bogdanor says: '[T]he electorate, it might be said, entrust their MPs as agents with legislative power; but they give them no authority to transfer this power.'[12] Bogdanor thinks that, from this principle of liberal constitutionalism, the case for referendums on constitutional questions naturally follows.[13] While these three theorists use slightly different language, the core commitment they communicate is the same: some kinds of constitutional questions are constitutive of constitutions, and therefore cannot conceptually be made by representatives.[14]

Two-track democracy has constitutional implications. If it is the case that there are some types of decisions which cannot be made by ordinary, elected representatives, then these decisions must be made by the people directly. While this picture appears emancipatory,[15] it is both misleading and limiting. The next three sections explain why the picture offered by two-track democracy is misleading, and the final section demonstrates the constraints that two-track democracy places on voters.

[9] '… Implicate the sovereign relations between people and their government.' Tierney (n 3) 360–61.

[10] ibid 360.

[11] B Galligan, 'Amending Constitutions Through the Referendum Device' in M Mendelsohn and A Parkin (eds), *Referendum Democracy: Citizens, Elites, and Deliberation in Referendum Campaigns* (Palgrave 2001) 109.

[12] V Bogdanor, *The People and the Party System* (Cambridge University Press 1981) 76.

[13] 'Such authority, it is natural to suggest, can be obtained only through a specific mandate, that is, a referendum. The idea that power is entrusted to the nation's representatives only for specific purposes reflects one of the central principles of liberal constitutionalism, and has its origins in Locke. "The Legislature", he claims, "cannot transfer the power of making laws to any other hands. For it being but a delegated power from the People, they who have it cannot pass it to others." There is thus a clear and principled justification for requiring a referendum to be called whenever it is proposed to transfer the powers of Parliament.' ibid 77.

[14] Tierney's approach here is also explicitly endorsed by Elkins and Hudson as '[a]n important theoretical insight, which may help us to understand better how citizens might view their responsibility in these different contexts'. Z Elkins and A Hudson, 'The Constitutional Referendum in Historical Perspective' in D Landau and H Lerner (eds), *Comparative Constitution Making* (Elgar 2019) 148.

[15] Although Kalyvas worries that this 'emancipatory promise' has already been lost. Kalyvas (n 7) 225.

III. Constitutions

Two-track democracy prioritises the textual nature of constitutions.[16] This is, of course, not the only way to think about constitutions, nor the only way in which constitutions have been understood. As Niesen helpfully explains, the idea that constitutions are grounded in texts arose alongside the idea that some decisions must be made by people directly through exercises of constituent power. Before the rise of constituent power, and the idea of two-track democracy, constitutions were not understood as texts. Constitutions were instead understood broadly as everything that happens.[17] The choice is, of course, not an 'either/or'. All constitutions, irrespective of whether they are codified, include both textual and non-textual elements. The question is instead how constitutions are constituted and whether the constitution of constitutions can be articulated in texts. Is it possible to clearly demarcate the decisions that must be made by voters and those which must be made by representatives? This chapter argues that this is not possible – the distinction between constitutive and constituted powers is deeply and constantly contested in constitutions. This section offers two reasons to think that the constitution of constitutions cannot be captured by texts. First, it is not possible to distinguish between constitutive matters which involve the allocation of authority and those which do not. Questions about rights, conscription, and even pensions and taxation directly implicate the fundamental relationships between voters and their government. Second, the allocation of authority in a democracy is fundamentally contested. It is not fixed, but is rather an ongoing process of negotiation. This includes the relationship between voters and representatives.

A. Distinguishing between Constitutive and Constituted Powers

Two-track democracy relies on the idea that it is possible to distinguish between constitutive and constituted powers. This is not possible. It is not possible to

[16] 'Constituent power is a modern concept. Its source can certainly be traced to debates in medieval political thought, but it emerges in a distinct form only with the establishment of modern institutions of the state. The concept is a product of the secularizing and rationalizing movement of late eighteenth century European thought known as the Enlightenment and it comes to occupy a central place in constitutional thought only after the late eighteenth century American and French Revolutions.' M Loughlin, 'On Constituent Power' in M Dowdle and M Wilkinson (eds), *Constitutionalism Beyond Liberalism* (Cambridge University Press 2017) 151.

[17] 'The language of *pouvoir constituant* demands that we distinguish between an older meaning of "Constitution" as the sum total of political circumstances and the new, revolutionary meaning of "constitution" as a written text that lays out the competences of government organs and can be changed at will. Only the latter qualifies as its object.' P Niesen, 'Extinguishing the Burning Embers: Rubinelli on Sieyès' *Verfassungsblog* (19 December 2020), verfassungsblog.de/extinguishing-the-burning-embers-rubinelli-on-sieyes, accessed 20 January 2021.

distinguish between those questions that amend 'sovereign relations' or 'transfer powers' and those that do not. This section considers four sets of questions which have been the subject of referendums were not classed as constitutive by the theorists above: questions about pensions, conscription, same-sex marriage, and suffrage. All these cases could defensibly be construed as modifying the sovereign relations between people and the government, yet they sit uneasily within the framework of two-track democracy. The existence of borderline cases does not, of course, mean that two-track democracy has no value. The number and scope of these counterexamples, however, suggests, that the distinction between constitutive and constituted powers is misleading and unhelpful.

Taking pensions first: this was one of the questions put to voters in the Russian constitutional referendum of 2020 alongside other questions about language and rights.[18] Pensions may appear to be ordinary policy issues, but they raise fundamental questions about the relationship between the citizen and the state. What responsibilities does the state have to care for its citizens when they can no longer work? If there is a social contract, pensions are at the heart of how contributions to, and benefits from, the state are understood. The question of whether the most vulnerable can live with dignity into old age directly implicates the legitimacy of a state and so it is at least arguable that this is a constitutive constitutional question. If this kind of policy question is constitutive, it raises the possibility that other similar questions such as access to affordable health care are also constitutive.

Conscription presents another example of the difficulties of distinguishing between constitutive and constituted powers. It cannot be the case that conscription is an ordinary policy issue that does not implicate in a fundamental way the relationship between voters and the government. The requirement to fight for one's country was put to a referendum in Australia in 1916 and 1917 and Canada in 1942. While this question is not about the allocation of authority in a democracy, it is difficult to imagine a more fundamental question about what it means to be a citizen of a country. Indeed, for the state to have control over someone's life inverts the relationship between voters and government on which democracy relies. It must be understood as constitutive of constitutions, as should any question about compulsory national or military service.

A third issue that puts pressure on the distinction between constitutive and constituted powers is suffrage. Suffrage is an important example because it articulates the paradox in the idea of constitutive powers themselves.[19] If it

[18] Indeed, just a few of the amendments in the 2020 Russian constitutional referendum were the indexing of pensions, along with same-sex marriage, making the minimum wage a living wage, and the constitutional status of the Russian language. 'Putin Strongly Backed in Controversial Russian Reform Vote' *BBC News* (2 July 2020), www.bbc.co.uk/news/world-europe-53255964.

[19] 'Modern constitutionalism is underpinned by two fundamental though antagonistic imperatives: that governmental power ultimately is generated from the "consent of the people" and that, to be sustained and effective, such power must be divided, constrained, and exercised through distinctive institutional forms. The people, in Maistre's words, "are a sovereign that cannot exercise sovereignty"; the power they possess, it would appear, can only be exercised through constitutional forms already

is the people who constitute constitutions, who are the people? Can the people define themselves in a profoundly undemocratic way that undermines the equality on which democracy relies?[20] Referendums are often used for questions of suffrage,[21] in ways that implicate the fundamental question of who counts as a member of a demos. The difficulty for two-track democracy is that it relies on the idea that 'the people' has already been, at least roughly, defined. Suffrage referendums put pressure on this idea, and so put pressure on the distinction between constitutive and constituted powers. Again, as with pensions and conscription, the example of suffrage invites further borderline cases. What about decisions making it compulsory to show identification in order to vote, or which make polling places inaccessible? All these cases demonstrate the difficulty in sharply defining a distinction between constitutive and constituted powers.

The previous three examples demonstrate that it is difficult to define with any precision what it means for sovereign relations to be modified between voters and the government. Additionally, in a referendum it is unclear whose sovereign relations are being modified, particularly in referendums about rights. Minorities whose rights are taken away, for instance the right to marry, through a referendum, could rightly and reasonably feel that their sovereign relations with the state had been compromised. Acts of discrimination or oppression of minorities by majorities implicate the relationships between citizens and the state in the most fundamental ways.

A reader might think that this worry, and the argument in this section in general, is taking the distinction between constitutive and constituted powers too literally. The value of the distinction is normative or metaphorical, it might be argued, rather than descriptive. While it is right to say the force of the distinction between constitutive and constituted powers is normative, the normative basis for this distinction is too narrow as well. The point is this: it is not possible to define one principled category of questions which implicate the sovereign relations between voters and their government, and another for those that do not. It is then unclear what two-track democracy is meant to track, and its normative and practical defensibility is weakened. This ambiguity in the relationship between

established or in the process of being established. This indicates what, in its most elementary formulation, might be called the paradox of constitutionalism.' M Loughlin and N Walker, *The Paradox of Constitutionalism: Constituent Power and Constitutional Form* (Oxford University Press 2007) 1.

[20] As persuasively discussed, for instance, in Dyzenhaus's analysis of Carl Schmitt. D Dyzenhaus, 'The Politics of the Question of Constituent Power' in M Loughlin and N Walker (eds), *The Paradox of Constitutionalism* (Oxford University Press 2007) 130–33.

[21] Indeed, referendums were used this way, including in the United States, to limit the expansion of suffrage. B Gamble, 'Putting Civil Rights to Popular Vote' (1997) 41 *American Journal of Political Science* 245, 246. There was a movement to use a referendum to block the expansion of women's suffrage in the United Kingdom. 'During the controversy over women's suffrage in the first two decades of the century, the anti-suffragists seriously considered whether they ought to call for a referendum on the issue. Lord Curzon, a leader of the anti-suffragists, composed a memorandum in February 1913, entitled 'Woman Suffrage and the Referendum' in which he debated this question … 53 peers signed a memorial letter to *The Times* calling for a referendum on women's suffrage.' Bogdanor (n 12) 34–35.

constitutive and constituted powers is symptomatic of a deeper problem for two-track democracy: its focus on constitutions as principally textual.

B. The Contestation of Constitutions

Two-track democracy supposes that it is both possible and desirable to lay out in a text where authority lies in a constitutional democracy. This approach is limiting because it places too great a focus on what Goldoni and Wilkinson call the formal constitution, at the expense of the material constitution. Goldoni and Wilkinson were not the first to identify the distinction between the formal constitution and the material constitution; the idea comes from Kelsen.[22] The formal constitution is the text of the constitution itself. The material constitution is the push and pull of forces and factors that shape and inform the legitimacy of a constitutional text.[23] The relationship between the formal and material constitutions is dynamic and in flux.[24] The material constriction is more complex, and is made up of ordering forces that are potentially in tension and pull in different directions.[25] Distinguishing between the formal and the material constitution adds enormous complexity to the constitution, but this complexity is illuminating. It is through the dynamic between society and the constitutional order that change occurs.[26]

Goldoni and Wilkinson's picture of constitutional change is so complex that it will not be the same across systems or even within systems. This approach, however, in all its ambiguity is an advantage in both the theory and practice of democracy. As Nick Barber rightly argues, constitutional ambiguities can help democracies to muddle through. This is because the purpose of constitutions is not to address all disagreement, but rather to act as sites for constructive disagreement.[27] This constructive disagreement is the material constitution, and as Goldoni and

[22] H Kelsen, *General Theory of Law and State* (Harvard University Press 1949) 124, discussed at ibid 569.

[23] Indeed, Wilkinson go even further to argue that '[t]he formal constitution is a feature, an instance *of* the material constitution. Without a corresponding material constitution, without political and social traction, a formal constitution remains a "dead letter", a list of wishful auspices, or even a "sham".' M Goldoni and M Wilkinson, 'The Material Constitution' (2018) 81 *Modern Law Review* 567, 593 (emphasis in original).

[24] 'Recognition of the material constitution has conspicuous consequences. It enriches constitutional enquiry by revealing the material relations between law, politics and society undergirding the formal constitution … The concept of the material constitution captures the internal relation between constitutional order and society without, however, eliding its conflictual and evolving nature. It is through this dynamic that constitutional change occurs.' ibid 596–97.

[25] 'The four ordering forces of the material constitution [are]: political unity, a set of institutions, social relations, and fundamental political objectives … because these ordering forces are multiple and in tension with each other, there is no single determining factor of constitutional development.' ibid 567.

[26] The material constitution prevents '[t]he collapse of the idea of constitutional change into the practice of formal constitutional amendment'. Goldoni and Wilkinson (n 23) 593.

[27] 'Ambiguities provide a compromise framework within which … inconsistent claims can co-exist.' N Barber, 'Against a Written Constitution' (2008) *Public Law* 11, 17.

Wilkinson helpfully demonstrate, constitutions cannot be understood without it. There will never be unanimity about, for instance, the relationship between legislatures and the judiciary in a constitutional democracy as cases such as *Cherry/Miller*,[28] *The Reference re Secession of Quebec*,[29] and *Marbury v Madison*[30] demonstrate in different jurisdictions. Indeed, the questions in democracy that are the most fundamental may well be the most contested. These debates are themselves best understood as part of the democratic process.[31]

This contestation of constitutions demonstrates how dynamic constitutions are. Writing about the English constitution in 1921, Lytton Strachey argued that it was an 'indescribable entity … a living thing, growing with the growth of men, and assuming ever-varying forms in accordance with the subtle and complex laws of human character. It is the child of wisdom and chance.'[32] If Strachey meant that the English constitution, or indeed any constitution, is constitution is *only* the child of wisdom and chance, he puts the point too strongly. Nevertheless, Strachey's view offers a helpful alternative to the textualist approach to constitutions which arose alongside the focus on the distinction between constitutive and constituted powers in the French and American revolutions. Mary Wollstonecraft wrote that the American Constitution demonstrates the possibility of escaping 'constitutions formed by chance and continually patched up'.[33] Americans, she argued, had shown that it was possible to start fresh with a new constitution 'on

[28] 'For the purposes of the present case, therefore, the relevant limit upon the power to prorogue can be expressed in this way: that a decision to prorogue Parliament will be unlawful if the prorogation has the effect of frustrating or preventing, without reasonable justification, the ability of Parliament to carry out its constitutional functions as a legislature as the body responsible for the supervision of the executive. In such a situation, the court will intervene if the effect is sufficiently serious to justify an exceptional course.' *R (on the application of Miller) v Prime Minister, Cherry (and Others) v Advocate-General For Scotland* [2019] UKSC 41 at para [50].

[29] 'Moreover, the Canadian Constitution does not insist on a strict separation of powers. Parliament and the provincial legislatures may properly confer other legal functions on the courts, and may confer certain judicial functions on bodies that are not courts.' *Reference re Secession of Quebec* [1998] 2 SCR 217 at para [15].

[30] 'Certainly all those who have framed written constitutions contemplate them as forming the fundamental and paramount law of the nation, and, consequently, the theory of every such government must be, that an act of the legislature, repugnant to the constitution, is void … It is emphatically the province and duty of the judicial department to say what the law is. Those who apply the rule to particular cases, must of necessity expound and interpret that rule. If two laws conflict with each other, the courts must decide on the operation of each.' 5 US 137 (1803) Chief Justice Marshall at 177–78.

[31] 'The concepts of liberty, democracy, and the rest function … as interpretive concepts of value: their descriptive sense is contested, and the contest turns on which assignment of a descriptive sense best captures or realises that value.' R Dworkin, 'Hart's Postscript and the Character of Political Philosophy' (2004) 24 *Oxford Journal of Legal Studies* 1, 9 (emphasis in original).

[32] King is in dialogue with Strachey at the beginning of a piece where he makes a provocative and persuasive case for the need for constituent constitutional assemblies in the United Kingdom. J King, 'The Democratic Case for a Written Constitution' (2019) 72 *Current Legal Problems* 1, citing L Strachey, *Queen Victoria* (Harcourt, Bruce and Company 1921) 153. King's account is discussed in the section on authorship below.

[33] M Wollstonecraft, *An Historical and Moral View of the Origin and Progress of the French Revolution and the Effect It Has Produced In Europe* (London 1794) 14.

the basis of reason.'[34] Wollstonecraft's approach to constitutions and authorship has informed the approach to constitutional referendums that is challenged here. Such an approach is deeply misleading. It suggests that constitutions are created in a static way, and that legitimate authority is static as well. While Wollstonecraft was excited about the emancipatory power of this idea, it constrains and limits voters' authority in indefensible ways.

IV. Legitimate Authority

The distinction between constituted and constitutive power is based on a particular view of what makes democratic authority legitimate. Sieyès's distinction between *pouvoir constituant* and *pouvoir constitute* was driven partly by his approach to the social contract.[35] The distinction, and the social contract, provided a way to maximise liberty and freedom.[36] Like the decision between constituted and constitutive powers, the idea of the social contract remains influential today. Loughlin helpfully and accurately captures this influence when he says: 'Constitutions today are generally conceived as contracts drawn up by "the people" to establish and limit the powers of governing institutions.'[37] While influential,[38] the idea that democratic authority is legitimate if and only if it is consented to and that constitutions articulate and establish that consent is taking a narrower approach to legitimate authority than is necessary. This is for three reasons. First, what will be called here the 'singularity thesis'. In modern, pluralist democracies, there are multiple sources of democratic legitimacy. Second, and substantively, the idea of the social contract has serious shortcomings. Third, the nature of democratic authority is constantly in flux. It is not established or changed by a single act but is continually changing because of shifting public standards of legitimacy. While, as Loughlin rightly says, the social contract is never meant to be taken literally, the figurative idea is itself unhelpful.[39]

[34] ibid.

[35] Rubinelli (n 2) 51–56.

[36] For Sieyès, Rubinelli says, 'The main pillar of his political theory was the principle according to which all men are free … individual freedom is the ultimate aim of every social and political arrangement.' ibid 50.

[37] M Loughlin, *The Foundations of Public Law* (Oxford University Press 2010) 275.

[38] In his comprehensive and influential study of constitutional amendment, Albert takes this as a given: 'In the modern tradition of representative government, amendment rules hold special status … they legitimatize higher and ordinary law as derived from the consent of the governed.' R Albert, *Constitutional Amendments: Making, Breaking, and Changing Constitutions* (Oxford University Press 2019).

[39] And for this and other reasons, Loughlin himself advocates moving beyond the contractual metaphor to the kind of authorship discussed at section V. ibid 310.

A. The Singularity Thesis

Under conditions of reasonable pluralism, there is no need for one single conception of what makes democratic authority legitimate.[40] Green has effectively shown that the conditions of pluralism are such that a piecemeal approach to legitimate authority is the most defensible approach.[41] There are all kinds of reasons that democratic authority may be justified, not just that voters consent to it or control it. Democracy authority may be justified for procedural reasons because it engages voters and reflects their views.[42] Or democracy may be justified for instrumental reasons,[43] because it makes better decisions than alternative systems.[44] Further, there is no need to choose between these two sources of legitimacy, and it is difficult to separate them anyway.[45] Political traditions of voluntarism may characterise democratic jurisdictions, but this is a contingent rather than a conceptual claim. Legal systems indeed require multiple types of rules,[46] but the social contract is neither necessary nor sufficient to establish those types of rules. This is all to say: even if a jurisdiction has a tradition of voluntarism in justifying legitimate authority, this cannot and should not be understood to be the only source of legitimate authority.[47] The legitimacy of a constitution, even in a country with a strong history of voluntarism, will still be shaped by its procedural legitimacy (how it engages voters) and instrumental legitimacy (is it making good decisions?) Legitimate democracy authority must be understood as plural; there is no need to see it as singular.

Readers might resist this argument move. The idea of the social contract has been hugely resilient in justifying constitutions. This is because the claim is so closely tied to the idea that voters are the ultimate source of authority in a

[40] '"Singularly in ground" is the name A.J. Simmons gives to the second assumption mentioned above, which, as a prelude to rejecting it, he states as "the requirement that there be one and only one ground of political obligation".' J Wolff, 'Political Obligation: A Pluralistic Approach' in M Baghramian and A Ingram (eds), *Pluralism: The Philosophy of Politics and Diversity* (Routledge 2000) 184, citing Simmons in AJ Simmons, *Moral Principles and Political Obligations* (Princeton University Press 1979) 35. Wolff also discusses the work of Klosko, who makes a similar claim: G Klosko, *Political Obligations* (Oxford University Press 2008) 4.

[41] 'Political bonds in the modern state are more complex and more attenuated than traditional theorists suggest.' L Green, *The Authority of the State* (Oxford University Press 1990) 248.

[42] S Hershovitz, 'Legitimacy, Democracy, and Razian Authority' (2003) 9 *Legal Theory* 201, 212.

[43] These kinds of decisions are significant. The quality of the vaccine rollout is as great a threat to the democratic legitimacy as the success or failure or success of the future of Europe conference on democratic renewal.

[44] ibid 212.

[45] 'An adequate doctrine of political fairness should make a place for both … [procedural and outcome-based] considerations.' C Beitz, *Political Equality* (Princeton University Press 1989) 95.

[46] 'The social contract defines a two-level set of rules. That is [an] elementary truth. The terms of the social contract form the basic law of a political association stipulating the rules, offices, and powers through which the practical task of governing takes place, as well as the principles of public life by which day-to-day measures of politics and policy are to be judged.' A Weale, *Modern Social Contract Theory* (Oxford University Press 2020) 418.

[47] Green (n 41).

democracy. The point of this book is not to challenge the claim that voters are the ultimate source of authority in a democracy. They are. The point is just that the picture of how this authority is exercised is not a singular or simple one. Further, the justification for that legitimate authority, if it exists, will vary between citizens and jurisdictions. Finally, the legitimacy of democracies is also in flux. It is changing all the time. Legitimate authority is constantly changing *because* of the supremacy of the people. In this way, the view of constitutions where voters delegate some authority to representatives on a limited, fixed, and finite basis, and revisit that arrangement periodically through referendums, limits rather than enhances voters' role in a democracy.

B. The Substantive Limitations of the Social Contract

The social contract is not merely a justification for legitimate authority; it is a cultural and political phenomenon.[48] The resilience of this idea is particularly impressive, given that challenges have been raised to it by Hume and others following. These questions include: 'Who consents? Can they be said to have consented if they had no choice? What about generational change?[49] In thinking about constitutive and constituted powers, one worry about the social contract is particularly salient: the relationship between voting and consent. Consent is a demanding normative idea and consequently does much normative work in justifying authority. It provides a clear, stable, intuitive justification of authority in publicly understandable terms. This approach relies, however, on voting as understood as an instance of individual or collective[50] consent. Can voting perform the role of individual or mass consent?

[48] M Lessnoff, *Social Contract Theory* (Blackwell 1990) 1.

[49] 'It is in vain to say, that all governments are, or should be, at first, founded on popular consent, as much as the necessity of human affairs will admit. This favours entirely my pretension. I maintain, that human affairs will never admit of this consent, seldom of the appearance of it; but that conquest or usurpation, that is, in plain terms, force, by dissolving the ancient governments, is the origin of almost all the new ones which were ever established in the world. And that in the few cases where consent may seem to have taken place, it was commonly so irregular, so confined, or so much intermixed either with fraud or violence, that it cannot have any great authority. My intention here is not to exclude the consent of the people from being one just foundation of government where it has a place. It is surely the best and most sacred of any. I only pretend, that it has very seldom had place in any degree, and never almost in its full extent; and that, therefore, some other foundation of government must also be admitted … Can we seriously say, that a poor peasant or artisan has a free choice to leave his country, when he knows no foreign language or manners, and lives, from day to day, by the small wages which he acquires? We may as well assert that a man, by remaining in a vessel, freely consents to the dominion of the master; though he was carried on board while asleep, and must leap into the ocean and perish, the moment he leaves her.' D Hume, 'Of the Original Contract' in *Essays, Moral, Political, and Literary* (EF Miller ed, Liberty 1777) 479.

[50] S Tierney, *Constitutional Referendums: The Theory and Practice of Republican Deliberation* (Oxford University Press 2012). 55.

Consent is a three-place transaction in which one actor (A) gives consent to do something (φ) – and this consent is always given to another party or agent (B). So, 'A consented (to B) to φ'.[51] In determining a constitutive constitutional question, what do these parts of the concept of consent stand for? Who is A – the voters, the voters as a metaphor of the people, or the franchise? All of these meanings raise problems depending on the meaning of φ. Often φ is understood to be A's consent to participate in the process of voting rather than to any particular outcome. It is not clear whether that is right, but even if it is accurate, it is unclear why if someone consents to a process, then normatively, they are consenting to an outcome. Imagine someone who votes as a protest even though that they know the system is rigged, for example, or that they think the underlying electoral system is unjust. At best, this is an indirect source of democratic legitimacy.[52] Turning to B: consent is being given to what or to whom when someone votes? A constitutional settlement, specific representatives, or the state? This is not to suggest that voting goes no way to demonstrating something like agreement. Voting does indicate that a majority, or perhaps plurality, of voters – on balance – support a political proposition. The point is that consent is doing a considerable amount of normative work, and it is not clear that voting is the kind of act that amounts to consent. Extrapolating voting to collective consent presents other problems, particularly of homogenising the pluralism which characterises modern liberal democracies. In sum: while voting may look something like agreement in certain circumstances, it is only part of the puzzle of democratic legitimacy. Voting does not go so far as to establish consent to constitutional settlements.

A reader might worry that this is all too literal; the work that voting is performing as an act of consent is metaphorical.[53] Abstraction does not, however, mean all these difficulties can be avoided. One of the ways that modern social contract theorists have avoided the challenges to the idea of the social contract raised by Hume is by moving towards tacit consent.[54] Another way of putting the idea of tacit consent is saying that, in voting, someone consents to participate in a process. The difficulty is that the distinction between constitutive and constituted powers requires the least persuasive version of the social contract. The difference between constitutive and constituted powers rests on the idea of explicit consent to constitutive constitutional questions, through an act such as a referendum. The choice for supporters of the social contract is an unenviable one. The idea of the contract is either so weak as to not do the requisite normative work in justifying constitutions, or it is so strong so as to be implausible.

[51] J Kleinig, 'The Nature of Consent' in F Miller and A Wertheimer (eds), *The Ethics of Consent: Theory and Practice* (Oxford University Press 2009) 5.

[52] As Wollheim famously argues in R Wollheim, 'A Paradox in the Theory of Democracy' in D Weiss, P Laslett, and WG Runciman (eds), *Philosophy, Politics, and Society* (Blackwell 1962).

[53] Lessnoff (n 48) 2.

[54] ibid 3.

C. Legitimate Authority is in Flux

Legitimate authority is based on public perceptions, and public perceptions are constantly in flux. Constitutions are documents, but they are not only documents and while their legality is textual, but their constitutionality is also not exhausted by texts. While, as a matter of law, the United Kingdom did not need to give notice of withdrawal from the European Union under Article 50 of the Treaty on European Union (TEU) after the 2016 Brexit referendum, this would not have been a constitutional issue. Indeed, the constitutional significance of the 2016 referendum is best understood in a broader context. The democratic legitimacy of membership of the European Union was not determined just in the 2016 referendum campaign but by the failure of the UK government to hold referendums before signing the Maastricht Treaty and Lisbon Treaty. It was impacted too by the change in the European Union's scope and evolution, from the European Economic Community to the European Union.[55] The development of the European Union demonstrates a broader and essential constitutional principle: constitutions that were once acceptable, for example those prohibiting the participation of certain genders, ages, and ethnicities, can come over time to be perceived as illegitimate and lose public support. The conventions around the exercise of the royal prerogatives in Commonwealth Countries did not change in one fell swoop but rather over time due to the social and political evolution of public perceptions of legitimacy and evolving institutions.[56] The broad public perception of the monarchy's legitimacy, for instance, shapes its constitutionality as head of state.[57]

One of the advantages of the distinction between constitutive and constituted powers is the distinction's supposed emancipatory power. The distinction embeds itself during a time of revolution and allows people to come together not as 'mere politicians' but in the name of 'we the people'.[58] This view is only superficially emancipatory. On this approach, if voters are lucky, they can undertake this kind of action perhaps once in a generation. While such an approach may appear emancipatory, this approach to constitutional authorship is profoundly limiting. Indeed, the next section argues that any conception of constitutions as 'authored' undermines voters' role in a democracy.

V. Constitutional Authorship

The idea of constitutional authorship has clear appeal. It offers a compelling vision of constitutions where voters are unambiguously in control. Nevertheless, this

[55] As discussed in greater depth when the case of Brexit is considered in detail at ch 6, section II.

[56] P Leyland, *The Constitution of the United Kingdom: A Contextual Analysis* (4th edn, Hart 2021), ch 4.

[57] ibid.

[58] Ackerman (n 1) 192.

section will argue that the idea of constitutional authorship is neither possible nor helpful as a constitutional metaphor. This is because it requires an intentional approach to constitutions, and constitutions cannot be created intentionally. This section has two parts. The first explains the metaphor of constitutional authorship and three possible meanings of the metaphor. The second part shows why, on these three possible meanings of intentional, the metaphor of authorship is unintelligible.

A. Three Possible Meanings of Authorship

Constitutional authorship is a metaphorical[59] rather than literal idea. The core commitment of authorship, as Michelman says, is the idea that constitutions are created 'intentionally', and this idea is incredibly difficult to escape.[60] No proponent of authorship thinks that constitutions are authored in the way that novels are authored, but supporters of authorship are committed to the view that constitutions are intentionally created through these acts of direct participation or ratification. Consider three models for how this authorship happens in practice: (i) the originalist view, (ii) the transtemporal view, and (iii) the presentist view. While all approaches to authorship rely on the idea of the intentional constitution, different accounts of authorship, to different degrees, take the idea of the intentional constitution literally. While these views treat the idea of intentionally created constitutions differently, they all argue that constitutions must be deliberate constructions by the people. Supporters of authorship are obliged to think this because, without intentionality, authorship cannot perform normative work in justifying democratic constitutions.

First, on the originalist view, a group of people really do author the content of constitutions on behalf of the people. The meaning of constitutions can only be understood through this original intent.[61] Originalism is driven by the idea that the purpose of the constitution is to entrench principles that will bind future generations, and those principles are intentionally constructed by a constitution's framers.[62] This is the most literal approach to intentionally creating constitutions, but it is not the only approach.

A more flexible approach to constitutional authorship is the second, 'transtemporal' view, or a third, even more abstract, 'presentist' view. On the second view, authorship is an ongoing dialogue between the original authors of a constitution

[59] 'I think the best case for a written constitution is the right of citizens to participate in the writing of fundamental law. This idea revolves around the metaphor of authorship.' King (n 32) 2.

[60] 'I examine … the impossible, unreliquisable idea of the intentional constitution, of constitution as legislation – or, as it has sometimes been put, as "writing" or "written".' F Michelman, 'Constitutional Authorship by the People' (1999) 74 *Notre Dame Law Review* 1605, 1606.

[61] DJ Goldford, *The American Constitution and the Debate over Originalism* (Cambridge University Press 2005) ix.

[62] ibid x.

and contemporary actors.[63] Constitutions are the result of these cross-generational relationships, as people engage in the ongoing process of determining their collective identity and the principles that should govern them.[64] This approach looks less like authorship of a novel or a poem but retains the intention to create constitutions in a deliberate way. On the third view – the presentist view, advocated by Michelman – constitutions are authored, but they are constantly authored in a contemporary context by an all-considered first-person judgement of its legitimacy and meaning.[65] Each moment of constitutional interpretation is revolutionary.[66] While this view clearly takes a more expansive conception of authorship, Michelman argues that it is impossible under the current paradigm of constitution law and theory to take a non-intentional approach to constitutions.[67]

B. The Strengths and Limitations of Authorship

The idea of authorship is rhetorical, but not only rhetorical. It is often the foundation of the preamble of constitutions, and these preambles have significant legal impact[68] and salience.[69] This intentionality also does normative work. It is the fact that constitutions are intentionally created that is central to their legitimacy.[70] The intentionality of authorship is both its advantage and its fatal flaw. The idea of authorship has legal and normative salience because it is a demanding idea. It suggests that this document is worthy of entrenchment because it was chosen to play that role.

The three different models of authorship outlined above raise different challenges of intentionality. The originalist model is too intentional to be plausible;

[63] As well as those philosophers and theorists on whom the original framers rely. PW Kahn, 'Political Time: Sovereignty and the Transtemporal Community' (2006) 28 *Cardozo Law Review* 259, 260.

[64] ibid 274.

[65] For a helpful analysis of Michelman's work and role in the literature see M Kuo, 'Cutting the Gordian Knot of Legitimacy Theory? An Anatomy of Frank Michelman's Presentist Critique of Constitutional Authorship' (2009) 7 *International Journal of Constitutional Law* 683, 685.

[66] F Michelman, 'Ida's Way: Constructing the Respect-Worthy Governmental System' (2003) 72 *Fordham Law Review* 345, 348.

[67] Further, Michelman argues, this reality is inextricably connected to the idea that there must be two tracks of decision-making in democracies: one for the people and one for politicians. He says: 'In order for popular self-government to exist or be the case, ordinary questions would have be reserved to the people.' F Michelman 'Always under Law' (1995) 345 *Constitutional Commentary* 227, 246.

[68] '"We the people" or its equivalent, appears in so many constitutions, all over the world, that "constitution" as a verbal form defined by that phrase – may be said to have become a literary genre. While it may sound like anachronistic revolutionary rhetoric, or worse, an empty demagogic cliché, "We the People" presents a substantial principle around which to organize discussion of the legitimacy of constitutional democracy.' Kuo (n 65) 683–84.

[69] 'At the centre of constitutional authorship in the vein of constructive reflexivity is the idea of the first person plural "we" which emerges from the process of constitutional deliberation.' ibid 685.

[70] 'We think of good constitutional charters or regimes not as blessings that luckily befall us as strength and health befall [an] animal, but as designed creations by responsible human authors and as laws … whose expressly legislated character is part, at least, of what gives them their claim on our allegiance.' Michelman (n 60) 1606.

conceptually grounding constitutional content in actions which may be profoundly undemocratic.[71] A constitution needs to be justified '*currently*',[72] and this need for a justification that holds today is what pushes theorists towards taking a transtemporal or presentist approach to constitutional authorship.

The difficulty with the transtemporal and presentist approaches to authorship is that the processes of dialogue between generations that they posit are not intentional enough to qualify as authorship. The originalist model is vulnerable to the question of how to connect the intentions of previous generations to a contemporary context. The transtemporal account, on the other hand, is an attempt to address this problem, but it is not clear why a dialogue between generations should be understood as sufficient to establish an intentional approach to constitutions. If it is not intentional, then it is not clear why it should be understood as an act of authorship, and have the normative force that authorship provides. The presentist approach to constitutional authorship is subject to the same worry as the transtemporal view. Further, as Kuo rightly says, this presentist approach still presupposes a transtemporal view of institutions which holds across time,[73] the legitimacy of which he cannot independently justify.

The idea of an intentional constitution creates both challenges and opportunities for constitutions. Opportunities because it offers a foundation of legal and political legitimacy, but it also creates challenges because the weaker the idea of intentionality, the less normative work the idea can do. Trying to address one problem with the idea of authorship, for example taking a transtemporal approach, solves one problem for the metaphor, but creates others. What is required in place of constitutional authorship is a broader understanding of the role for public participation in constitutions.

VI. Participating in the Material Constitution

Letting go of the metaphor of authorship does not entail letting go of the idea that voters should participate in constitution-making processes. It does not follow from the argument that voters are the ultimate source of authority in a democracy that have 'a right … to participate in the writing of fundamental law'.[74] Voters exercise this authority in a range of ways, this chapter has argued, and they exercise this authority all the time through their perceptions of legitimacy. This does not mean the absence of good reasons to include voters in the creation and changing

[71] This is Michelman's worry: that intentional approaches to constitutions like this lead to unpersuasive doctrines such as originalism. ibid 1628.

[72] ibid 1617 (emphasis in original).

[73] '[Michelman] cannot fully account for the commonly chosen, authoritative dispute-settling public institutions whose legitimacy lies at the core of his presentist view of legitimacy, without presupposing a transtemporal view of identity.' Kuo (n 65) 714.

[74] King (n 32) 2.

of constitutional texts. Chapter four outlines many such good reasons, and chapter five shows how to design referendums to maximise voter participation. The point is twofold: (i) that this participation in the creation of a constitutional text is not conceptually required by democracy, (ii) even when such participation occurs, it should be understood as the beginning rather than the end of voters' constitutional roles in a democracy.

Participation in the creation of texts should be understood as the beginning, rather than the end of voters' roles in a democracy, because prioritising the writing of fundamental constitutional law will leave people out rather than include them. The pace is too slow. The most that approaches like King's, where voters have a right to participate in the creation of fundamental law, can offer is generational change.[75] This approach is vulnerable to literalist critiques. By arguing that every person really does have a right to participate in creating a constitution, through representatives in a citizens' assembly that is ratified in a referendum, there is the potential to leave out plenty of participants.[76] More fundamentally, though, King's approach is too limiting. Voters exercise control over their constitutions by what they determine to be legitimate. They constantly let their representatives know what is legitimate through opinion polls, elections, letter-writing, or even by seeking to become representatives themselves and running for office. Constitutions are weaker, not stronger, for carving up decision-making into ordinary tracks for representatives and exceptional tracks for voters.[77]

A spark for constitutional change is often generated by economic hardship.[78] The American revolution was, at least in part, precipitated by the British raising taxes on stamps and then imports;[79] for the French revolution it was the price of

[75] 'The Constitution is something that should belong to each generation in the important sense of authorship. ibid 33.

[76] King's proposal is for: 'a constituent assembly featuring a combination of party members and members of the general public … the constitution should be … entrenched and amendable through an Act of Parliament and a referendum … and come up for complete revision about once a generation'. ibid 35.

[77] King employs the language of Ackerman discussed in section II. He is clear he is drawing on Ackerman's work saying the advantage of popular mandates through '… acts of writing, deciding, and legislating provide the opportunity – a "moment" to borrow Bruce Ackerman's imagery – to confront big constitutional questions and decide.' ibid 12.

[78] 'In and around 1990, citizens took to the streets of the capital cities in some sixteen sub-Saharan African countries to express discontent with economic hardship and political representation to demand civic reforms. In response, between November 1989 and May 1991, at least twenty-one governments adopted significant reform measures to permit greater pluralism and competition within the polity.' M Bratton and N van de Walle, 'Popular Protest and Political Reform in Africa' (1992) 24 *Comparative Politics* 419, 419.

[79] 'The first significant post-war tax imposed on the colonists was the Stamp Act of 1765 … A second attempt at raising revenue followed through a series of acts called the Townshend Acts of 1767. Individually, they were the Revenue Act of 1767, the Indemnity Act, the Commissioners of Customs Act, the Vice Admiralty Court Act, and the New York Restraining Act. The Townshend Acts were a little bit different than the Stamp Act since they were indirect taxes on imports. Since the colonists didn't directly bear the costs, King George III assumed that they would be less offensive to the colonists, but he was wrong.' K Erb, 'On July 4, How Taxes, Tariffs, and Tea Led to American Independence'

flour and salt.[80] The trigger for constitutional reform in Chile was protest over bus fares, which were symbolic of broader systems of inequality.[81] All of these examples are just to underline Goldoni and Wilkinson's points above about the relationship between the formal and material constitutions. Both the text and the practice of a constitution are important, but the material constitution must be lexically prior to the formal one. 'The formal constitution is a feature, an instance *of* the material constitution. As Goldoni and Wilkinson say: '… without political and social traction, a formal constitution remains a "dead letter", a list of wishful auspices, or even a "sham".'[82] Goldoni and Wilkinson are right about this: while the relationship between the formal and the material constitution is iterative, it is the material constitution which gives the formal constitution meaning. This chapter has argued that two-track democracy has prioritised voters' participation in the formal constitution while underplaying their logically prior role in the material constitution.

VII. Conclusion

This chapter challenged the possibility of two-track democracy. It began by defining both two-track democracy and constitutive constitutional questions. Two-track democracy is the claim that democracy requires two types of decision-making: one for 'we the people' and one for politicians. Two-track democracy argues that constitutive constitutional questions must be made by voters. Constitutive constitutional questions are questions that are fundamental because they amend sovereign relations, transfer powers, or concern the allocation of authority in a democracy. These constitutive questions are usually argued to include secession, devolution, or joining supranational bodies, but this chapter rejected the framing of this category of constitutional topics, arguing that it is neither possible nor helpful to distinguish between constitutive and constituted powers. The chapter argued that drawing the distinction between constitutive and constituted powers relies on an approach to (i) constitutions, (ii) democratic authority, and (iii) constitutional authorship that is too narrow.

In challenging the conception of constitutions on which two-track democracy rests, this chapter made two arguments. It first raised four examples of cases which are not ordinarily understood to be constitutive, and so put pressure on

(Forbes 2018), www.forbes.com/sites/kellyphillipserb/2018/07/04/on-july-4-how-taxes-tariffs-tea-led-to-american-independence/?sh=1de42ad7296d, accessed 31 August 2023.

[80] 'More serious disruption occurred in the spring of 1788 when the price of bread began to rise dramatically. Riots demanding lower prices for bread were the traditional reasons for urban disorders in the Ancien Régime because bread constituted the most important part of the diet.' S Neely, *A Concise History of the French Revolution* (Rowman and Littlefield 2007) 72.

[81] As will be discussed in ch 6, section IV.

[82] Goldoni and Wilkinson (n 23) 593.

the distinction between constitutive and constituted powers. These examples were pensions, conscription, suffrage, and civil rights. Second, the chapter argued that the constitution of constitutions is always contested and in flux, and that this is a feature not a bug of democratic constitutions. It challenged the helpfulness of clearly demarcating authority in a constitutional text.

The second part of the chapter challenged the approach to legitimate authority on which two-track democracy relies. It argued that no single conception of legitimate authority, particularly the social contract built on its conception of consent, could provide a basis for legitimate authority in a contemporary, plural democracy. It drew on the work of Green to challenge the idea that legitimate authority could be static or singular. It advocated instead for a piecemeal and plural conception of legitimate authority. On this plural view, there are all kinds of good reasons to hold referendums, but the claim that some decisions cannot be made by representatives is the wrong kind of reason. Some of the right kinds of reasons to hold referendums, following from this piecemeal view of legitimate authority, will be identified in the next chapter.

The third part of the chapter challenged the possibility that constitutions could be created intentionally through acts of authorship. It argued that the idea of authorship is so demanding as to be incoherent, or so weak as to be meaningless. More fundamentally, it challenged this agential approach to constitutions as documents that can be controlled through texts. While such an approach appears emancipatory, authorship confines participation to exceptional constitutional moments. This limits, rather than realises, the principle that voters are the ultimate source of authority in a democracy.

The final part of the chapter offered an alternative account of what it means for voters to participate in constitution-making. It drew on Goldoni and Wilkinson's account of the material constitution to argue that two-track democracy has prioritised voters' participation in the formal, text of a constitution while underplaying their logically prior role in the material, practice of a constitution. The distinction between the formal and the material constitution, as Goldoni and Wilkinson persuasively show, is not sharp. This fluidity is a further reason to let go of the idea of two-track democracy.

Above all, this chapter has sought to show that challenging the idea of two-track democracy does not mean challenging the idea that voters are the ultimate source of authority in a democracy. The claim made here is just that voters' ultimate authority is also exercised through participation in the material, rather than the formal, constitution. This participation in the material constitution is shaped by and shapes participation in the formal constitution, but participation in the material constitution is lexically prior. In this way, letting go of two-track democracy is the logical conclusion of accepting, not abandoning, the claim that voters are the ultimate source of authority in a democracy.

3

Why Referendums on Fundamental Constitutional Matters Cannot be Directly Democratic

I. Introduction

The previous chapter argued that there cannot be two decision-making paths in democracies: one for the people and one for representatives. Even if all the arguments in chapter two failed, however, it would still be the case that referendums on fundamental constitutional questions are not a way for the people to make decisions instead of decisions being made by representatives. This chapter argues that it is not possible descriptively, and not helpful metaphorically, to understand referendums as higher-order processes, ie exceptional processes of democratic law-making.

This chapter has three aims. First, to demonstrate the power and significance of the claim that referendums on fundamental constitutional questions must be exceptional ways to allow people to make decisions instead of representatives. Second, the chapter breaks the claim that 'in referendums on fundamental constitutional questions voters come together to make decisions instead of decisions being made by representatives' into parts and challenges it. The first idea challenged is that in referendums *the people* come together to make decisions instead of decisions being made by representatives, focusing on the possibility and helpfulness of the concept of the people. The second challenge in this chapter is to the claim that the people *come together* in referendums to make decisions. It argues that the electorate is not a kind of group that can come together to decide. The third challenge that the chapter raises is to the nature of decision-making. It argues that the people cannot come together to *make decisions*. A vote in a referendum is better understood as a choice about a decision made by representatives, rather than a decision made from first principles. The fourth section argues that the people cannot come together to make decisions *instead of decisions being made by representatives*, demonstrating how closely the actions of representatives and voters are connected; even when answering fundamental constitutional questions. Third and finally, the chapter explores the question of whether the claim that voters make decisions instead of decisions being made by representatives is literal or metaphorical. Either way, the chapter concludes, the claim cannot succeed.

II. The Case for Referendums as Exceptional

This section demonstrates the close connection between the claims of two-track democracy, developed in the last chapter, and the case for referendums as exceptional exercises in higher-order law-making. The view that referendums can be exercises of higher-order constitutional authorship rests on a view of referendums that goes like this: it is possible in referendums for the people to come together to make decisions instead of decisions being made by representatives. The underlying motivation is the claim, made in different ways by different theorists, that it is necessary to distinguish between the constituent power to create constitutions, and the constituted power of ordinary representatives to act under those constitutions.[1] This idea has become, as Tuck rightly says, the 'basic fact' or 'default constitution of modern states'.[2] This is not to suggest every constitution has been approved through referendums, or requires referendums for fundamental constitutional change. As Blount helpfully demonstrates, however, 40 per cent of the constitutions created since 1975 have been approved through referendums.[3] Clearly, referendums are in widespread use in processes of constitution-making all over the world.

Tuck is also correct about the degree of influence the distinction between constitutive and constituted powers has on the case for referendums. The distinction between constitutive and constituted powers is motivated by the social contract, which as the previous chapter argued is the dominant way of understanding the legitimacy of constitutions.[4] With respect to referendums with constitutive constitutional content, the Lockean version of the social contract is particularly influential.[5] Locke's powerful idea is that representatives cannot properly make

[1] This is argued in ch 2, section II drawing particularly on the version of the distinction drawn by Sieyès. Rubinelli explains Sieyès's view in English in the following way: 'Sieyès's idea of constituent power not only refers to a specific way of conceiving popular power but also underpins a precisely defined political project – one in which popular authority is restrictively defined as an authorising power, exercised in two moments. The first is the moment of foundation. It enshrines the authority of the people to create the political order and express itself in the ex ante authorisation of a constitutional text written by extra-ordinary elected representatives. The second corresponds to moments of ordinary politics and reduces popular power to the elections of ordinary representatives authority to act within the limits set by the constitution.' Lucia Rubinelli, *Constituent Power: A History* (Cambridge University Press 2020) 73. Many other theorists, as ch 2, section II demonstrated, also offer versions of this claim including Locke and Rousseau in JJ Rousseau, *Of the Social Contract and Other Political Writings* [1762] (Penguin 2012) 6; and J Locke, *The Second Treatise of Government* [1689] (CB Macpherson ed, Hackett 1980) §141.

[2] Both the influence of this idea, and its exceptions, are discussed in ch 1, section II. R Tuck, 'Democratic Sovereignty and Democratic Government' in R Bourke and Q Skinner (eds), *Popular Sovereignty in Historical Perspective* (Cambridge University Press 2016) 141.

[3] At least as of his study in 2011: J Blount, 'Participation in Constitutional Design' in T Ginsburg and R Dixon (eds), *Comparative Constitutional Law* (Edward Elgar 2011) 37.

[4] As Loughlin says, today's constitutions are usually understood to be contracts: 'Constitutions today are generally conceived as contracts drawn up by "the people" to establish and limit the powers of governing institutions.' M Loughlin, *The Foundations of Public Law* (Oxford University Press 2010) 275.

[5] Rousseauean arguments tend to make a case that referendums are necessary for all questions and strong democracy. The claim is made because once the people are represented, they are no longer free,

some decisions, and so they must instead be made by the people directly and together. Locke says: '[T]he *legislative cannot transfer the power of making laws* to any other hands: for it being but a delegated power from the people, they who have it cannot pass it over to others.'[6] This division of labour is necessary, Locke says, because '[t]he power of the legislative, being derived from the people by a positive voluntary grant and institution, can be no other than what that positive grant conveyed'.[7]

On Locke's view, the positive voluntary grant of authority from the people is a 'trust that cannot be delegated'.[8] The power of this idea is clear and straightforward.[9] The people are the ultimate source of authority in a democracy. The only way for the people to be the ultimate authority in a democracy is to control the location of authority. Representatives cannot make decisions about the allocation and location of this authority, and this authority cannot be transferred on, because that would make the acts of representatives *ultra vires*. Representatives never had the authority to make fundamental constitutional decisions because these decisions must rest in the people.

The significance of two-track democracy for understanding referendums on constitutional questions, is that referendums are thought to be a way for the people to make decisions instead of the representatives. Claims that referendums can play this role are argued to follow inexorably from Locke's argument about representatives. Bogdanor makes a case for constitutional referendums in explicitly Lockean terms, saying the case for referendums follows naturally from Lockean principles of liberal constitutionalism. Bogdanor says:

> The electorate, it might be said, entrust their MPs as agents with legislative power; but they give them no authority to transfer this power. Such authority, it is natural to suggest, can be obtained only through a specific mandate, that is, a referendum. The idea that power is entrusted to the nation's representatives only for specific purposes reflects one of the central principles of liberal constitutionalism and has its origins in Locke. 'The Legislature' he claims 'can not transfer the power of making laws to any other hands. For it being but a delegated power from the People, they who have it cannot pass it to others.'[10]

as in B Barber, *Strong Democracy: Participatory Politics for a New Age* (University of California Press 1984) 261.

[6] Locke (n 1) 141 (emphasis in original).

[7] ibid.

[8] The influence of this idea may be seen in practice in, for example, the arguments of the Berkshire Constitutionalists who Lenowitz argued 'generated their demand for popularly created constitutions by combining social contractualism with a new understanding of constitutions … the Constitutionalists isolated constituent power in the authorization process and defined the right to ratify as inalienable.' J Lenowitz, '"A Trust That Cannot Be Delegated": The Intention of Ratification Referenda' (2015) 109 *American Political Science Review* 803, 804.

[9] '[The Berkshire Constitutionalists] … espoused an early theory of constituent power, the idea that only the people have the unique moral ability to make and unmake the set of fundamental laws that undergird their state.' ibid 810.

[10] V Bogdanor, *The People and the Party System* (Cambridge University Press 1981) 76.

Bogdanor goes on to conclude that Locke's principles of authority establish 'a clear and principled justification for requiring a referendum to be called whenever it is proposed to transfer the powers of Parliament'.[11] Similarly, Galligan invokes Locke directly in making a case for constitutional referendums. Like Bogdanor, he thinks the case for constitutional referendums is a 'natural extension' of Locke's arguments. Galligan says:

> According to the early champion of liberal politics, John Locke, only a government that has the consent of the governed is legitimate. While Locke did not advocate popular referendums and was no democrat, his theory of legitimate government is based squarely on the consent of those governed, and in a constitutional democracy, the appropriate mechanism for consent, by way of extending Locke, is the constitutional referendum.[12]

It follows that, on Galligan's view, referendums are ways that the people come together to express their sovereignty. He says that in referendums the people 'express their democratic sovereignty through consent and in so doing they constitute themselves as the sovereign body that makes authoritative decisions about their system of government'.[13] Tierney does not draw explicitly on Locke.[14] Tierney does, however, take an analogous view to Galligan and Bogdanor of referendums as devices of constitutional amendment and authorship. Tierney is clear, however, that he is only talking about constitutive constitutional referendums. He distinguishes between ordinary and constitutional referendums saying:

> At the first-order level of ordinary legislation, politicians and political institutions represent the people functionally in terms of will-formation and expression. And at the constitutional level … the institutions of the constitution come to represent the people in acts of will-formation and expression when the constitution is amended by institutions in place of and in the name of the people.[15]

This passage from Tierney distinguishing between ordinary and higher-order law-making is helpful and important because it demonstrates the connections between three ideas. These ideas are thought to flow logically and necessarily from each other. These three ideas are, first, that democracy requires two decision-making paths: one for the people and one for politicians. Second, that referendums are decision-making exercises for the people. Third, that when voters make these kinds of higher-order decisions they must be exercises in direct democracy. It is the aim of this chapter to challenge every move in this argument.

[11] ibid 76–77.

[12] B Galligan, 'Amending Constitutions Through the Referendum Device' in M Mendelsohn and A Parkin (eds), *Referendum Democracy: Citizens, Elites, and Deliberation in Referendum Campaigns* (Palgrave 2001) 111.

[13] ibid 109.

[14] Although he does mention Locke's influence on these matters generally: S Tierney, 'Constitutional Referendums: A Theoretical Enquiry' (2009) 72 *Modern Law Review* 360, 369.

[15] ibid 367.

In connecting the case for two-track democracy and the case for referendums as acts of higher-order law-making, there is one more important link: the idea of referendums as acts of democratic consent. Tierney says: 'the one job that a referendum can do that no other device can is to provide the legitimacy that comes with a mass act of consent'[16] and that:

> We have observed that one way to understand the role of referendums is to envisage them as a means by which representation is itself supplanted, returning direct power to the people; in order words as some kind of reversal of the original act of transference, or at least a temporary return of power to the people.[17]

Here, Tierney is not arguing that referendums literally displace representatives. He is rather making the case for normatively understanding referendums as providing a higher-level of legitimacy by returning decisions back to voters. Similarly, Galligan thinks that constitutional referendums are closely connected to the idea of democratic consent. Galligan says that constitutional referendums are the 'appropriate mechanism for consent'.[18] Bogdanor uses a more Lockean phrase, saying that constitutional referendums '[transfer] powers' to parliament.[19] Lenowitz also draws on Locke to agree that 'only the direct consent of the majority can give life to a constitution'.[20] While consent is widely understood to be significant, as the previous chapter argued it is nevertheless a misleading way to think about legitimate authority. This chapter builds on the last to offer a further reason why consent is such an unpersuasive foundation for the social contract. Referendums are not democratic processes whereby the people, rather than representatives, can come together to make decisions and amend the social contract. If referendums cannot play this role, it is difficult to imagine what can. The remainder of this chapter challenges every part of the idea that, in referendums on fundamental constitutional issues, the people come together to make decisions instead of decisions being made by representatives.

III. *The People* Coming Together to Make Decisions Instead of Decisions Being Made by Representatives

The necessity for referendums on questions of constitutive constitutional content is thought to follow logically from the idea that 'the people' is a 'logical pre-requisite

[16] S Tierney, *Constitutional Referendums: The Theory and Practice of Republican Deliberation* (Oxford University Press 2012) 55.

[17] Tierney (n 14) 367.

[18] Galligan (n 12) 110.

[19] Bogdanor (n 10) 77.

[20] Lenowitz (n 8) 805. Moreover, Lenowitz demonstrates how the idea of referendums as consent has 'widespread acceptance'. He describes this consent-based rationale for constitutional referendums as now 'ubiquitous'. ibid 814.

for democracy'.[21] This first section challenges the possibility of 'the people'. 'The people' is not only a powerful theoretical idea, but it has legal salience too. It is legal insofar as serves as the foundation[22] of the constitutions of, to name just a few examples, the United States,[23] France,[24] and Germany,[25] and multiple constitutional instruments in the United Kingdom.[26] The difficulty both in theory and in practice with the idea of 'the people' is that for both its strongest proponents like Canovan,[27] and the sharpest sceptics like Weale,[28] it is a myth. 'The people' may or not be a democratic ideal: for Canovan, it is[29] and for Weale, it is not,[30] but either way, the idea is a 'hazy'[31] and a 'many-sided political project'.[32] It causes problems, especially for referendums, because on the view of referendums as higher-order law-making, they are a manifestation of the exercise of popular sovereignty. The problems with the myth of 'the people' are many and familiar. Who counts as part of 'the people'?[33] How, or why should the electorate be treated as a proxy for the members of a political community as a whole? Can 'the people' exist statically or is this constantly in flux?[34]

[21] Tierney (n 14) 376.

[22] While references to 'the people' are often made in constitutional preambles, Orgad shows that these are increasingly influencing questions of constitutional interpretation and design. L Orgad, 'The Preamble in Constitutional Interpretation' (2010) 8 *International Journal of Constitutional Law* 714, 714.

[23] The American constitution begins, for example: 'We the People of the United States, in Order to form a more perfect Union, establish Justice, insure domestic Tranquility, provide for the common defence, promote the general Welfare, and secure the Blessings of Liberty to ourselves and our Posterity, do ordain and establish this Constitution for the United States of America.' Preamble, Constitution of the United States, 1788 (spelling reflects original).

[24] 'The French people solemnly proclaim their attachment to the Rights of Man and the principles of national sovereignty as defined by the Declaration of 1789, confirmed and complemented by the Preamble to the Constitution of 1946, and to the rights and duties as defined in the Charter for the Environment of 2004.' Preamble, Constitution of France, 2008.

[25] 'Conscious of their responsibility before God and man, Inspired by the determination to promote world peace as an equal partner in a united Europe, the German people, in the exercise of their constituent power, have adopted this Basic Law.' Preamble, German Basic Law, 1949.

[26] '... It is declared that the Scottish Parliament and the Scottish Government are not to be abolished except on the basis of a decision of the people of Scotland voting in a referendum.' Scotland Act 2016, s 63A(3). '... It is declared that the Assembly and the Welsh Government are not to be abolished except on the basis of a decision of the people of Wales voting in a referendum.' Wales Act 2017, s 1(3).

[27] 'The challenge still facing democrats is to devise institutions for representing the people-as-population that live up to the expectations generated by "the People" as myth.' M Canovan, 'The People' in J Dryzek, B Honig, and A Phillips (eds), *The Oxford Handbook of Political Theory* (Oxford University Press 2008) 359.

[28] A Weale, *The Will of the People: A Modern Myth* (Polity 2018) 3.

[29] Canovan (n 27) 352.

[30] Weale (n 28) xi.

[31] Canovan (n 27) 352.

[32] ibid.

[33] 'We are ... faced with the problem of boundaries: how do we delimit the group within which, for purposes of making particular decisions, votes are to be counted and majority preference identified?' F Whelan, 'Prologue: Democratic Theory and the Boundary Problem' (1983) 25 *Nomos* 13, 14.

[34] 'The people as process is a source of democratic legitimacy that moors state institutions but is compatible with change, surprise, and innovation. It can both sustain democratic institutions and accommodate people's indeterminacy because it does not seek a predetermined goal.' P Espejo,

Assume for sake of argument though, that the idea of 'the people' can get off the ground. The argument that referendums with constitutive constitutional content are exceptional does not inexorably follow from this idea. It is misleading to say that the idea of 'the people' is a logical perquisite for democracy. Not all theories of democracy rely on 'the people' in its collective capacity, with liberalism focusing on the 'many' instead.[35] The idea of the 'many' is sufficient for liberal theories of democracy where popular sovereignty can be demonstrated as control of office-holders.[36] Finally, as a normative matter, the idea of 'the people' can be a homogenising device, rounding down the edges of reasonable pluralism.[37] To sum up: it is not clear that the people as a collective 'we' is a necessary starting point for thinking about legitimate democratic authority or referendums. Even if 'the people' was a coherent and helpful democratic myth, however, it would not be a helpful one on which to base a theory of constitutive constitutional referendums. Referendums are not the kind of democratic process by which a people can come together to make decisions.

IV. The People *Coming Together* to Make Decisions Instead of Decisions Being Made by Representatives

Even if there were a people, it is not clear that it is right to think of the people as *collectively* intending to decide through a referendum. There are a wide range of models of collective intentionality, but the core condition that must be satisfied is that participants must have all directed their minds towards a particular end. The kinds of collective intentionality that philosophers of action usually focus on are on a small scale, like playing for a sports team or singing a duet, for example. Theories of collective intentionality do not lend themselves to massively shared agency.[38]

The Time of Popular Sovereignty: Process and the Democratic State (Pennsylvania State University Press 2011) 13.

[35] McCormick raises these possibilities to challenge Carl Schmitt's claim that a unified people is a conceptual necessity for democracy in J McCormick, 'Identifying or Exploiting the Paradoxes of Constitutional Democracy? An Introduction to Carl Schmitt's Legality and Legitimacy', *Legality and Legitimacy* (Duke University Press 2004) xxxii.

[36] 'Popular sovereignty as the multitude's power to control office-holders is a democratic achievement.' M Lane, 'Popular Sovereignty as Control of Office-Holders: Aristotle on Greek Democracy' in R Bourke and Q Skinner (eds), *Popular Sovereignty in Historical Perspective* (Cambridge University Press 2016) 72. Although this will not be enough for some who take liberalism to be a weak form of democracy. One particularly compelling version of this concern is expressed in A Somek and M Wilkinson, 'Unpopular Sovereignty' (2020) 83 *Modern Law Review* 955. The response to this concern is offered as part of the case for understanding referendums as representative democracy in ch 5, section IV.B.

[37] Tierney raises this concern as a possibility, but he thinks that deliberative democracy is a way to overcome this risk saying: 'A strong case for referendums might be made … but it is here that we see the significant risk of hegemony that they entail.' Tierney (n 14) 374.

[38] 'The world we have gained … is characterised by the enormous scale of social life … and yet, philosophy has no viable theory for analysing these ubiquitous activities.' S Shapiro, 'Massively Shared

Shapiro offers two reasons why collective intentionality has been construed too narrowly to accommodate massively shared agency. First, in groups characterised by collective intentionality, participants are highly committed, and this does not hold for massively shared agency.[39] Second, massively shared agency tends to be characterised by central, powerful authorities to organise behaviour, and this does not lend itself to collective intentionality either.[40] Shapiro nevertheless thinks that these obstacles can be overcome and that a theory of massively shared agency is possible. His approach argues that authorities can establish shared plans through which people participate on a massive scale, but that this process cannot look like the kind of hyper-committed collective intentionality possible in small groups. He says that this is possible if everyone accepts that they are part of a plan, and 'do not interfere with others playing their part'.[41] Shapiro's account is useful because it demonstrates the possible paths forward in thinking about voting and massively shared agency. To maintain that voters do collectively intend the process to 'succeed', or to take Shapiro's more diffuse approach and to say it is enough for voters to play their part and to not interfere with others playing their part too. This chapter will argue that in the context of voting in a referendum, neither approach can succeed. Consequently, it is misleading to think of the people as coming together to decide.

Kutz is an example of the theorist who takes the first, and more demanding, approach to massively shared agency. He maintains that voting is a fundamentally collective endeavour. He argues that voting is fundamentally a joint exercise, and that individual voting is only reasonable when voting is understood collectively.[42] Is Kutz right about this? Is voting an effort to figure out, together, what we ought to do? Accept for sake of argument that everyone does understand themselves as part of a 'we' and are not alienated or excluded from their political system. Must that be all voters' intentions when they vote? Is voting fundamentally a joint exercise? Well, it cannot be that voters intend a particular *outcome*. When deciding to participate in the voting process, it cannot merely be that they intend for the proposition they support to win. If this were the case, then they would not have the requisite 'we' intention if the proposition they support fails. The intention must be something else. The most popular idea is something like: voters intend to participate in the process of deciding what we ought to do. Lots of people hold this view. Steinberger,[43] for instance, says that when voting, 'participation itself is

Agency' in M Vargas and G Yaffe (eds), *Rational and Social Agency: The Philosophy of Michael Bratman* (Oxford University Press 2014) 258.

[39] ibid 259.

[40] 'Without some centralised control over behaviour, the odds that many people will organise themselves towards the same objective and resolve their conflicts in an efficient manner is apt to be low.' ibid.

[41] ibid 278–88.

[42] Voting, for Kutz, is an attempt to work out a collective judgment of what we together ought to do. C Kutz, 'The Collective Work of Citizenship' (2002) 8 *Legal Theory* 471, 491.

[43] Steinberger is not alone in making this claim. Plamenatz says something similar, arguing: 'Surely, to put a cross against the name Smith on a ballot paper at an election is to express the wish that Smith

a consent-constituting activity'.[44] He thinks this because voting in an election is like sitting down at a poker table, and sitting down at the table 'indicates not only active acceptance of winnings, should I win, but also an active acceptance of losses should I lose'.[45]

Even if Steinberger is right and every citizen were engaged in the voting process as if they were sitting down at a poker table, which is very doubtful, it would remain the case that the strong version of voting as massively shared agency cannot succeed. This view cannot succeed because it is necessary to distinguish between the *act* of voting and the *intentions* voters have when voting. While it is right to say that the act of voting is an act of participation, and voting is an act that it only makes sense for groups to do, the whole point of voting is that voters may vote for any reason or no reason at all. Voters certainly do not need to accept the legitimacy of a system to participate. They may believe the system to be rigged, or that their vote will not change the end result. They may think, for instance, that the entire method of 'first past the post' representation is flawed; concluding that their vote for an unpopular option will make no difference. Voters may well believe that the question asked is itself fundamentally flawed and so there is no way for the process to succeed.

Even if every person did intend to participate in collective decision-making, however, it would still make no difference. Intentions in voting are not like intentions when playing cards or participating in duets. Voting is an aggregative process. The whole point of voting is to separate the vote from the voter's intentions; every vote looks the same when it is counted. Rather than thinking of all voters as players in one big orchestra, the better view is that casting a vote is like running a marathon. The *act* of the marathon is shared – everyone runs 42.2 km – but they do it in their way, at their own pace, potentially even at very different times and places. Voters' intentions remain distinct when voting, even if the act is shared.

Further, sometimes voters may want to undermine shared plans. This is entirely defensible. They may cast protest votes, destroy their ballots, or write-in candidates on the ballot paper. While these cases are marginal in numbers, they demonstrate something important about the disaggregated nature of voting. Voters can intend whatever they want, or nothing at all – that is their prerogative. So, both the small and large-scale accounts of collective intentionality do not lend themselves to the act of voting in a referendum.

To wrap up this section: while the idea of voting as a collective constitutive act is popular, it is not the only one on the table. There is a tradition running back to

should hold the office for which he is a candidate? But the voter may not want Smith to hold the office; he might think that Smith has no chance of getting elected and may vote for him only for the sake of preventing the election of Brown. Yet, if Smith were in fact elected, it would be odd to say of anyone who had voted for him that he did not consent to him holding office.' J Plamenatz, *Consent, Freedom and Political Obligation* (2nd edn, Oxford University Press 1968) 168.

[44] PJ Steinberger, *The Idea of the State* (Cambridge University Press 2004) 219.

[45] ibid.

Aristotle in which popular sovereignty consists of control over office-holders.[46] This kind of approach continues to be reflected in liberal approaches to voting today. Gardner takes this view, for example, in responding to Kutz. Gardner argues that when voters are thinking about the actions and intentions of others it is a sign not that democracy is succeeding but rather that it is failing.[47] Gardner says that voters act like limits on the actions of representatives the way cogs do in a machine:

> Voters, it seems to me, are best regarded as individual petty bureaucrats who each play an individual role as a tiny individual cog in a huge political machine, each serving as a distinct check and balance on the overmightiness of other larger cogs (such as the legislature and the executive.)[48]

What is helpful about Gardner's view is how it can be true that voting is both an interconnected set of acts, like cogs in the machine, and also a process whereby individual votes are distinct from each other. The tradition of voting as limits on the actions of representatives is advocated by Schumpeter[49] and Riker.[50] In sum: while it is right to say that voting as a physical act connects voters on a massive scale, it certainly does not necessarily follow that voting is an act of collective intentionality.

V. The People Coming Together to *Make Decisions* Instead of Decisions Being Made by Representatives

What is a decision? The literature stresses several connected features. To decide is to form an intention as a result of deliberation.[51] It is widely held that deliberation is a necessary condition for decision-making.[52] Part of the power of a decision is

[46] Lane (n 36) 72.

[47] 'When democracy is faring well, mutual voter ignorance and the consequent impossibility of adjusting one's intentions to other people's intentions (let alone having *joint* intentions) are a strength of the system not a weakness … The importance of there being a large number of cogs with widely different views and attitudes is sufficient to justify the existence of a social rule … that all are to vote. It is also a reason for each voter to vote irrespective of whether he or she is aware of the case for its existence. Conformity to the rule works as an invisible hand mechanism.' J Gardner, 'Reasons for Teamwork' (2002) 8 *Legal Theory* 495, 509.

[48] ibid 509.

[49] J Schumpeter, *Capitalism, Socialism, and Democracy* (George Allen & Unwin Ltd 1943) 241.

[50] Riker explicitly calls this the liberal view. W Riker, *Liberalism Against Populism* (Freeman and Company 1982) 11.

[51] This is a minimal conception of what it means to decide, it is not meant to be exhaustive. The book adopts this approach to decision-making because I hope it is acceptable both to those who think that voting is an instance of voters acting together, and those who are doubtful about that proposition. This account of decisions as reasons rightly places the crux of disagreement at the nature of deliberation. This is the most productive point of disagreement in debating the significance of referendums on fundamental constitutional questions.

[52] R Weatherford, 'Choosing and Deciding' in T Honderich (ed), *The Oxford Companion to Philosophy* (2nd edn, Oxford University Press 2005). PH Nowell-Smith, 'Choosing, Deciding and Doing' (1958) 18 *Analysis* 63.

in its finality – in its power to stop deliberation and for decision-makers to take action.[53] Finality is what gives decisions their normative and practical force, so if the purpose of a decision is to stop deliberation and act, it makes sense that deliberation would be a pre-requisite for decision-making. So, to determine whether votes in referendums are instances of collective decision-making, it is necessary to ask whether and how deliberation occurs before the act of voting in a referendum. For the decision to be collective, the underlying deliberation must be collective.

The first problem that is encountered in establishing the relationship between voting and deliberation is the direction of travel. There is a close relationship between deliberation and voting, both on an individual and a collective level. But it works both ways. As Mackie argues, 'voting shapes deliberation and deliberation shapes voting'.[54] There is also, he argues, deep confusion about the relationship between deliberation, decision, and voting, and they are often – wrongly – treated synonymously.[55] Instead, they are logically independent of each other.[56] Deliberation is, in its broadest form, 'bringing to mind ideas or images meant to have some rational relation to the topic being considered, in the service of reaching a conclusion about what to think or do'.[57] The difficulty is that the kind of deliberation possible on a small scale is not possible on a large scale; this is the problem of large numbers. Tierney helpfully explains the problem of large numbers for deliberation saying:

> The kind of discursive deliberation that can take place within a small group is not possible, at least not in the same way, at the macro level. But still, there is the possibility that people can be encouraged to reflect on the issues, to learn more about them, and then to engage in a more attenuated national process of communicative deliberation.[58]

Tierney is almost completely right here. He is right that the kind of deliberation that takes place on a small and local scale is different from debates at a national level. Where Tierney is not quite right is in arguing that 'reflection on the issues' or an 'attenuated national process of communicative deliberation' should count as deliberation. While such processes of reflection and debate are significant in understanding the role and significance of referendums, they are not enough to count as deliberation for purposes of making a decision.

It may well be that voters individually deliberate before they cast their ballots, but this is not necessarily true. As seen above, it is the prerogative of voters to vote

[53] Although note that Chambers says that this finality has the potential to undermine deliberation too if the stakes are too high. S Chambers, 'Constitutional Referendums and Democratic Deliberation' in M Mendelsohn and A Parkin (eds), *Referendum Democracy: Citizens, Elites, and Deliberation in Referendum Campaigns* (Palgrave 2001) 251.

[54] G Mackie, 'Deliberation and Voting Entwined' in A Bächtiger and others (eds), *The Oxford Handbook of Deliberative Democracy* (Oxford University Press 2018) 233.

[55] ibid 224.

[56] ibid 229.

[57] N Arpaly and T Schroeder, 'Deliberation and Acting for Reasons' (2012) 121 *Philosophical Review* 209, 212.

[58] Tierney (n 16) 213.

for any reason or no reason at all. Even if each individual act of voting were an act of deliberation, however, it would not follow that adding up all these individual instances of deliberation would amount to collective deliberation. And if deliberation exists, it precedes a series of individual actions that are aggregated. Adding up millions of instances of deliberation does not amount to a collective decision.

A distinction may help make this idea clear: if voters individually deliberate in a referendum, each vote may count as a decision. When they debate and discuss with others how they will vote, however, that deliberation is *about* a decision; it is not deliberation which will *make* a decision. Deliberative democrats rightly stress the importance of deliberative, participatory processes in democracy for precisely this point. Deliberative democrats are right to argue that voting cannot be a deliberative act.[59] Deliberative democrats think this because they rightly argue that voting is an aggregative activity. To say voting is an aggregative activity is to say that votes are deliberatively decoupled from intentions. In the final, anonymous tally, a voter's intention and ballot come apart. This decoupling of intentions and votes is essential to understanding why referendums cannot be processes of collective decision-making.

Not all intentional acts require deliberation in the way decisions do. There are other candidates for what kind of process voting is. One possibility is that a vote in a referendum is a choice. The idea of choice is compatible with the aggregative nature of voting. Raz, Oldenquist, and Meiland all think that there is a difference between decisions and other intentional acts such choices, and they mostly agree on what the difference is. Some decisions are choices; not all choices are decisions. Choices are a less demanding sort of activities that do not necessarily require deliberation. Choices may involve deliberation, but they do not rely on deliberation in the way that decisions do. Raz and Oldenquist – in different ways – use the example of Jones and the martini to illustrate the difference between decisions and choices.

> If Jones is offered a tray of different kinds of drinks and takes a martini it would be correct to say that he chose the martini but not that he decided to take the martini. If Jones decided to take the martini, then we expect that prior to the action there was deliberation, or that at least preference and resolution, and *that between the time he decided and the time reacted we could correctly say that he intended to take the martini.*[60]

The example of Jones and the martini draws out some of the differences between decisions and choices. The same is true of voting. A voter may well have deliberated and decided to vote for the 'Wolf in Sheep's Clothing' party: but not necessarily. Voters need not have deliberated and decided how to vote. They might have flipped

[59] Mackie (n 54) 218.

[60] J Raz, 'Reasons for Action, Decisions and Norms' (1975) 84 *Mind* 481 (emphasis in original); Oldenquist similarly argues 'in the preceding example Jones did not *decide* to take a martini because decision is more closely tied to deliberation and intention than is choice'. A Oldenquist, 'Choosing, Deciding, and Doing' in P Edwards (ed), *The Encyclopedia of Philosophy* (Collier-MacMillan 1967) 98.

a coin; they might have chosen randomly. It is the prerogative of voters in democracies that they can decide for any reason they like or no reason at all. If I do decide to vote for a particular candidate or particular party, though, I make that decision individually. How will *I* vote; in which box will *I* place an X? Even if I think I have a duty to vote in the best interests of the country, the decision I reach about how to vote is my decision about what I think is best. It is not what my community or family think is best for everyone: although those decisions might overlap, that is not what my choice is when I vote myself. Whatever other processes are happening in a democracy, no matter how deliberative, the act of voting is itself a choice that is distinct from those processes. Again: those processes may well involve deliberation *about* a decision, but this is not deliberation to *make* a decision.

The distinction between choices and decisions better reflects the options and opportunities voters had to deliberate when they vote. When I vote, I cannot propose the candidate I wish were on the ballot or answer the referendum question I think ought to have been asked. I am not deliberating from first principles; I am making a choice given the options available to me. These choices are some of the most important actions a person can take. To label these as choices is not to argue against their significance. To call votes choices is to take seriously the limitations of the act of voting, and the impossibility of them being directly democratic processes that bypass representatives.[61]

This section has argued that the decision to hold a referendum requires deliberation. This deliberation can be performed by a range of bodies such as citizens' assemblies, legislatures, the executive, or electoral commissions. This prior triggering action by representatives is not a choice,[62] it is a decision requiring intention and deliberation about what to do. Deliberation underlines the logical necessity of representatives for the process of voting in referendums, and consequently, the impossibility of higher-order law-making by the people directly that is distinct from actions by representatives. Representatives are a necessary and logical prerequisite in all kinds of practical and conceptual ways, as the next section will demonstrate.

VI. The People Coming Together to Make Decisions *Instead* of Decisions Being Made by Representatives

The idea that in referendums the people are coming together to make decisions instead of decisions being made by representatives is part of the claim that

[61] Lenowitz also concludes that voting in referendums are best understood as choice, but he concludes that such choices cannot be meaningful. J Lenowitz, *Constitutional Ratification Without Reason* (Oxford University Press 2022) ch 6.

[62] Or not *only* a choice. It might be a choice in jurisdictions where referendums are triggered automatically when constitutional change is proposed.

referendums are directly democratic. Sometimes direct and representative democracy are placed on a spectrum,[63] Moreover, sometimes they are put in different categories altogether.[64] Sometimes a combination of both approaches is taken. Schiller and Setälä, for instance, argue that both direct and democracy are mediated, but that a distinction can be drawn between these two different types of mediation.[65] The subtlest approach is that taken by Uleri, who argues that referendums are reliant on representatives,[66] but, nevertheless, that processes of direct and representative democracy can be 'analytically and empirically distinguished'.[67] This section, in particular, and this book overall, will argue that processes of representative democracy cannot be distinguished either empirically or conceptually from 'direct democracy'. *Pace* Schiller and Setälä, the types of mediating processes in representative democracy cannot be distinguished from those of direct democracy. Empirically, they cannot be distinguished because the process of aggregating political preferences both in legislation and referendums by representatives are fundamentally the same. Further, in both the processes of elections and referendums, voters are voting for representatives and giving guidance to representatives. All this holds, both descriptively and normatively, even for referendums on the most fundamental constitutional questions.

While it is not precisely clear what mediation is, it must in some way, refer to the aggregation of preferences. The label 'direct democracy' is used to identify some closer connection between voters and outcomes than is possible in practices of representative democracy. The connection may be because the content and (or) form of preference aggregation are different. The case for the use of the label 'direct democracy' relies on what is on the ballot. The *prima facie* appeal of this argument is straightforward. There does initially seem to be something narrower or more specific shown on the ballot in a referendum as opposed to an election. The aim of this chapter is not to contest this; it is instead to argue that this specificity should not be taken to indicate that referendums do not involve

[63] 'Participation and representation not as two alternative forms of democracy but on a continuum.' N Urbinati, 'Representation as Advocacy: A Study of Democratic Deliberation' (2000) 28 *Political Theory* 758, 759.

[64] 'Therefore even the categorisation of legislative referendums as an instance of direct democracy as opposed to representative democracy is perhaps something of an oversimplification. In playing a role within a broader representative system of government where the authority of these referendums is clearly subsidiary to those constitutional institutions which retain the competence to create and change hierarchical rules, they should perhaps more accurately be portrayed as part of being part of that representative system, since the effect given to the outcomes they produce is ultimately subject to the representative competence of constitutional institutions, most obviously legislatures, but also courts.' Tierney (n 14) 364.

[65] 'It is possible to make a distinction between the mediation of people's opinions in decision-making through the institutions and organisations of representative democracy on the one hand and through the institutions of direct democracy on the other.' T Schiller and M Setälä, *Referendums and Representative Democracy: Responsiveness, Accountability, and Deliberation* (Routledge 2009) 4.

[66] 'The referendums phenomenon considered as a decision-making process is not an autonomous and independent phenomenon.' P Uleri, 'Introduction' in M Gallagher and P Uleri (eds), *Referendums in Europe* (Macmillan 1996) 2.

[67] 'The two sets of decisional mechanisms and processes can be analytically and empirically distinguished.' ibid 2.

the mediation of preferences through representatives. There are a range of ways in which the term mediation may be used, and the actual process of mediation takes several forms. Barreyro identifies a range of these when she helpfully asks: 'Why are direct democratic institutions called *direct* if they, as law-making mechanisms are mediated by elites, political parties, and mass media, and shaped by electoral law?'[68] Consider now the significance of some of these actors as mediating forces in referendums. They demonstrate that referendums should not be described as unmediated democratic exercises in practice for three reasons. First, the role of elites and representatives in shaping and aggregating political will. Second, what voters cast their ballots for is mediated in a strong sense by what is on the ballot. Third, the broader representative context which is required for referendums to operate at all. This broader representative context can never be decoupled from the referendum process itself, and so the label 'unmediated' or 'direct' is misleading and unhelpful.

A. Referendums as Mediated by Representatives

A perennial worry about referendums is that they are merely tools to be manipulated by elites. Walker's study of referendums, for instance, argues that referendums are tools used by elites to achieve their goals,[69] Moreover, referendums are particularly useful political tools for executives to use against legislatures.[70] Worries about representatives are expressed by Mendelsohn and Parkin too, who also think that referendums are tools used by elites to achieve their agendas.[71] Even those like Tierney who are more optimistic about the use of referendums are clear that elites play an essential role in the agenda-setting stage of referendums.[72] There is a debate in the social scientific literature, for example, about whether voters are more likely to vote for the status quo; so it matters what is being voted 'for' or 'against'.[73] The role of elites plays out differently depending on the role that referendums

[68] Her answer to this question is that the debate between representative and direct democracy is between two different fictions: the people in their collective capacity and representatives acting on behalf of the community. M Barreyro, '"Direct Democratic Institutions": Direct and Democratic' (2019) 10 *Jurisprudence* 313, 315 (emphasis in original).

[69] 'Referendums are part of a bargaining process between elites who have their basis of power in different institutional settings.' M Walker, *The Strategic Use of Referendums: Power, Legitimacy, and Democracy* (Springer 2003) 3.

[70] 'Executives can better position themselves than legislatures along a policy spectrum to win when introducing referendums.' ibid 3.

[71] M Mendelsohn and A Parkin, 'Introduction', *Referendum Democracy: Citizens, Elites and Deliberation in Referendum Campaigns* (Palgrave Macmillan 2001) 3.

[72] 'This … requires that the referendum be broken down into a number of process components: the initiation stage begins the process, but we must also consider a second agenda-setting stage, which encompasses question-formation and process planning and including timing issues; and, third, the campaign process itself, embracing the campaign rules, provision of information to voters, funding and expenditure rules etc.' Tierney (n 16) 99.

[73] S Fisher and A Renwick, 'Do People Tend to Vote against Change in Referendums?' *The Constitution Unit* (22 June 2016), constitution-unit.com/2016/06/22/do-people-tend-to-vote-against-change-in-referendums, accessed 1 November 2019.

perform in a system of constitutional and policy change. In a system where referendums are automatically used to approve constitutional reforms, representatives have a significant impact on the content of what is voted on.[74] In *ad hoc* systems such as the United Kingdom,[75] representatives may abuse referendums. This does not mean mediation or intervention by representatives in the referendum process is necessarily sinister. As Tierney argues, the better view is that representatives simply, necessarily shape the agenda-setting process.[76] Agenda-setting is unavoidable. The voting stage of the referendum process offers voters a limited number of options; the decisions underlying referendums dictate those options. This mediation process is central to understanding how a referendum operates in practice. Further, the quality of this underlying mediation process – the question of whether proposals are helpful or divisive, for example – sets them up for success. This essential role for representatives is the first reason to challenge the label of referendums as 'unmediated'. It is misleading to use 'narrow' or 'specific' as synonymous with 'unmediated' because to do so places representatives on the periphery of the process. This agenda-setting role for representatives in referendums does not disappear just because referendums are considering fundamental constitutional questions. Indeed, in those circumstances where outcomes will be deeply entrenched, understanding the way that representatives shape the choices that voters are offered may be even more important.

B. Ballots as Mediators of Political Will

Representatives determine both the form and the content of preference aggregation in referendums. Part of the distinction drawn between referendums and elections is that referendums are votes for policies and elections are votes for representatives. Consequently, referendums are not mediated by representatives, and elections are. This distinction is unhelpful. Votes in referendums lend credibility to representatives, and representatives are elected on the basis of policies. Again, social scientific literature shows that referendum campaigns are often shaped by whether voters want to support or send a message to certain political parties or elected officials.[77] Successful campaigns inevitably give legitimacy to those who propose and support the winning policies. My point is not that referendums are

[74] In Australia, for instance, s 128 of the Constitution holds that changes to the Constitution must be passed by an absolute majority in both Houses of Parliament. Once passed by both Houses, it is then put to a referendum.

[75] The Political Parties, Elections and Referendums Act 2000, s 101 holds that enabling legislation is required for referendums. However, the form of that enabling legislation varies on a case-by-case basis.

[76] Tierney (n 16) 55.

[77] 'Risk assessments, emotional reactions to EU membership, and leader image heuristics were other major proximate forces driving the choices voters made.' H Clarke and others, 'Why Britain Voted for Brexit: An Individual-Level Analysis of the 2016 Referendum Vote' (2017) 70 *Parliamentary Affairs* 439, 453–54.

only about voting for representatives. There will necessarily always be an overlap between voting for propositions and people. To cast the relationship between referendums and elections as either voting for policies or representatives is misleading. Once again, it is fair enough to say that what is on the ballot in a referendum is *narrower* or more *specific* than in an election. The idea of unmediated does not follow from narrowness or specificity. Despite the narrowness of what is on the ballot, in practice, it is the prerogative of voters that they may vote for any reason they wish (or no reason at all). Indeed, the more specific the propositions on the ballot, the *more* mediated that referendums are, in that more work has been done to construct political preferences. Thus the guidance given to representatives about how to execute those preferences is narrower too.

Even if referendums could offer voters a closer connection between voters and outcomes than elections do, this connection could only hold for those who support the winning proposition. There can not be a privileged, unmediated connection between voters and an outcome if voters voted explicitly against an outcome. There is some relationship between voters who did not support the winning proposition and outcomes. There may well be compelling reasons to support the outcome, perhaps because of a voter's general confidence in a democratic system. As Wollheim says, however, this reasoning can only be explained *indirectly*.[78] Supporting an outcome that one disagrees with requires a broader appeal to the principle of democracy. As soon as this argumentative move is made, there is a gap in the connection between voters and outcomes. A democratic process is doing the work of mediating the content of preferences. This claim is both descriptive and normative. It is descriptively the case that there cannot be a 'direct' connection between voters and outcomes when some voters did not support those outcomes. The claim is a normative one because this indirect connection between voters and outcomes better captures the rationale for referendums and democracy. The whole point of democracy is to manage disagreement and to deal with the fact that people will not get their own way all the time. Nevertheless, democracy gives people an indirect reason to support successful proposals, even if they disagree with them. The indirectness of this justification is foundational to the justification of democracy.

C. Referendums as Part of a Larger Democratic Context

'Unmediated' does not capture what is going on in referendums, either descriptively or normatively. The whole point of referendums (and of democracy) is

[78] 'Now I think it should be clear that my suggestion, if accepted, would resolve our paradox by the only means still available to us, i.e. by showing that the two limbs of the conjunction are not inconsistent. For – to return to the example – "A ought to be enacted" is asserted by the citizen who has been outvoted as a direct principle, whereas "B ought to be enacted" is asserted by him as a derivation from an oblique principle, i.e the principle of democracy.' R Wollheim, 'A Paradox in the Theory of Democracy' in D Weiss, P Laslett, and WG Runciman (eds), *Philosophy, Politics, and Society* (Blackwell 1962) 86.

mediation in the strong sense. Democracy is a method of group decision-making, so the aim is necessarily to aggregate the views of a range of voters. This process of aggregation is best understood as a demanding form of mediation. Democracy is, by definition, a decision-making process involving a wide range of actors. In the process of aggregation, compromises and concessions are made even for those who prevail. If there is a direct connection of any kind between one person or group's preferences and a particular outcome, this is likely to have meant that something has gone very wrong. To describe referendums as unmediated is antithetical to their purpose as processes whose function is to help address disagreement. If referendums are mediated democratic processes, it then makes sense to understand them as exercises in representative democracy.

Admittedly, understanding referendums as representative processes requires a broader account of representation. It requires decoupling the idea of representativeness from elections. As Pitkin says, an expansive account of representation is the better view.[79] Those who are not elected, such as monarchs, judges, and civil servants, can stand for and act for others in a range of ways.[80] They may be symbolically[81] or descriptively[82] representative. Representation and mediation are not synonymous; an actor may purport to represent a community without ever being responsive to others or mediating political preferences. The claim instead goes like this: referendums require two representatives to perform two types of mediating roles. The first is representation *within* a referendum process itself. Call this agenda-setting mediation; deciding what votes will be about and how they will work. The second type of mediation that requires representatives is bridging representation. Bridging representation connects referendums to an overall democratic system. This section will now consider the practical importance of each of these types of representation before turning to their normative significance.

Preferences are not aggregated in a vacuum. There are three reasons that representatives are needed in order to connect referendums with the overall process of representative democracy. The first is that representatives are needed to maintain the coherence of decisions. In cases where voters choose both to X in 2000 and then to not-X in 2005, for example, this is necessary.[83] Second, there is a need to implement the decisions that are taken by referendum. There is no point in having

[79] 'No doubt the contemporary popularity of the concept depends much upon its having become linked with the idea of democracy, as well as with ideas of liberty and justice. Yet through much of their history both the concept and the practice of representation have had little to do with democracy or liberty. Representation need not mean representative government. A king can represent a nation as can an ambassador. Any public official can sometimes represent the state. Thus, institutions are practices which embody some kind of representation are necessary in any large and articulated society, and need have nothing to do with popular self-government.' ibid 2.

[80] ibid.

[81] ibid 11.

[82] ibid.

[83] The challenges of the initiative system in California are an excellent example of this and the gridlock created by directing the legislature both to X and to not-X. P Schrag, *Paradise Lost: California's Experience, America's Future* (University of California Press 2004) 188.

a decision unless it is executed, and this is not something that voters can do themselves. All political questions are necessarily indeterminate. Executing decisions requires judgement; it is not just a mechanical process. Finally, and also because of this indeterminacy, there is a need to adjudicate the meaning of voters' choices. Taken together, the need for coherence between decisions, as well as the execution and implementation of decisions, mean that referendums rely on representatives to connect them to the representative democracies upon which they depend.

Decisions can never be wholly determinative in a referendum process. Decisions need to be interpreted and executed. Any democratic decision is an ongoing process rather than a static event. This connection between referendums and other actors such as judges and civil servants is not peripheral to the referendum process; it is better understood as part of the referendum process. As Tierney rightly argues, a referendum is more than the voting stage.[84] It is a series of processes that include a variety of types of deliberation and disagreement. These cannot be separated from the referendum process itself because people are voting for outcomes. It is impossible to say anything about the connection between outcomes and preferences without taking a broader view of referendums.

So far, the challenges have been to the descriptive helpfulness of the term misleading. Supporters of the label 'direct democracy' may still make a different kind of claim. They may argue that while descriptively mediation is necessary for referendums, it is essential for normative reasons to treat referendums as if they are direct. Put differently: the myth of direct democracy is a useful fiction. Indeed, Barreyro,[85] drawing on Kelsen[86] and Pitkin,[87] makes the argument that representatives act together legislatively is also a myth. Barreyro is right to suggest that this must be the kind of argument that some supporters of the label direct democracy are making. Even if Barreyro is right that these are different myths, some types of myths are more useful than others. As argued in chapter two, even if the claim that referendums are unmediated exercises in direct democracy is a myth, it is not a helpful myth. It does not capture the nature of constitutions, legitimate authority, or constitutional authorship. The myth of 'direct democracy' argues that the purpose of referendums is to get representatives out of the way, and this can undermine representative democracy.

This section has advocated for a expansive conception of representation. Representation should not be taken in the narrow sense to mean that voters elect others to act on their behalf. If representative meant elected, then monarchs

[84] 'Thus we need to envisage the referendum process as a longer and more complex democratic engagement than it is often considered to be. It can in fact be seen as a series of stages'. Tierney (n 16) 51.

[85] '... We distinguished public indirect law making, which relies on the fiction that representatives act as *organs of the community*, from public direct law making, which relies on the fiction that the electorate act *as the community itself*.' M Barreyro, '"Direct Democratic Institutions": Direct and Democratic' (2019) 10 *Jurisprudence* 313, 333.

[86] H Kelsen, *General Theory of Law and State* (Harvard University Press 1949) 289.

[87] H Pitkin, *The Concept of Representation* (University of California 1967) 86.

and ambassadors would not be representatives.[88] There are a range of ways that actors and institutions can act on others' behalf. Both because they are elected, and also because they aid in the process of aggregating, articulating, interpreting, and executing political will. These processes should also be understood as mediating in a strong sense. They are essential to both the form and the content of the aggregation of political will, and they shape the connections between voters and outcomes. Above all, representatives make decisions, and the public then makes choices about those decisions when they vote. Representatives are not only essential descriptively for how referendums work in practice; this necessary relationship between voters and representatives captures what is good about referendums too.

VII. Conclusion

This chapter had two aims. First, to demonstrate the connections between the idea that referendums with fundamental constitutional content are processes where voters come together, literally, or metaphorically, to make decisions instead of representatives, and three other claims. These three other connected claims are that (i) it is a conceptual requirement of democracy that it is has tracks, one for voters and one for representatives; (ii) voting in a referendum on an exceptional constitutional issue is an act of consent; and finally (iii) voting in a referendum on a constitutional question is an exercise in direct democracy. This chapter challenged the idea that in referendums on significant constitutional issues voters come together to make decisions instead of decisions being made by representatives, as well as the three claims connected to it.

After introducing these claims, and demonstrating who holds them, this chapter first put pressure on the possibility of defining the concept of 'the people', and the helpfulness of this idea in for thinking about constitutional referendums. 'The people' is, at most, a myth. The helpfulness of this myth is contentious, particularly concerning referendums because they are where abstract political theory and the practice of constitutional development intersect. While the idea of 'the people' might have merits, it is not a strong enough conceptual foundation on which to base a theory of referendums, and constitutive constitutional referendums also demonstrate the weakness of the myth of 'the people'. The second aim was to challenge the idea that voters were the kind of group that could serve as a collective agent or make decisions in any kind of literal or philosophical way. The main difficulty encountered here is the aggregative nature of voting. Voting is the kind of process which deliberately decouples votes from the voter's intentions and

[88] 'A king can represent a nation as can an ambassador. Any public official can sometimes represent the state. Thus institutions are practices which embody some kind of representation are necessary in any large and articulated society, and need have nothing to do with popular self-government.' Pitkin (n 87) 2.

puts everyone's preferences in a big pile. The aggregative nature of voting makes it conceptually tricky for voters to be the right kind of group and voting for the right kind of action, to be a collective decision or exercise in constitutional authorship. Finally, the chapter contested the idea that, even if all of this were possible, referendums are instances of voters making decisions instead of decisions being made by representatives. It introduced the possibility instead that votes are choices about decisions made by different kinds of representatives. It then teased out the many ways that voting for representatives is inseparable from voting for specific propositions, and so questioned the contrast between representative and direct democracy. It argued that this contrast is helpful even when thinking about fundamental constitutional questions.

Challenging the helpfulness of characterising referendums as directly democratic is not an end, but rather a means to dispute the possibility that referendums are instances of higher-order law-making. If votes in referendums are inextricably connected to many different representative processes, it is difficult to place them on a higher democratic plane. Supporters of the view that referendums are instances of higher-order law-making are likely to argue that this chapter has taken their views too literally. They are not describing the act of constitutional authorship; they are justifying it normatively. This is probably true – the argument that referendums are instances where voters make decisions instead of representatives is principally doing normative work. The claim does not, however, do the right kind of work to justify the use of referendums in mass pluralist democracies. The next chapter puts forward a piecemeal, plural justification for the use of referendums on fundamental constitutional questions. On this view, there are all kinds of good reasons to hold referendums depending on the context. The claim that referendums must be held because some decisions cannot be made by representatives, however, undermines rather than supports representative democracy.

4

Referendums as Representative Democracy

I. Introduction

So far, this book has offered three reasons to doubt the argument that referendums on fundamental constitutional issues are exceptional democratic processes. The book has challenged (i) the distinction between constitutive and constituted powers; (ii) the idea that in referendums the people make decisions directly and together; and (iii) the possibility of constitutional authorship. This chapter begins to offer an alternative account of referendums on fundamental constitutional questions as ordinary exercises in representative democracy. It argues that, rather than votes on matters of policy, referendums should be understood as processes where voters provide direction to representatives. This means that, even on fundamental constitutional issues, referendums are just one way among many that voters provide direction to representatives.

In making a case for this alternative, this chapter has five sections. Section I explains this alternative account of referendums as providing direction to representatives. This alternative account is defined by four commitments: (i) referendums are negotiation processes; (i) referendums cannot be distinguished from elections; (iii) referendums are not bare votes; and (iv) referendums on constitutional issues are not 'overriding' in any way. Section II explains why this alternative requires understanding referendums as representative democracy and the benefits of this approach. Section III offers a normative rationale for understanding referendums as exercises in representative democracy. The central claim is this: the rationale for referendums should be the same as that for ordinary democratic processes. Section IV gives an account of the right kinds of reasons to hold referendums. Section V anticipates the worry that the definition of referendums outlined here is too demanding. While the account offered here does set a high standard for what counts as a referendum, this demandingness is defensible. Referendums are not the same as bare votes. More should be required of a democratic process than just a vote on a matter of policy if that process is to count as a referendum.

II. Referendums as Providing Specific Direction to Representatives

The standard view of referendums is that they are popular votes on matters of policy. This chapter argues instead that referendums are processes of providing direction to representatives. This section will explain this alternative by making three claims: (i) referendums are not votes, they are longer processes of negotiation between a range of democratic actors; (ii) referendums cannot be distinguished from elections, and neither elections nor referendums are directly democratic; and (iii) referendums on constitutional issues are not overriding in any sense, they are just one way among many that voters provide direction to representatives.

A. Referendums as Negotiation Processes

Referendums are usually defined as popular votes on matters of policy.[1] Sometimes referendums are distinguished as particular kinds of popular votes, for example those triggered by representatives, but, overwhelmingly, referendums are treated as synonymous with votes.[2] The opinion that referendums are votes is most frequently expressed by those who take the view that constitutional referendums are exceptional democratic processes, but others may also take that view. Referendums are principally discrete, static acts. Most theorists and lawyers think that a vote is a necessary and sufficient condition for a referendum, but it is not enough to ensure a good referendum.[3] There is broad agreement that for effective referendums longer processes of consultation and engagement with voters are needed, but that a popular vote on a matter of policy provides the necessary and sufficient conditions for a referendum.

An alternative starting point for thinking about referendums is the word itself: the meaning of the word referendum comes from the word *referre*, which means 'to refer back'.[4] This is a better starting point for thinking about referendums than viewing them as popular votes for three reasons. The first is that voting is a limited way of participating in a process of constitutional change, even during referendum processes. Indeed, best practices in comparative constitutional law demonstrate

[1] M Setälä, *Referendums and Democratic Government* (Macmillan 1999) 4.

[2] The definition of referendums is discussed in greater detail in ch 1, section IV.

[3] Tierney, for instance, offers the most persuasive account of referendums as exceptional, but he is clear that there many different stages of effective referendums. S Tierney, *Constitutional Referendums: The Theory and Practice of Republican Deliberation* (Oxford University Press 2012) 50–52.

[4] 'The word "referendum" comes from the Latin neuter of *referendus*, gerundive of *referre*, "to refer back".' M Qvortrup (ed), *Referendums Around the World: The Continued Growth of Direct Democracy* (Palgrave MacMillan 2014) 2.

that constitutional conventions,[5] public polls,[6] and substantive consultations,[7] are just a few of the ways that the public may be engaged in constitution-making as part of referendum processes. As Landemore rightly argues, substantive participation in constitution-making is now the rule rather than the exception. She says: 'Public participation in constitution-making is now both an established international norm and a widespread practice.'[8] Landemore is correct, and her insights are significant. The legitimising force of referendums does not just arise from votes. This is clear too in Amaral's account of referendums on peace treaties. Amaral stresses that negotiation is where the actual peace-making process takes place, and that the consensus-building power of referendums does not arise at the voting stage.[9] Amaral's studies demonstrate that referendums do not make peace – people do. Moving away from referendums as one-off votes, and instead seeing them as ongoing processes of referral and consultation with voters is the better view both practically and normatively. As Altman helpfully argues: '[r]educing the world of direct democracy to popular votes is a myopic approach' and the relationships between referendums and representative institutions are 'dynamic'.[10] Altman is entirely right about this. Treating referendums as popular votes is an unhelpful starting point. Once the idea that referendums are votes are abandoned, however, the consequences for constitutions are significant. It is the aim of this book to grapple with those consequences.

Treating referendums as votes is what makes it possible to cast them as processes where voters make decisions *instead* of representatives. If referendums are not votes, and instead a dialogue with representatives, this puts pressure on the whole conceptual framework of distinguishing between constitutive and constituted powers. The dialogue or negotiation that happens in referendums occurs on many levels. It occurs between voters, as they determine how to vote. It also occurs between voters and representatives, as voters provide direction to representatives. Third and finally, as argued in chapter three, representatives play a necessary agenda-setting role in referendums. In doing so, representatives exercise

[5] Electoral Reform Society, 'Constitutional Conventions', www.electoral-reform.org.uk/campaigns/democratic-innovations/constitutional-convention, accessed 23 September 2020.

[6] Public polling or 'peace polls' were used in Northern Ireland in 1998. C Irwin, 'The People's Peace Process: Northern Ireland and the Role of Public Opinion Polls in Political Negotiations' (1999) 30 *Security Dialogue* 305, 305.

[7] 'A first wave of participatory constitutional processes thus took place in Nicaragua in 1986, Brazil in 1988, Uganda in 1995, South Africa in 1996, and Kenya in 2001.' H Landemore, 'When Public Participation Matters: The 2010–2013 Icelandic Constitutional Process' (2020) 18 *International Journal of Constitutional Law* 179, 179.

[8] ibid.

[9] 'When referendums are held to ratify a peace agreement, the process of their negotiation and mediation needs to be well thought out from the start. As a tool of democratic politics, peace agreement referendums must be preceded by inclusive negotiations involving a broad spectrum of political stakeholders and civil society, and must engage the public at an early stage of the process.' J Amaral, *Making Peace with Referendums* (Syracuse University Press 2019) 138.

[10] D Altman, *Citizenship and Contemporary Direct Democracy* (Cambridge University Press 2018) 11.

control over referendum processes. Referendums are, bottom-up and top down, horizontal and vertical democratic processes. They are ways both that voters seek to control representatives, and ways that representatives seek to harness popular legitimacy to achieve political goals.[11] This is the picture Altman is painting above. On this approach, referendums are the result of a fluid set of relationships between constitutive and constituted powers. Further, this multifaceted account of referendums suggests that the line between elections and referendums is not as sharp as is often thought.

B. The Indistinguishability of Referendums from Elections

Referendums are often defined by what they are not. They are directly democratic, so the argument goes, because they are not elections. Processes are directly democratic when they involve votes for propositions rather than the selection of representatives. Referendums are not the only processes given this label. Presidentialism, primaries, initiatives, and recall[12] are treated as processes of direct democracy too.[13] What connects these different processes? What makes them direct? It seems to be the idea that they are unmediated by representatives in a material way. In presidential systems, for instance, the democratic process is 'direct' because the executive is chosen by voters rather than the legislature. The claim that direct democracy is unmediated has varying degrees of strength. Minimally, it says that there is a privileged connection between voters and outcomes. However, this minimalist view is so thin that it cannot provide much guidance on the meaning of mediation. Maximally, it says that voters entirely and literally must bypass representatives.[14] Here, mediation will be understood in an ecumenical way. To say a democratic process is unmediated is, at the very least, to say that it can be 'analytically and empirically distinguished'[15] from those that are mediated, where there is no privileged connection between voters and particular outcomes.

[11] 'Political actors use referendums to achieve their goals.' M Walker, *The Strategic Use of Referendums: Power, Legitimacy, and Democracy* (Springer 2003) 1.

[12] A Lijphart, *Patterns of Democracy: Government Forms and Performance in Thirty-Six Countries* (Yale University Press 1984) 198.

[13] While the argument here is narrower in scope, making a case only that referendums are instances of representative democracy, the argument does hold for these other processes too. At root, these processes also are about mediation of political will in a strong sense, and so providing direction to representatives. Consequently, they are not exercises in direct democracy.

[14] Barber argues that strong, or direct democracy, requires '[u]nmediated self-government by an engaged citizenry. It requires institutions that will involve individuals at both the neighbourhood and legal level in common talk, common decision-making and political judgement, and common action.' B Barber, *Strong Democracy: Participatory Politics for a New Age* (University of California Press 1984) 261.

[15] P Uleri, 'Introduction' in M Gallagher and P Uleri (eds), *Referendums in Europe* (Macmillan 1996) 2.

So, what is the difference between how elections and referendums are mediated? There are at least two possibilities. One might be that the *content* of the preferences being aggregated are different. Referendums are about particular policy or constitutional questions. The thought might be this makes votes in referendums less mediated than, say, voting for a manifesto. These preferences are aggregated from voters directly. A second possibility is that referendums are directly democratic because the *form* of preference aggregation is different. This is to say that, in referendums, the structure of preference aggregation is different. This means the scope of consideration is different than in elections because referendums are considering matters of policy rather than which representative to select.

While it is right to say that there are differences between elections and referendums, these differences are overstated. If there are differences in the kind of mediation that happens in referendums and elections, those differences are matters of degree rather than kind. Neither the form or content of preference aggregation between referendums and elections is demonstrably different. Take the question of form first. In referendums, voters vote for issues, but also for those who are advocating for these issues. It is clear, for example, that the popularity of governments and broader economic conditions make a significant difference to how people vote.[16] It is clear too in referendums that issues and those advocating for them are regularly conflated.[17] While referendums do not usually involve selecting or choosing between representatives, they do lend legitimacy to those representatives who are advocating for certain issues and arguments.[18] In secession referendums in particular, mandates to secede are not only for the proposition of secession, but those who advocated for secession in the first place. Further, when referendums authorise the beginning of processes of constitutional change, they may then involve the selection of representatives to conduct that negotiation.[19] It is

[16] Qvortrup persuasively shows that at least concerning referendums on European integration; the longer governments are in power, the less likely they are to win referendums. He says: 'Overall, the outcome of referendums tends to be associated with the number of years the government has been in office, the state of inflation at the time of the vote, whether the vote in question pertains to accession and [who] is part of the "no"-campaign.' M Qvortrup, *The Referendum and Other Essays on Constitutional Politics* (Hart 2019) 107–08.

[17] Think of the referendum in Italy in 2016 and Prime Minister Matteo Renzi deliberately conflating the constitutional reforms on the ballot with his personal mandate, for instance. 'The referendum was more than a vote on constitutional reform; it was widely regarded as a chance to reject establishment politics. It was a resounding victory for the No camp, a medley of populist parties headed by the Five Star Movement, which capitalised on Mr Renzi's declining popularity, years of economic stagnation, and the problems caused by tens of thousands of migrants arriving in Italy from Africa.' 'Matteo Renzi's Referendum Defeat Risks Italy Political Crisis', *BBC News* (5 December 2016), www.bbc.co.uk/news/world-europe-38204189, accessed 15 November 2023.

[18] After surveying the use of referendums in France, Chile, the Soviet Union and the Post-Soviet states, Walker concludes: '(1) That referendums are part of a bargaining process between elites who have their basis of power in different institutional settings. (2) Referendums give political actors the political legitimacy to pursue change and potentially alter status quo institutions.' Walker (n 11) 91.

[19] As was the case with the referendum question in Québec in 1995: D Millette, M-E Lambert, and GL Gall, 'Quebec Referendum of 1995' (*Encyclopedia Britannica*) www.britannica.com/topic/Quebec-referendum-of-1995, accessed 15 November 2023.

also misleading to suggest that the content of preference aggregation is different in elections as opposed to referendums. Voting for the 277-page Lisbon Treaty, for example, involved a wider range of considerations than many government manifestos.[20] Equally, parties may run to be elected on a single issue. This is all to say: the kind of mediation that happens in referendums and elections varies enormously depending on the circumstances, and the differences between these two kinds of democratic processes is nowhere near as sharp as is often suggested.

The real difference between referendums and elections is that the direction being given to representatives in referendums *may* be more *specific*,[21] or *narrower* than it is in elections. Note, however, that the word specific has a different meaning from the word direct. While the intuition that there is something direct about referendums is right, the word direct is unhelpful. Direct suggests a privileged connection between voters and outcomes, and the term 'specific' does not. What often, albeit not always, makes referendums different from elections is that voters are providing a narrower range of guidance to representatives than they do in elections. As noted above, however, this may not necessarily be the case. Referendum outcomes may be comprehensive or open-ended, providing a broad and (or) inchoate direction to representatives. The word 'specific' allows that a referendum can, at least potentially, consider a narrower question than that which is at stake in an election. The idea of 'direct' democracy is troubling because it suggests some sort of shortcut or straightforward path around representatives. This creates the possibility that referendums can be exceptional democratic processes, where decisions can be made by voters *instead* of by representatives.

Despite being persuaded of the unhelpfulness of the term 'direct democracy', readers might nevertheless still think that there is something significant about the word 'direct' in direct democracy. There is something direct, they might insist, about voting for a proposition in a referendum as opposed to voting for a candidate or political party. Further, this directness is central to the case for referendums; they disrupt the rigidity of party structures and opinion by allowing people to weigh in on a narrower question. A reader might agree that the term 'direct democracy' is unhelpful, and still resist the proposition that referendums are representative. While it is right to think that something distinct is happening in elections as opposed to referendums, this is incorrectly cast as one process being mediated and the other unmediated. Mediation comes in different degrees and kinds, and there is no fundamental difference between what is happening in elections and referendums. To the extent that there is a difference between elections and referendums, the question is a matter of the *specificity* of content rather than bypassing representatives altogether. In this way, the instinct behind the idea of

[20] JC Piris, *The Lisbon Treaty: A Legal and Political Analysis* (Cambridge University Press 2010) 21.

[21] Altman takes a slightly different approach. He holds onto the term direct democracy but uses the idea of specificity to define directness. 'I define a *mechanism of direct democracy* as a publicly recognised, institutionalised process by which citizens of a region or country register their choice or opinion on specific issues through a ballot with universal and secret suffrage.' Altman (n 10) 6.

direct democracy is helpful. However, the use of the term has led to deep normative and practical misunderstanding about referendums.

C. Distinguishing Referendums from Bare Votes

The account of referendums as 'providing direction to representatives' distinguishes referendums from bare votes. One consequence of the view put forward here is that a vote on a matter of policy is a necessary condition for a referendum, but it is not a sufficient condition. Referendums, to count as referendums, must have a relational element. This relational element is providing direction to representatives. There are two important consequences of this approach. First, it sets the bar higher for when a popular vote will count as a referendum. Second, it means the boundaries of what counts as a referendum may be fuzzier. The approach taken here moves away from a descriptive standard for referendums and introduces an evaluative standard instead. These consequences may worry readers. Even if a reader is broadly sympathetic to the claim that referendums should be understood as exercises in representative democracy, they might nevertheless resist distinguishing referendums from bare votes. However, while distinguishing referendums from bare votes introduces complexity, treating referendums as synonymous with bare votes has risks too. This section identifies the risks of treating referendums as synonymous with bare votes, and then advocates for setting a higher, blurrier standard for referendums.

The way that referendums are currently distinguished from bare votes is, essentially, by distinguishing between referendums and plebiscites. Plebiscites are distinguished from referendums both by their content, their bindingness, and their democratic credentials. The aim in distinguishing referendums from plebiscites is to say that, for any number of reasons, this vote is not as authoritative as a full-blooded referendum. The limitation with the plebiscite versus referendum approach is that it does not properly draw this contrast. This is a vote-centric approach to distinguishing between democratic processes. The work that this distinction needs to do is to separate those processes which meet a higher democratic standard and to explain why. Referendums as providing direction to representatives can accomplish this in two ways. First, by making sure that voters are controlling the process. That is to say: voters are providing direction to representatives, not the other way around. Second, by making sure that the content that voters prefer is clear.

The direction of travel is important too. It is essential in referendums that voters provide direction *to* representatives, not the other way around. This is at the heart of many of the worst abuses of referendums. If a popular vote has been used to consolidate a dictator's power, rather than meaningfully solicit feedback from voters, it does not deserve the label of referendum. When a process is labelled a 'referendum' or an 'election', that lends it power and legitimacy. The question is what threshold needs to be reached to satisfy that process. This section has argued that a vote alone is not enough to satisfy that threshold. Treating referendums as equivalent to bare votes would be the same as treating a process as an election when the process is rigged. This is for three reasons: the process has not provided direction to or control of representatives; the process has not achieved its purpose; and the process it does not deserve the democratic legitimacy that the term conveys.

The standard view – ie treating referendums as synonymous with votes on matters of policy – has clear appeal. Voting has much to commend it. Voting has low barriers to entry; it is a simple process with straightforward publicity of involvement.[22] Voting offers enormous normative power because it helps supply the equality on which democracies relies. Nevertheless, voting has its limitations. Voting, as demonstrated in chapter two, is at most a process of authorisation or ratification. On its own voting does not offer the opportunity for voters to provide substantive input in referendum processes. Voting is only one of many tools in the democratic toolbox. A vote without any kind of meaningful consultative process, one that does not refer a question back to voters, does not deserve the label 'referendum'. It might be argued that the case has been made here for the definition of a *good* referendum, not merely for a referendum. This is not the case. An election has failed if it does not result in the selection of representatives. That is what an election is: its purpose is to select representatives. If a referendum has not provided direction to representatives, both in terms of content and control, it should not be given the label of referendum.

Referendums are powerful, and the term 'referendum' is powerful. Referendums demonstrates support for propositions[23] in addition to, as argued in chapter two, providing support for representatives. In this way, input from voters on specific issues is a significant legitimising force for both representatives and issues. This potential for referendums to shore up individual personal legitimacy for representatives makes them dangerous democratic processes. Only those popular votes which meaningfully provide direction to representatives deserve the label 'referendum'. Inevitably, this alternative approach will create some borderline cases. These borderline cases are the necessary cost of doing business, however, in preventing manipulation by the elites and ensuring that all processes labelled referendums deserve the name.

D. Referendums as not Overriding

On the standard view of referendums as exceptional democratic processes, referendums are overriding. Even if a referendum is not legally binding, on the exceptionalist view this referendum still demonstrates a will of the people that is immutable. If, however, referendums are processes of negotiation, and indistinguishable analytically and empirically from elections, then they cannot be overriding

[22] J Evans, *Voters & Voting: An Introduction* (Sage 2004) 1.
[23] This is the mandate theory of voting.

processes. They cease to exist on a higher democratic plane and become one of the ways in which direction is provided to representatives in a democracy. To say referendums are not overriding is not to say that they can never be *dispositive*. For any number of legal and political reasons, they may be entrenched as outcomes. The point is just this: if referendums are processes which are indistinguishable from elections, they are not automatically and necessarily binding irrespective of whether circumstances change. That is because, on the alternative offered here, the purpose and rationale of referendums are different. The aim is not to displace representatives. Referendums are not distinct decision-making processes. The objective of referendums is not to make decisions for all time. It is to ensure that voters' preferences constrain the actions of representatives. So long as voters' preferences reflect referendum outcomes, they continue to provide direction to representatives. If voters preferences change, however, there is nothing overriding about the result of a referendum simply because it is a referendum. Such democratic decisions should not be understood to exist on a higher democratic plane.

This view that referendums are not overriding is in sharp contrast the exceptionalist, two-track view of referendums and democracy. On the exceptionalist view, referendums on constitutive constitutional questions are once-in-a-generation events where voters make decisions, instead of representatives. While this approach might appear appealing, Chambers offers an effective critique. She argues that rather than clarifying or supporting deliberation, treating referendum as once-in-a-generation higher-order events instead has the effect of undermining the quality of democratic processes.[24] Chambers is right about this – the separation of constitutional debates in referendums from the ordinary iterative processes of democracy undermines participation and accountability. Chambers argues that in these circumstances, the stakes are so high that debates become polarised and unhelpful.[25] Chambers rightly argues for an approach to referendums as ongoing processes of constitutional consultation.[26]

It might be argued that treating referendums as overriding is one of the ways that voters maintain their role as having ultimate authority in a democracy. While this approach appears emancipatory, the reverse is true. Understanding referendums as ongoing processes where voters provide direction to representatives gives voters more power to shape their constitutions, and provide direction to

[24] 'Referendums present the voter with the image of inflexibility (debate cannot alter the framing of the question) and irreversibility (constitutional proposals are entrenched outside the ongoing interative processes of normal politics. These factors are disincentives to adopt a deliberative point of view.' S Chambers, 'Constitutional Referendums and Democratic Deliberation' in M Mendelsohn and A Parkin (eds), *Referendum Democracy: Citizens, Elites, and Deliberation in Referendum Campaigns* (Palgrave 2001) 232.

[25] She contrasts the kinds of deliberation that occur in two types of juries, those that are 'evidence' driven and those that are 'verdict' driven. She shows that juries that were evidence-driven came to decisions that were 'perceived as more legitimate and had a stronger sense of efficacy.' ibid 248.

[26] 'It would be better if discrete democratic decisions were not presented as the last word on the matter. If referendums are used, we should consider making them part of an ongoing process of consultation rather than a once-and-for-all ratification.' ibid 251.

representatives, on an ongoing basis. Further, if it is the case that the purpose of referendums is to provide direction to representatives, it follows that there is the strongest case for referendums when that direction is most required. That is to say, the case for referendums is the strongest when there is the greatest gap between the views of voters and those of representatives.[27] Again, the approach offered here proposes a more expansive role for voters than the exceptionalist view does. The following section turns to the implications of characterising this alternative account of referendums as representative.

III. The Constitutional Implications of Treating Referendums as Representative

While the commitments outlined above are controversial, the broader implications of understanding referendums as exercises in representative democracy are even more significant. While this is by no means the first book to express dissatisfaction with the term 'direct democracy', the book is distinctive in wrestling with the consequences of the impossibility of direct democracy for democratic constitutions. Even though many books on referendums begin with asides about how the term is deeply misleading, still – for simplicity – the authors concede that they will use it anyway.[28] A range of alternative terms such as hybrid,[29] quasi,[30] or semi-direct[31] democracy have been used in a range of ways, but none have achieved widespread use. There is growing literature challenging the plausibility of the term, particularly descriptively.[32] Altman has long argued convincingly that the distinction between representative and direct democracy is oversimplistic. All this literature is helpful and important, and the aim of this book is to use this literature to challenge the default approach to democratic constitutions.

As argued in chapters two and three, the aim and advantage of arguing that referendums are representative is to challenge the conceptual claim that,

[27] This is a kind of 'safety valve' rationale for referendums that Qvortrup helpfully offers at Qvortrup (n 4) 4.

[28] Kobach recognises that using the term direct democracy is inaccurate; he means semi-direct democracy, but he uses direct democracy because it is too unwieldy to explain what semi-direct democracy means. K Kobach, *The Referendum: Direct Democracy in Switzerland* (Dartmouth Publishing Company 1993) 58.

[29] 'Most Americans live in a "hybrid democracy." That is, they live where processes of both direct and representative democracy coexist as part of state government.' S Bowler and A Glazer (eds), *Direct Democracy's Impact on American Political Institutions* (Palgrave 2008) 1.

[30] B Ackerman, *We the People, Volume 2: Transformations* (Belknap Press 1998) 83.

[31] Kobach (n 28) 58.

[32] A el-Wakil and S McKay, 'Disentangling Referendums and Direct Democracy: A Defence of the Systemic Approach to Popular Vote Processes' (2020) 56 *Representation* 449, www.tandfonline.com/doi/epdf/10.1080/00344893.2019.1652203, accessed 15 November 2023; R Van Crombrugge, 'Are Referendums Necessarily Populist? Countering the Populist Interpretation of Referendums through Institutional Design' (2020) 57 *Representation* 109, www.tandfonline.com/doi/full/10.1080/00344893.2020.1720789, accessed 10 August 2020.

metaphorically, in referendums decisions are made by voters rather than by representatives. This is the version of direct democracy found in normative arguments for constitutional referendums such as those made by Galligan[33] and Tierney.[34] Crucially, for Tierney and Galligan, 'direct democracy' is the right label only for very specific types of constitution-changing referendums.[35] This normative argument only holds for constitutive constitutional referendums.[36] Since the people are the ultimate source of authority in a democracy, it must be the case (so the argument goes) that decisions about the allocation of powers should be made by the people directly and together.[37] This final point about togetherness is essential too. It is the fact that voters make these decisions in their *collective capacity* instead of decisions being made by representatives that makes processes directly democratic.[38] In sum, the aim and advantage of challenging the directness of

[33] 'Constitutional referendums are also fundamentally significant as a legitimating mechanism for democratic government. Through collectively deciding upon the system of government under which they love, the people express their democratic sovereignty. In so doing they constitute themselves as the sovereignty body that makes authoritative decisions about their system of government.' B Galligan, 'Amending Constitutions Through the Referendum Device' in M Mendelsohn and A Parkin (eds), *Referendum Democracy: Citizens, Elites, and Deliberation in Referendum Campaigns* (Palgrave 2001) 109.

[34] Referendums are a 'means by which representation is supplanted, returning direct power to the people; in other words as some kind of reversal of the original act of transference, or at least a temporary return of power to the people.' S Tierney, 'Constitutional Referendums: A Theoretical Enquiry' (2009) 72 MLR 360, 367.

[35] 'Even the categorisation of legislative referendums as an instance of *direct* as opposed to *representative* democracy is perhaps something of an oversimplification. In playing a role within a broader representative system of government, where the authority of these referendums is clearly subsidiary to those constitutional institutions which retain the competence to create and change higher-order rules, they should perhaps more accurately be portrayed as being part of that representative system, since the effect given to the outcomes they produce is ultimately subject to the representative competence of constitutional institutions, most obviously legislatures, but also courts. In contrast, the people's direct democratic capacity to act as, or at least to influence the location and distribution of, the supreme source of constitutional law within a polity, distinguishes constitutional referendums as, potentially at least, true conduits of popular determination.' ibid 364 (emphasis in original).

[36] 'There are four ways in which referendums are used today at the constitutional level: to found new states; to create or radically change constitutions; to establish complex new models of sub-state autonomy; and to transfer sovereign powers from the state to international institutions. What connects these four types of referendums is that they each address the location or distribution of ultimate lawful authority within the polity and in doing so, implicate the sovereign relations between people and government.' ibid 360.

[37] 'Constitutional referendums are also fundamentally significant as a legitimating mechanism for democratic government. Through collectively deciding upon the system of government under which they live, the people express their democratic sovereignty. In doing so they constitute themselves as the sovereign body that makes authoritative decisions about their system of government ... Constitutional referendums, while also being instruments of direct democracy, have as their fundamental purpose the originating and changing of the system of government.' Galligan (n 33) 109–11.

[38] Madison says that what makes direct democracy direct is that The People exercise their 'collective capacity' to govern. 'It is clear that the principle of representation as neither unknown to the ancient nor wholly overlooked in their political constitutions. The true distinction between these and the American governments, lies IN THE TOTAL EXCLUSION OF THE PEOPLE, IN THEIR COLLECTIVE CAPACITY, from any share in the LATTER, and not in the TOTAL EXCLUSION OF THE REPRESENTATIVES OF THE PEOPLE from the administration of the former.' A Hamilton, J Madison, and J Jay, *The Federalist Papers* (Penguin Classics 1987).

referendums is descriptive, but the descriptive challenges are in service of a larger aim. This larger aim is understanding legitimate authority in a democracy as plural and in flux, rather than expressed discretely through referendums. By drawing on this alternative approach to legitimate authority, this book offers an alternative justification for referendums as well, which is considered in the following section.

IV. Justifying Referendums as Representative

Representative democracy requires giving direction to representatives. The direction given to representatives in democracies may take many forms. In addition to voting in a referendum, actions such as protests, voting in elections, writing letters, and lobbying representatives are examples of representative democracy in action. This broad definition requires, however, understanding the meaning of representation. There are many ways of being a representative. A person can be a representative descriptively or symbolically, and different approaches can be taken to being a representative, for example because that representative is a delegate or a trustee. Pitkin's influential definition of representative says that to be a representative is to independently act on behalf of someone else in a manner responsive to their interests.[39]

Pitkin's approach is the right way to think about representation, because of the tension built into the definition, and Pitkin's view is shared by Urbinati and Christiano. It is a different way of formulating Christiano's argument that representation is 'discretion within limits'.[40] Similarly, Urbinati suggests understanding representation as driven by this tension too: 'The tension between commitment to the electors' cause and a representative's autonomous judgement, which animates advocacy, exemplifies the character of representative democracy.'[41] Pitkin, Christiano, and Urbinati are correct about this. On the one hand, representatives must act independently, but they must be responsive to their constituents too. In this way, direction from constituents is a necessary part of representation and representative democracy, but representation is necessarily more than taking direction from one's constituents too. Different representatives in different democracies will respond to this tension in different ways on different issues. It will never be resolved in one direction or another.[42] Going too far away from responsiveness

[39] 'Representing … means acting in the interest of the represented, in a manner responsive to them. The representative must act independently; his actions must involve discretion and judgement; he must be the one who acts.' H Pitkin, *The Concept of Representation* (University of California 1967) 209.

[40] T Christiano, *The Rule of the Many* (Westview Press 1996) 2.

[41] N Urbinati, 'Representation as Advocacy: A Study of Democratic Deliberation' (2000) 28 *Political Theory* 758, 774.

[42] Pitkin's account of representation does not take a side in the delegate trustee controversy, although it does rule out the extreme versions of both views. I think this is a strength of her account of representation and shows that the trustee-delegate debate should not be seen in either-or terms. Part of what it is to be a representative is to find a balance between independence and responsiveness, too far in either

to constituents, or exercising no independent judgement, means an actor ceases to be a representative at all.[43]

Striking this balance between responsiveness and independence is not only what happens in elections; the same process happens in referendums too. This balance must be struck because of the inchoate nature of referendum questions. The nature of law, constitutions, and language are such that votes in referendums will never be exhaustive. Some type of representation is necessary to determine the content of referendum outcomes and execute them. Referendums, as in elections, are authorising individuals to undertake a set of actions. The direction given to representatives in referendums ranges in degree, volume, content, and scope. Further, representation is not only an act, but it is systemic. As Pitkin says, referring to a system as 'representative' means 'saying something broader and more general about how it operates as an institutionalised arrangement … even the representing done by an individual legislator must be seen in such a context, as embodied in a whole political system'.[44] The essential point Pitkin is making here is that representation must be understood in the round. Representation is not a feature of any one event or institution, but rather how they connect and fit together. Referendums are reliant on, and inextricable from exercises in what is ordinarily called representative democracy. They require representatives both to connect them to a broader representative system and other democratic institutions, and to execute their outcomes. Taken together, this suggests that referendums are best understood as regular exercises in representative democracy.

This section has argued that referendums on fundamental constitutional issues *are*, descriptively, exercises in representative democracy. This raises the risk that this argument makes the naturalistic fallacy; deriving an 'ought' from an 'is'. That is not the move here. While it is the case that referendums in practice are representative, they should not be understood as representative merely *because* they are representative. Referendums should be understood as processes in ordinary, representative democracy because that best captures the reasons to hold referendums in the first place. Further, the idea that referendums are exceptional democratic processes has a narrow conceptual basis. Understanding referendums as representative allows for a plural, and persuasive, way of justifying the use of referendums. That piecemeal justification for the use of referendums, in contrast to a justification grounded in the social contract, is considered in the next section.

direction and an actor ceases to be a representative at all. Pitkin (n 39) 166; Urbinati says this too; she argues that thinking about representation in this way is 'an alternative to the dichotomy of representative as delegate or representative as trustee'. Urbinati (n 41) 777.

[43] 'The conceptual principle sets the limits of representation, of what we are willing to recognise as representing (or a representative) and what no longer qualifies. If a state of affairs deviates too much in one direction or another, we shall say that it is no longer representation at all, there is room for a variety of views on what a good representative should and should not do.' Pitkin (n 39) 166.

[44] ibid 221.

V. Procedural and Instrumental Arguments for Referendums

The arguments made by those who think referendums are exceptional democratic processes often come to the right conclusions about when referendums should be used, but they do so for the wrong reasons. It is right to argue, as those who treat referendums as exceptional do, that referendums are helpful tools in processes of constitutional change. This is not, however, because such decisions *cannot* be made by representatives. Just as there are many justifications and purposes for representative democracy, so too are there many arguments for referendums as democratic processes. There are innumerable defences of democracy, and particular democratic processes. There are two broad traditions of justifying representative democracy: procedural and instrumental reasons, and both sets of reasons are applicable to justifying referendums too. These justifications for referendums inform the right kinds of reasons for their use.

The instrumental-procedural distinction is not hard and fast, and most theorists support both approaches to some extent. These two traditions are not mutually exclusive[45] and they may be labelled in different ways.[46] Proceduralists argue that democratic decisions are good principally because of the way democratic decisions are made. Instrumentalists take a different approach, arguing that democracy is valuable because of the quality of the decisions it reaches. Instrumental and procedural arguments focus on two different rationales for democracy and emphasise different features. As Dworkin says, each tradition offers different answers to the question 'what is good about democracy?'[47] 'Are good … democratic outcomes good because they are democratically chosen, or are they democratically chosen because they are good?'[48]

What is good about referendums? It depends. Referendums, even on fundamental constitutional issues, may be justified for both instrumental and procedural reasons. They may be instrumentally valuable because they help address specific problems, for instance the divisiveness or intractability of a question. They might be procedurally valuable because they help voters participate in a process to address intractable issues. Referendums are procedurally valuable to the extent that they offer meaningful, inclusive processes for coming to those outcomes. They are instrumentally valuable insofar as they help come to better decisions than

[45] 'Democratic decision-making has two very different evaluative aspects that sometimes collide but usually complement each other to some degree. On the one hand, we judge democratic decisions from the quality of outcomes. We concern ourselves with whether the outcomes are just or efficient or protect liberty and promote the common good. On the other hand, we evaluate decisions by the quality of the procedure. We are concerned to decide a way that includes everyone who by right ought to be included and that is fair to all participants.' T Christiano, 'The Authority of Democracy' (2004) 12 *Journal of Political Philosophy* 266, 266.

[46] ibid 266–67.

[47] R Dworkin, *Is Democracy Possible Here?: Principles for a New Political Debate* (Princeton University Press 2008) 66.

[48] ibid.

would have otherwise been possible. Crucially, the instrumental and procedural value of referendums will vary from case to case, but this variation is a strength of this way of justifying the use of referendums across contexts.

VI. A Piecemeal Case for Referendums

A single justification for referendums is unnecessary and undesirable. Referendums offer legitimacy to authorities for all kinds of reasons and may themselves be justified for all kinds of reasons. This section explores this range of reasons. The aim is to begin to offer an alternative, piecemeal account of how and why the use of referendums may be justified. These differences reflect that democracies have different histories, traditions, and levels of cohesion.[49] Instrumentally good outcomes are also a source of legitimate authority. Referendums may be authoritative because they offer just or satisfactory solutions to questions of allocating authority in a democracy. A referendum that radically amends a constitution might have legitimacy because, among other things, it is aligning the content of a constitution more closely with the prevailing social morality; for example, concerning the rights of LGBTQ+ people. Good outcomes can be achieved by coming to conclusions that bridge differences or help build understanding. These kinds of outcomes are particularly important for successful peace referendums. Unless a referendum comes to a conclusion which instrumentally addresses the concerns of those in disagreement, and does so in a consociational way, it will not be perceived to be legitimate.[50] Additionally, a referendum may provide an instrumentally new defensible constitutional settlement. Referendums on subsidiarity, for example, may be valuable because they strengthen local communities. This subsidiarity may be both intrinsically and instrumentally valuable, and it may be impossible to distinguish these two types of value. Referendums on electoral reform and suffrage are best justified not on an *ultra vires* basis, where the decision is constitutive and never one for representatives to make, but rather on a conflict-of-interest basis. The problem is not that legislators do not have the power to pass authority further, but that they are biased in the result. Referendums with a strong deliberative culture may be procedurally valuable, perhaps because they enliven associational relationships. In this way, referendums could arguably offer second-order instrumental or procedural legitimacy in the form of re-engaging voters in democracies,[51] The referendum

[49] This diversity is true for proto-democratic political communities too in the case of self-determination.

[50] Amaral (n 9). She contrasts it with Cyprus in which Tierney also argues that this is the paradigmatic case of a successful referendum. Tierney (n 3).

[51] 'Although risky, I do not want to say, however, that referendums are always out of the question from the point of view of deliberation and democratic legitimacy … Furthermore, Ackerman is right to say that referendums contain a potential galvanising impetus to get citizens concerned and involved.' Chambers (n 24) 250.

in Scotland in 2014 was, for instance, sometimes argued to have had this effect.[52] These examples demonstrate the many types of instrumental and procedural value that referendums may have, and how these sources of instrumental and procedural value are often inseparable from each other.

A piecemeal case for referendums is essential too because, within political communities, members are situated in different ways with respect to authorities and referendums. The content of referendums – even within the category of constitutive constitutional referendum – varies a great deal. Legitimacy is also a question of degree and maybe over-determined in some cases. There may be more than one type of legitimacy provided by a constitutional referendum. The referendum is a varied democratic phenomenon, and this piecemeal approach to their normative justification attempts to tease out some of this diversity. The fact that the normative case for referendums with constitutive constitutional content varies, however, does not mean that nothing can be said about referendums in general. It means only that the rationale for, and the success and legitimacy of, referendums will vary. The singularity thesis, in other words the idea that there is only one justification or reason to hold constitutive constitutional referendums – because such decisions cannot be made by representatives – is both unnecessary and undesirable. There are all kinds of very good reasons to hold referendums on significant constitutional questions. The point is only that holding such referendums are not a conceptual requirement that follows from the legitimacy conditions of democratic constitutions.

VII. The Right Kind of Reasons to Hold Referendums

While the idea that there are some decisions which cannot be made by representatives is the wrong kind of reason to hold a referendum, there are all kinds of good reasons to hold a referendum. The reasons put forward here are not conceptual requirements – they are context-dependent and cannot be exhaustively listed. The rationale will depend on the issue. These reasons will hold to different degrees and may well be over-determined. There are at least three reasons, though, which do have general and significant application: the importance of entrenchment; the need to provide direction to representatives; and the ways in which referendums can help to address disagreement.

[52] 'The referendum is not a perfect device, and if not properly regulated it can indeed be manipulated by elites. But if the process is properly designed we now know it can work well. The Scottish referendum has not changed the borders of the UK but it has challenged the boundaries of our imagination. Constitutional politics may never be the same again.' S Tierney '"And the Winner Is … the Referendum": Scottish Independence and the Deliberative Participation of Citizens' *Centre on Constitutional Change* (29 September 2014), www.centreonconstitutionalchange.ac.uk/opinions/and-winner-referendum-scottish-independence-and-deliberative-participation-citizens, accessed 25 August 2020.

A. Entrenchment

While this book has argued that the distinction between referendums and elections has been cast too sharply, there is one essential way in which referendums are distinct from elections. Unlike elections, the outcomes of referendums tend to be entrenched, at least in the medium-term. This is because one of the reasons referendums may be held is that they are intended to be the last word on a subject, at least for a while.[53] This presents challenges that are distinct from the challenges experienced in elections. Referendums may happen *repeatedly*, but they do not happen *periodically*. The repeated nature of elections is an in-built accountability mechanism. If elected representatives do not keep their promises, they will not survive the next election. There is no such possibility with referendums. Where outcomes will be entrenched, referendums are helpful to ensure that the decisiveness or an outcome is an advantage, rather than a disadvantage, of holding a referendum.

Entrenchment is the process of making a conclusion more difficult to change. In this way, entrenchment is a kind of commitment device. Entrenchment it says that this outcome cannot be changed without some kind of extra-good reason. The fact that people voted in a referendum is itself a good reason to entrench an outcome. It is a good reason not because voting is an instance of voters expressing their authority, but because votes in a democracy matter,[54] and when the time has been taken to establish broad support for a proposition, that is a reason to treat it as decisive. This kind of decisiveness is particularly important in processes of constitutional because constitutional changes may create new relationships and institutions which in turn change laws. Think of joining the European Union or creating a devolution settlement, for instance. These possible spin-off effects of constitutional changes are all reasons to hold referendums to make very sure that voters support the proposed change, and have an opportunity to weigh in. All these reasons can be distinct from the claim that such decisions are higher-order constitutional questions.

B. The Need to Provide Direction to Representatives

Sometimes, it is unclear how voters think representatives should act. This is a good reason to hold a referendum, particularly – as noted above – when an outcome has significant, far-reaching, irreversible, or entrenched consequences. Imagine a scenario where war has been declared by a country since the past election, and it is

[53] Chambers (n 24) 251.

[54] '... Each of us, each individual voter (and non-voter) does make a difference through our voting behaviour to this feature of the electoral outcome: the strength of the elected representative's *manifest normative mandate*.' A Guerrero, 'The Paradox of Voting and the Ethics of Political Representation' (2010) 38 *Philosophy and Public Affairs* 272, 275 (emphasis in original).

unclear how broad support is for military intervention. Particularly when military action will have far-reaching economic social consequences, for instance because of major tax rises or compulsory military service, there is a very good reason to make sure that the views of representatives align with the views of voters. None of this is to say that it is impossible for representatives rather than voters to make this kind of decision, the point is only this: the fact that it is unclear what voters think about such a consequential issue is a good reason to hold a referendum. It may not be a dispositive reason to hold a referendum, but it is an essential consideration to be borne in mind.

C. Referendums May Help to Address Disagreement

While referendums have been used as devices of 'dictators and demagogues',[55] they have also been successfully used to address disagreement. In their comprehensive study of referendums on peace treaties, Levy, O'Flynn, and Kong persuasively demonstrate that referendums can be tools for achieving conflict settlements and helping those settlements endure by establishing shared agreement on public values.[56] While Levy, O'Flynn, and Kong do not establish, and do not seek to establish, the conceptual necessity of peace referendums, they persuasively show the impactful role referendums can play in establishing new norms in political communities. New norms and public values, the authors argue, require buy-in not just from elites but from voters as well. Participation in a process such as a referendum, may help to establish those shared values. Where there are good reasons to think that referendums may help to establish those shared values, that may be a good reason to hold a referendum.

While this book has expressed scepticism about the claim that the voting stage of referendums is an exercise in deliberative democracy,[57] referendums may still help to address democratic deficits. The key point is that referendums do not help to respond to democratic deficits by removing or replacing representatives. Referendums respond to democratic deficits by connecting voters to representative democracy and its commitments, including by helping to establish shared public values.

[55] This is an infamous formulation of referendums by Margaret Thatcher, then Leader of the Opposition, speaking against the 1975 referendum on remaining in the EEC. 'History shows, as Clem Attlee pointed out with terse force in 1945, [a referendum] is a splendid weapon for demagogues and dictators.' EEC Membership (Referendum) (Hansard, 11 March 1975) 307, hansard.millbanksystems.com/commons/1975/mar/11/eec-membership-referendum, accessed 6 September 2017.

[56] R Levy, I O'Flynn, and HL Kong, *Deliberative Peace Referendums* (Oxford University Press 2021).

[57] As discussed in ch 3 in reply to Tierney's arguments. Tierney says: 'At least in undivided societies, the referendum can be a successful constitutional instrument provided that adequate legal regulation serves to promote and protect a deliberative environment in which citizen participation can be fostered.' Tierney (n 3) 284.

D. Further Wrong Kinds of Reasons to Hold Referendums

In addition to the claim that some decisions cannot be made by representatives, and must be made by voters, there are also other wrong kinds of reasons to hold referendums. In his essential contribution constitutional theory, Lenowitz persuasively shows that ratification is optional, rather than conceptually required by democracy constitutions.[58] Lenowitz is similarly sceptical that constituent power can be expressed through ratification processes including but not limited to, referendums.[59]

While his book is not about referendums specifically, Lenowitz argues that there are three context-dependent reasons to employ processes of ratification. These are (i) a reparative justification; (ii) a bargaining advantage justification; (iii) a citizen-belief justification; and (iv) a deadlock breaking justification. Lenowitz also thinks that citizen ignorance is a good reason not to ratify a constitution through a process such as a referendum.[60] Finally, Lenowitz's argument differs from the argument made in this book in that he does not think there is sufficient evidence to suggest that ratification should be understood as part of best constitutional practice.[61]

Lenowitz's work is helpful and important, and he is right to challenge the necessity of ratification for democratic constitutions. He does not, however, successfully demonstrate persuasive reasons to hold referendums as processes of ratification. First, it is difficult to see how the reparative justification for referendums can be persuasive. This argument is that even if constituent power is not expressed through an earlier democratic process, it might be possible for a latter process to remedy this shortcoming with its strong democratic credentials. The paradigmatic case here for Lenowitz is the Berkshire constitutionalists. Lenowitz says 'for those convinced by a theory of constituent power, the concept might give reason to use ratification in this instance'.[62] This is a puzzling rationale because if arguments from constituent power are not persuasive at an earlier stage of ratification, it is

[58] J Lenowitz, *Constitutional Ratification without Reason* (Oxford University Press 2022).

[59] Although there are deep differences with the arguments made here and those advocated by Lenowitz. Lenowitz still thinks the core Lockean argumentative moves are correct, citizen belief in constituent power is a good reason to hold a referendum, and that ratification can 'repair' earlier processes which did not demonstrate constituent power. Lenowitz thinks the process of ratifying the American Constitution by the Berkshire Constitutionalists is an example of this reparative rationale in action. In contrast to the arguments made here, Lenowitz argues that it is by adopting two-track democracy that the challenges of expressing constituent power through referendums can be avoided. ibid 168.

[60] 'The standard of meaningful choice is unlikely to be met because voters will be too ill-informed, for the information required to evaluate a constitution in accordance with meaningful choice is technical, hard to obtain, and of little value in normal circumstances. Since one should expect voters to be able to make a meaningful choice, ratification referendums cannot be understood as the moment when the popular sovereign takes its decision.' ibid 201.

[61] '[Ratification] has no place in the best practices of constitution-making.' ibid 311.

[62] ibid 315.

unclear why they would be dispositive in a secondary, reparative context. Lenowitz says that the problems with expressing constituent power are not as relevant at the latter stage because 'most of the constituent-making process has already transpired'.[63] It really is not clear why this makes a difference, and grounds a reparative reason to hold a referendum. If a process of ratification cannot be an expression of constituent power in the first stage of a process of ratification, it is unclear why that rationale should hold at a later stage in that same process.

This answer, I think, to why Lenowitz thinks there might be a reparative reason to ratify a constitution later in the process connects to his third argument for ratification: the citizen-belief justification. For Lenowitz, the fact that voters believe processes of ratification to be expressions of constituent power may be a reason to ratify a constitution. Lenowitz is clearly right that this view is widely held, and that voters really do believe they have inalienable rights to ratify their constitutions. Further, the fact that voters hold these views may shape political realities. This idea is sometimes called the Thomas theorem: myths can offer legitimacy because actions are real if they are real in their consequences.[64] While Lenowitz is right to flag this argument, and right that it must be confronted in the realities of ratification, it is not the right kind of reason to hold a referendum. The fact that the claim that voters rather than representatives must make certain decisions is influential does not make it correct, and does not it make it helpful. Arguing that such an approach is the right kind of reason to hold a referendum is vulnerable to the naturalistic fallacy: it derives an 'ought' from an 'is'.

The second of Lenowitz's reasons why ratification may be justified are its role in establishing a bargaining advantage. Lenowitz is clearly right that this is an important consideration for elites to bear in mind when holding ratificatory processes, and to factor into designing constitutions, but it is not a reason to hold a referendum which supports the purpose of democracy. It is only Lenowitz's fourth and final reason – breaking deadlocks – which offers the right kind of reason to hold a referendum. This kind of reason supports the broader rationale for democracy – coming to decisions that voters have reason to accept irrespective of whether they agree with them – and connects to the arguments made here about addressing disagreement.

One final note is necessary about Lenowitz's views before proceeding. Lenowitz thinks that referendums, and other processes or ratification, cannot be instances of the people expressing their democratic sovereignty because voters are not informed enough to make a meaningful choice. Lenowitz makes it clear he does not consider voters to be blameworthy in this sense, it is simply that the institutional role of voters is such that it is impossible to have the right kind of information to make an informed decisions.[65] This is the wrong kind of reason *not* to hold a referendum.

[63] ibid.

[64] The Thomas theorem was originally formulated in WI Thomas and DS Thomas, *The Child in America: Behavior Problems and Programs* (AA Knopf 1928).

[65] ibid 308.

The standards Lenowitz sets for being informed are such that I am doubtful that any legislator, or even the Berkshire constitutionalists, could satisfy it. The 'meaningful choice' standard set by Lenowitz is not one that applies for processes to be legitimate in other democratic processes such as elections, and it is not clear why it should apply in processes of ratification. One of the strengths of democracy is that voters may vote for any reason, or no reason at all. While Lenowitz is right that (i) in referendums it is not the case that voters come together to make decisions instead of representatives; (ii) and right that this reality is a necessary consequence of mass, pluralist democracy; and (iii) correct as well that a vote in a referendum is a choice not a decision, the nature of democracy is such that it is for voters to decide what a 'meaningful choice' is for themselves on their own terms. If the question of what amounts to a meaningful choice could be determined for voters, the commitment to equality on which democracy rests would collapse.

E. The Right Action for the Right Reasons

In law, as in life, it matters not only that the right action is taken, but that the right action is taken for the right reasons. This is both because the reasons why people act are normatively significant, but also because reasoning shapes and impacts the outcomes of choices. This book argues that the idea that some decisions cannot be made by representatives is the wrong kind of reason to hold a referendum. This kind of thinking divides up democracy into tracks where voters decide exceptional questions on, at best, a generational basis, and representatives making decisions in the meantime. This section has defended the importance and value of public participation, and has instead offered three context-dependent, over-determined, and non-exhaustive reasons to hold referendums. It is a very good idea to hold a referendum when (i) outcomes will be deeply entrenched; (ii) where an issue is particularly divisive amongst voters or between voters and representatives; and (iii) there may be an especially large gap between what voters think and representatives think about a question. This approach takes a piecemeal approach to justifying referendums, relying on both instrumental and procedural rationales. The next chapter demonstrates how these reasons to hold referendums may be put into practice in a principled way.

VIII. The Trickiest Case: Secession

Arguing that referendums are not conceptually required for fundamental constitutional questions involves challenging the dominant paradigm of constitutional law and theory. This means that the arguments made in this book may be unintuitive to readers. Of all the unintuitive consequences of the argument made in this book, the idea that referendums are not required for secession is the trickiest of all. A reader might just about be able to accept that many constitutions have been created, and treaties transferring powers have been ratified, or authority has been devolved without referendums. But even on fundamental constitutional questions – those which supporters of the two-track view of democracy take to be constitutive of constitutions – one might think that the creation of a new state is in its own class altogether. Secession is the clearest expression of the intuitions behind two-track democracy. So, while secession might appear to be the trickiest case for the argument that referendums are best understood as exercises in representative democracy, the opposite is true. Secession offers the strongest case for the importance of understanding that, in referendums, voters cannot – and normatively should not be understood to be – acting instead of representatives.

The reason the secession case is so tricky is that marks the transition from one demos to another. So, it might be understood as being about the constitution of the constitution of constituent power. This thinking is misleading. Even, or perhaps especially, in cases of secession, voters are still casting ballots to select those who will act on their behalf. Acts of secession involve the creation of a whole new set of institutions, or a group to create those institutions on behalf of voters. Secession referendums are constitutionally consequential, and so the actions of representatives are institutionally influential and important. However, the contingent reasons to hold referendums advocated above are even more compelling in the context of secession. Nothing can be more deeply entrenched than the creation of a new state; the downstream consequences are enormous. This is a very good reason to hold a referendum. Secession may well be divisive, and in the creation of a new political community is it a very good idea to make sure buy-in is as widespread as possible.

Finally, understanding secession referendums as exercises in representative democracy helps to anticipate arguments against their use. Understanding referendums as ways of giving direction to representatives, decouples the creation of a homogenous demos from the exercise of self-determination. It turns a referendum into a helpful exercise in clarifying voters' intentions and avoids the risks of homogenising people and excluding minorities.[66] Referendums should almost certainly be held on questions of secession, but this is not a conceptual requirement of secession, such a conceptual approach is misleading. Two things can be true: it can both be nearly impossible to hold a secession referendum without a referendum, and also that such a referendum is not conceptually required by the logic of democracy.[67] Further, secession referendums would work better in practice without this motivating rationale.

[66] 'Self-determination, through its contribution to the creation of numerous post-Cold War states, contributed not to a dramatic increase in the number of democracies, but rather, to the tragically undemocratic climate in which ethnic-nationalism, advancing under the names of self-determination and democracy, has blossomed into a new, totally credible force.' Tierney (n 3) 608.

[67] Imagine a scenario where there is complete agreement by both the national and subnational bodies, and among the population, that secession is the right way forward. In such a case, there would be no need to hold a referendum.

IX. Conclusion

This chapter has argued that referendums are best defined one of many ways that direction is provided to representatives in a democracy. This alternative account requires three major changes to the way referendums are understood: (a) referendums are not votes, rather they are processes of negotiation; (b) any differences between elections and referendums are matters of degree rather than kind; and (c) the results of referendums are not 'overriding' in any sense. Referendums should be understood as representative both because this is a stronger normative justification, and it better captures descriptively how referendums work in practice. Like democracy itself, referendums require both instrumental and procedural justifications and may be valuable for both instrumental and procedural reasons. Indeed, referendums have multiple rationales, and these rationales may conflict with each other. They are best understood as having piecemeal sources of legitimacy, rather than being justified narrowly by the basis of the social contract. On the exceptionalist, two-track view, referendums are required on fundamental constitutional issues because there are some decisions that cannot be made by representatives. This chapter argued instead that there are all kinds of normative reasons to hold referendums, even on fundamental constitutional issues, and those reasons will vary from case to case. In particular, referendums should be used when decisions will be deeply entrenched, there is a gap between the views of voters and representatives (or as between representatives), or referendums can help to address deep disagreement. This pluralistic approach to justifying referendums means there are all kinds of reasons to use them, and that makes the case for their use more nuanced and compelling.

5

Principles for the Use of Referendums

I. Introduction

This book is an answer to the question 'Why should referendums be used?' It argues that referendums should be used not because they are exceptional exercises in constitutional authorship or higher-order law-making, but rather to help provide direction to representatives. This alternative rationale for referendums leads to a different account of how they should be used. The aim of this chapter is fourfold. First, to identify four ways that referendums can more effectively provide direction to representatives. The overarching aim of these methods is to establish a role for referendums, even on fundamental constitutional questions, that does not try to bypass representatives or to place referendums on a higher democratic plane. The second aim of the chapter is to draw a connection across these methods by challenging the claim that referendums are a remedy to the failings of representative democracy. The chapter argues instead that representative democracy is a remedy to the failings of referendums. The third purpose of the chapter is to demonstrate the payoff of these methods. These methods anticipate both the practical and conceptual arguments against the use of referendums. These methods make the case for the use of referendums stronger, not weaker. Fourth and finally, this chapter identifies the success conditions of referendums. While success is a matter of degree, not all uses of referendums are created equal. When the use of referendums is guided by the principles of representative democracy, they are more successful than when they are treated as exceptional democratic processes.

Before proceeding, a few quick clarifications are required about the methods put forward in this chapter: none are necessary or sufficient for the successful use of referendums. There is no hierarchy of methods, but some do follow from others, and they overlap in various ways. The list is not meant to be exhaustive but rather illustrative. Of course, context and jurisdiction make a great deal of difference; some guidelines will be more relevant to some countries and some referendums rather than others. This is particularly the case where referendums are required on certain issues as a matter of law. Nevertheless, this chapter demonstrates that there are some broad principles and methods for the use of referendums that hold in general.

II. Making Referendums Representative

The overriding idea in this book is that the purpose of referendums, even on fundamental constitutional questions, is to provide direction to representatives. All referendums, to some extent, provide direction to representatives, but this section explains how this direction can be provided more effectively. Maximising the representativeness of referendums requires attending to understanding referendums wholistically as composed of different stages (section II.A); drawing on a broad range of reasons to hold referendums to address disagreement (section II.B); treating voting in referendums as a process of ratification (section II.C); and finally, employing special majority requirements (section II.D). Each of these methods will be considered in turn.

A. Disambiguating the Stages of Referendum Processes

The first step in improving the quality of direction that referendums provide to representatives is disambiguating the different stages of the referendum process. Recall, as argued in chapters two and three, that voting cannot occur in a vacuum. It is contingent on prior actions by representatives. Therefore, it is essential that referendums be understood as a series of stages, of which voting is only one part. Referendums can only be understood in the round. Other accounts of referendums, even from those like Tierney who think constitutive referendums are exceptional, break them down into different stages. Tierney argues that the three stages of referendum include: (i) the pre-voting stage which frames the issue; (ii) the agenda-setting stage; and (iii) the campaign stage itself.[1] While Tierney is right about these stages, and the importance of distinguishing between them, this way of thinking about referendums remains too narrow. These stages of the referendum are still centred around the progress of voting rather than the broader and deeper process of providing direction to representatives. Further, it is crucial that the prior negotiation, and the subsequent negotiation stage, are understood as part of the referendum process. The bounds of what counts as part of the referendum process should not be set by the mechanics of establishing and organising a vote. Instead, the scope of a referendum should be set by what it is for: providing direction to representatives on how to address disagreement. One consequence of this view is that there will be no clear line where referendums stop, and everyday democratic processes begin. This consequence is not an argument against this approach. That is the point of this approach. The processes of representative, and what is conventionally called 'direct', democracy, cannot be conceptually or

[1] S Tierney, *Constitutional Referendums: The Theory and Practice of Republican Deliberation* (Oxford University Press 2012) 51.

empirically separated.[2] The benefits of understanding referendums as composed of a series of stages are manifold.

The first reason to disambiguate different stages of the referendum process is that they serve different purposes. Just as referendums are only one tool in the democratic toolbox, the different stages of a referendum are themselves individual tools in the referendum toolbox. The voting stage of a referendum is only one part of the process of addressing disagreement and providing direction to representatives. As the case studies in the next chapter will demonstrate, the most successful referendums are those with the richest, broadest, and deepest negotiation processes. In successful referendums, voting is merely the icing on the cake of a comprehensive process of consultation and compromise. Further, the significance of these processes of compromise and negotiation are not that they are 'pre-voting' parts of a referendum.[3] They have meaning and distinct from voting. Voting is doing some of the normative work in successful referendums, but it is neither necessary nor sufficient to achieve the referendum's overall aim: addressing disagreement in a way that provides direction to representatives.

The second reason to disambiguate the stages of a referendum processes is to take seriously the extraordinary agenda-setting power that elites have in referendums. The way in which questions are asked and how and when makes an enormous difference. Qvortrup has convincingly shown that the rate of inflation are indicators of how successful a referendum is likely to be.[4] Additionally, Hollander has persuasively shown that referendums are used as tools by the executive to strengthen their position against a legislature.[5] This all means that referendums may well be tools of elite manipulation, for which they are rightly and regularly criticised as democratic processes.[6] Emphasising that referendums are more than votes, and clarifying the role of representatives, helps to expose and articulate elite manipulation. It also forces referendum processes to articulate their meaning and consequences. While, as argued in chapter two, it is never entirely possible to separate voting for propositions and representatives, it is still helpful to attempt to disambiguate these two acts. For example, and as the next chapter will demonstrate, the first two votes in the Chilean process of constitutional reform in 2020 asked two questions: should there be a new constitution and, if so, which

[2] D Altman, *Citizenship and Contemporary Direct Democracy* (Cambridge University Press 2018) 6.

[3] This is a compelling argument that Chambers makes. She uses different models of juries to show that voting undermines, rather than supports, deliberation. S Chambers, 'Constitutional Referendums and Democratic Deliberation' in M Mendelsohn and A Parkin (eds), *Referendum Democracy: Citizens, Elites, and Deliberation in Referendum Campaigns* (Palgrave 2001) 233.

[4] 'Overall, the outcome of referendums tends to be associated with the number of years the government has been in office, the state of inflation at the time of the vote, whether the vote in question pertains to accession and whether [relevant parties] are part of the no campaign.' M Qvortrup, *The Referendum and Other Essays on Constitutional Politics* (Hart 2019) 107–08.

[5] 'Most referendums held in EU countries in fact serve the political elites, most notably the executive.' In S Hollander, *The Politics of Referendum Use in European Democracies* (Palgrave Macmillan 2019) 3.

[6] 'Political actors use referendum to achieve their goals.' M Walker, *The Strategic Use of Referendums: Power, Legitimacy, and Democracy* (Springer 2003) 1.

representatives should participate in the convention to write it. This is an extreme example, but it nevertheless articulates the importance of the choices made at the agenda-setting stage of referendums. If the agenda-setting power of elites in referendums is confronted directly, it is more likely to be mitigated and controlled by other parts of the referendum process.

B. Broadening the Reasons to Hold Referendums to Address Disagreement

Those who hold the view that referendums are exceptional democratic processes stress they are talking about only one kind of referendum: referendums on constitutive constitutional content. Referendums have, of course, been used for all kinds of other questions. These questions include, but are not limited to seatbelts,[7] pub-opening hours,[8] which side of the road to drive on,[9] and the use of nuclear power.[10] Having argued that referendums are ordinary democratic processes, the reasons that referendums are used to address these other kinds of policy questions are the same reasons to hold referendums on fundamental constitutional questions. There should be no difference between the justification of the use of referendums in these different categories. This means questions may be put to a referendum if, *inter alia*, they are irreversible, significant, far-reaching, and there is deep disagreement about them. Essentially, referendums should be used if, on balance, they can help to address disagreement by providing direction to representatives. This is a much better, and contextually contingent, set of reasons to hold referendums, as discussed in chapter four. These reasons to hold referendums, however, are more useful for processes of constitutional design than the view that they are exceptional democratic processes. If a referendum is being used because an issue is significant, divisive, and far-reaching, a referendum must then include consultative processes to help address that disagreement.

Note, though, that those who think there should be referendums on fundamental constitutional questions are right for the wrong reasons. It is true that significant constitutional questions tend to be significant, irreversible, with deep disagreement; however, these are the reasons to hold referendums, not because those questions cannot conceptually be answered by representatives. Note too that there may be contingent features of fundamental constitutional questions which mean that referendums might be especially helpful. Significant constitutional changes provide further justification for referendums in that their use often leads to entrenchment, and if matters are to be entrenched, it makes sense to ensure the

[7] As in Nebraska in 1986 and South Dakota in 1994.
[8] As in Wales in 1961.
[9] As in Sweden in 1955.
[10] As in, among other places, Austria in 1978, Sweden in 1980, Italy in 1987, and Lithuania in 2008.

broadest possible support for changes through referendums. The point is just this: there are all kinds of reasons to use referendums to help address disagreement fundamental constitutional issues. There are a cluster of reasons that tend to come up – irreversibility, significance, influence of decisions, entrenchment, and the need for a broad consensus – but these issues will vary depending on the context, and they are not fundamentally different from the reasons to hold referendums on other policy issues.

The questions that are best suited to be put to a referendum are those where additional direction is required for representatives. If there is universal agreement on a fundamental constitutional issue, there might be a case to put a relevant question to a referendum, but the case is weaker than if there is disagreement that needs to be resolved. Some additional features of disagreement which mean additional direction for representatives may be required include: (i) there is a disagreement between groups that might have been expected to be in agreement, particularly disagreement between representatives and the public, or internal disagreement within a political party; (ii) disagreement is particularly entrenched and inhibiting agreement on other issues, and a way is required to break the impasse; (iii) when ordinary representatives benefit directly from changes and so there is a conflict of interest, for instance issues such as Freedom of Information Act requests, expenses, and electoral reform. Note too, though, that these are all reasons to hold extra democratic processes in addition to elections, the question of whether a referendum is the right process to help address this disagreement does not necessarily follow and is a context-specific question.[11]

Finally, the nature of disagreement is significant because it helps identify the kinds of processes that should not be put to a referendum. Disagreements on questions of fact are not the kind of disagreement that referendums can resolve. Such questions are not appropriate because they are not political questions. A political question, as Pitkin rightly identifies, requires both expertise and judgement.[12] Questions of fact – is climate change happening, for example – are matters of expertise. The kind of disagreement at stake should drive the content of what kinds of questions should be put to a referendum, and whether that disagreement can be resolved in a way that provides direction to representatives. Considering a broader range of reasons to hold referendums leads to better processes of constitutional design, and therefore improves the quality of direction given to representatives.

[11] Including the question, of course, are referendums legally required.

[12] 'Political issues, by and large, are … not likely to be as arbitrary as a choice between two foods; nor are they likely to be questions of knowledge to which an expert can supply the correct answer. They are questions about action, about what should be done; consequently, they involve both facts and value judgements both ends and means. And, characteristically, the factual judgements and the value commitments, are inexplicably intertwined in political life.' H Pitkin, *The Concept of Representation* (University of California 1967) 212.

C. The Voting Stage of Referendums Must be Understood as a Process of Ratification

The simplest way for referendums to provide better direction to representatives is to ensure that the voting stage is being used as a process of ratification. This improves the quality of direction provided to representatives for two reasons. First, as argued in chapter two, voting must be a choice. It cannot be a decision because it cannot be deliberation from first principles. Voting is a responsive act, and it is impossible to remove representatives from the decision-making process. Second, and more importantly, it is normatively desirable for the voting stage of referendums to be processes of ratification. When this happens, voters are providing guidance to representatives on a specific proposal. This, rather than an open-ended mandate to negotiate, provides better direction to representatives.

This ratificatory role for voting should be reflected in the wording of the referendum question itself. For example, 'Do you agree with the proposals for X?'[13] or 'Do you think the X Act should be implemented?'[14] With both questions, voting in referendums is being used as a process of approval. Of course, approval itself is a spectrum ranging from government white papers to fully fledged bills which have already been passed by legislatures.[15] The content of instructions to representatives will always necessarily be indeterminate, even in the most detailed proposals. The direction offered by referendums as devices of approval is a matter of degree rather than kind. However, the more developed the proposal, the better the direction that can be given to representatives. Proposals of the form 'Should there be X?' are too abstract. They do not give direction to representatives but instead license representatives to pursue a broad set of possibilities. When voting in referendums initiates processes of reform, it is giving power to representatives rather than to voters.

Admittedly, it is not always possible for the voting stage of referendums to ratify constitutional or policy change. Sometimes, perhaps especially in secession referendums, it is necessary for there to be a vote that begins a process of other consultations, bookended by another vote in which votes can play a ratificatory role.[16] Provided it is clear up front that multiple votes are being held, this is an

[13] 'Are you in favour of the Government's proposals for a Greater London Authority, made up of an elected mayor and a separately elected assembly?' Constitution Committee, 'Referendums in the United Kingdom' (2009) 12th Report of Session 2009–10, 10.

[14] Take for instance the devolution referendums in the United Kingdom in 1979. They asked: 'Do you want the provisions of the Scotland Act 1978 to be put into effect?' and 'Do you want the provisions of the Wales Act 1978 to be put into effect?' ibid 9.

[15] An instance of this is the Northern Ireland referendum in 1973 in which there was a move to attach the UK government's white paper on Northern Ireland to the referendum question to avoid turning it into a sectarian headcount. The white paper was not attached, and 98.5 per cent of republican voters boycotted the referendum.

[16] 'Sometimes a referendum may be needed … to initiate intergovernmental negotiations. In such cases, the government should set out the precise plans for what will be done in the event of a vote change; the enabling legislation would set out a two-referendum process, for use in the event that the

excellent way to conduct a referendum. This will be demonstrated through the case study of Chile in the next chapter. Additionally, this potential need for multiple votes demonstrates the necessity of decoupling the definition of referendums from the definition of a vote. Referendums cannot be understood as just votes, singular, because they may very well need to involve votes, plural.

A reader might challenge this argument by suggesting that the reverse is true. The more comprehensive and complex the proposal, the more difficult it is for voters to engage. When voting on treaties on European integration, such as the Lisbon Treaty, for instance, referendums arguably became about superficial issues rather than the content of the treaty itself.[17] This concern is correct because there is no guarantee that by affirming, rather than initiating, constitutional changes that voters will receive a clear sense of what those changes are. This only further serves to demonstrate, however, the limits of the voting stage. Voting is not a process which necessarily entails deliberation, and it is not a process of content-setting in any sense. The need to engage voters in the content of proposals must come through consultation and compromise. Putting a matter to a vote is inviting voters to respond for any reason, or no reason at all, it is not an opportunity to modify or impact the substance of a proposal.

D. The Need for Special Majority Requirements

To provide effective direction to representatives, there is always a case for employing special majority requirements in referendums. This is not to undermine or limit the majoritarian nature of referendums, but rather to maintain the integrity of majoritarianism. This requirement may surprise readers. Referendums may appear, superficially, to be the most straightforwardly majoritarian processes. The simplicity and equality they offer through voting – everyone gets one vote on one issue – is facially the essence of majoritarianism. Indeed, this simplicity and equality are often argued to be central to the appeal of referendums. This appearance is misleading. The voting stage of a referendum cannot automatically offer the simplicity and equality of majoritarianism without special majority requirements.

settlement does not deliver what was promised.' UCL Constitution Unit, 'Report of the Independent Commission on Referendums', www.ucl.ac.uk/constitution-unit/sites/constitution-unit/files/ICR_Final_Report.pdf, accessed 30 October 2023.

[17] While the review of reasons to vote for the Lisbon Treaty in Ireland were shaped by the content of the Treaty itself, for instance, domestic political factors and incorrect views about what the Treaty held were also relevant. 'In particular, low levels of overall knowledge of what was in the treaty had a very powerful effect on increasing the NO vote.' R Sinnott and JA Elkink, 'Attitudes and Behaviour in the Referendum on the Treaty of Lisbon: Report prepared for the Department of Foreign Affairs' (6 March 2009), www.researchgate.net/publication/265305810_Attitudes_and_Behaviour_in_the_Second_Referendum_on_the_Treaty_of_Lisbon, accessed 30 October 2023. JC Piris, *The Lisbon Treaty: A Legal and Political Analysis* (Cambridge University Press 2010).

The meaning of a majority appears simple enough, but it is deceptively tricky. A simple majority may demonstrate a *plurality* of support for a proposition rather than majority support.[18] The idea, and normative force of majoritarianism, is central to the project of self-government. Alexander Hamilton said it is 'the fundamental maxim of republican government' that 'the sense of the majority should prevail'.[19] The idea of majoritarianism is closely connected to the idea of democracy itself. Indeed, Weale thinks that they are the same: 'to be a democrat is to be a majoritarian'.[20] The case for majoritarianism is powerful. Weale puts it like this: 'democracy implies political equality, and political equality implies majority rule'.[21] Likewise, for Waldron, while majoritarianism[22] is imperfect,[23] it remains the best way to give effect to the connected principles of equality and self-determination.[24] Like Weale, Waldron thinks that majoritarianism is 'according equal weight or equal potential decisiveness to individual votes [as] a way of respecting persons'.[25] The benefit of this equality and simplicity of majority voting is that meant to be that it is impartial as between individuals and alternatives. The most popular account of what a majority means is simply: more votes for a proposition than against.[26] Call this the simple majority requirement. The simple majority requirement is not, however, the only way of defining a majority. Special majority requirements set the threshold for what counts as a majority in a range of different ways, for example through turnout thresholds of different kinds.[27]

The main argument against special majority requirements is that they undermine the equality that majoritarianism requires. As Weale argues, it is necessary for majoritarianism that decisions are taken 'only by reference to the numbers favoring one side rather than another … [this] captures the principle of equality of participants'.[28] The difficulty with this is that, as shown in the first part of the book, is that the voting stages of referendums do not occur in a vacuum. Candidates and propositions always have in-built advantages. There are all kinds of ways that voting is partial, as between individuals and alternatives. The incumbency advantage, for example, is real.[29] Furthermore, participation in democracy

[18] 'Extraordinary Majority Requirements and the Equal Protection Clause' (1970) 70 *Columbia Law Review* 486, 486.

[19] A Hamilton, J Madison, and J Jay, *The Federalist Papers* [1788] (Penguin Classics 1987), No 22 at 193.

[20] A Weale, 'Three Types of Majority Rule' (2019) 90 *Political Quarterly* 62, 64.

[21] A Weale, *The Will of the People: A Modern Myth* (Polity 2018) 49.

[22] While Waldron is making a case for majoritarianism in the context of legislation, not referendums, but the same principles still apply.

[23] J Waldron, 'The Core of the Case Against Judicial Review' (2006) 115 *Yale Law Journal* 1346, 1372.

[24] ibid 1374.

[25] J Waldron, *Law and Disagreement* (Oxford University Press 1992) 114.

[26] 'Only by reference to the numbers favoring one side rather than another.' Weale (n 20) 65.

[27] I explore the implications of these different kinds of special majority requirements, their meaning, and implications for referendums on constitutional questions elsewhere with Matt Qvortrup, in M Qvortrup and L Trueblood, 'The Case for Supermajority Requirements in Referendums' (2023) 21 *International Journal of Constitutional Law* 187.

[28] Weale (n 20) 65.

[29] A Gelman and G King, 'Estimating Incumbency Advantage without Bias' (1990) 34 *American Journal of Political Science* 1142.

is not equal across demographics. Women, minorities, and the poor are consistently disenfranchised.[30] On the simple majority view alone, this is not a threat to majoritarianism, but the conception of equality on which the simple majoritarian view is built is too thin.[31]

The point is this: the idea of simple majoritarianism is too thin to sustain equality and address disagreement. Simple majoritarianism means more voters cast their ballots to support one proposal rather than the other, but this is not the same as saying that there is greater support for one proposition than the other. There is always a case for using special majority requirements in referendums. This is because referendums tend to be used for (i) significant questions, asked (ii) in a way which is not periodically revisited, and (iii) are meant to be decisive. The greater degree that referendums are used for significant, decisive questions that are difficult to reverse, the greater the case for special majority requirements. Using special majority requirements serves two purposes. First, it helps provide better direction to representatives because outcomes are clearer. Second, special majority requirements provide better direction to representatives because they provide reasons for those who do not support an outcome reason to support the overall process. There must have been at least some effort to engage other constituencies as well.[32] Indeed, this clarity, and the existence of reasons to support outcomes one disagrees with, are the minimal success conditions for referendums.

III. The Success Conditions of Referendums

Not all referendums are created equal; some referendums are more successful than others. There are many ways that referendums can succeed. For example, they can help to resolve disagreement, they may modernise constitutions to address historic injustices, or they may aid processes of self-determination. Minimally, however, this section argues that there are at least two success conditions of referendums. First, referendums succeed – at least to some extent – when their outcome is clear. Second, referendums succeed when they provide members of a political community with reasons to support outcomes they disagree with. This section will explain why these are success conditions for referendums and provide examples of how these conditions are met in practice. While these are not sufficient success conditions for successful referendums, this section will argue that they are necessary conditions for successful referendums.

[30] B Blessett, 'Disenfranchisement: Historical Underpinnings and Contemporary Manifestations' (2015) 39 *Public Administration Quarterly* 3.

[31] Beitz persuasively argues that the conception of equality informing majoritarianism is 'implausibly narrow.' C Beitz, *Political Equality* (Princeton University Press 1989) 95.

[32] Qvortrup and I argue elsewhere that there are more fundamental, conceptual reasons to require referendums for questions of constitutional change. Qvortrup and Trueblood (n 27).

A. Clarity of Outcomes

Whatever else referendums are, referendums are decisions. While the voting stage of a referendum alone cannot be a decision, voting at most is a choice, when considered holistically, a referendum is a process of decision-making. This is because the purpose of referendums is to come to conclusions, even if the conclusion is 'maintain the status quo' or 'revisit an issue later'. This is the purpose of decisions too; decisions are taken to 'cut off' considerations. Indeed, that is the root of the word 'decision' itself.[33] This idea of decisions as 'cutting off' captures something essential about referendums.[34] The previous chapter argued that referendums should be understood to have instrumental and procedural value. That is to say: referendums should be justified both because they include voters in the decision-making process and because they come to better outcomes than alternative systems. Clarity, as a success condition of referendums, has these instrumental and procedural dimensions. It has procedural dimensions insofar as it is clear what the process is meant to achieve, and is instrumentally valuable in that it is helpful to know what the outcome of a process is. That is to say: clarity as a success condition of referendums draws out what makes referendums both instrumentally and procedurally valuable and demonstrates the plurality in referendums' rationale.

If referendum outcomes are unclear, because the question itself is unclear, or the outcome is contested, for instance, then by definition – at least in one respect – the referendum has not been successful. One referendum which demonstrates the dangers of a lack of clarity is the referendum question in Québec in 1995, the implications of which were deeply contested.[35] Issues of campaign malfeasance too can undermine the clarity of outcomes.[36] These issues of clarity are also success conditions in elections, but in elections the stakes are lower. When election outcomes are unclear, there are consequences for those who manipulated rules. When election outcomes are unclear, there are ongoing processes for voters to make their views known. This is not true of referendums, particularly when they

[33] The word decision has the Latin root *decidere*, to cut off, according to the definition of 'decide' in the *Oxford English Dictionary* (2nd edn, Oxford University Press 1989).

[34] 'To make a decision is to put an end to deliberation. It is also to refuse to go on looking for more information and arguments and to decline to listen to them when they crop up in one's mind or are suggested by other people. No doubt in most cases the refusal to re-open the case is not absolute. Usually, it is accompanied by some unspecified rider – provided no new information becomes available, or, more strongly, provided no major change occurs, etc. Not all decisions are of the same strength, not all of them are subject to the same escape clause. But all of them are exclusionary reasons and it is this which distinguishes between them and mere intentions to act.' J Raz, 'Reasons for Action, Decisions and Norms' (1975) 84 *Mind* 481, 490–91.

[35] 'Do you agree that Québec should become sovereign, after having made a formal offer to Canada for a new economic and political partnership, within the scope of the Bill respecting the future of Québec and of the agreement signed on 12 June 1995?' M Lambert, GL Gall, and D Millette (2016, September 20). 'Quebec referendum of 1995', *Encyclopedia Britannica* (20 September 2016), www.britannica.com/topic/Quebec-referendum-of-1995, accessed 30 September 2020.

[36] This will be discussed in the case of Brexit in ch 6.

are cast as exceptional democratic processes, making clarity as a success condition even more important.

To say that an outcome must be clear for a referendum to be successful does not mean that a decision must be final for all time. The kinds of questions that are put to referendums, including foundational constitutional questions, are likely to be ongoing and contested. Constitutions are sites of deep disagreement, but that is a feature of constitutions, not a problem to be solved.[37] The point of clarity as a success condition of referendums is only to say that the outcome of a particular referendum must be unambiguous.

Whether one takes an exceptionalist view of referendums, where the aim is to voters to clearly demonstrate their will, or the view advocated in this book where the purpose of referendums is to provide unambiguous direction to representatives, clarity is all-important. There is no point in holding a referendum without coming to a clear decision. If this is the case, then clarity must be a success condition for a referendum. That is not to say clarify is a sufficient condition for a successful referendum – in some of the most abhorrent uses of referendums it was clear what dictators were doing – but it must be a necessary one.

B. Voter Support in the Absence of Agreement

The second minimal success condition for referendums is related to the first. A referendum is successful if members of a community have reason to accept a substantive outcome irrespective of whether they agree with it. This is true both for referendums, and for democracy in general. Whatever else democracy is, it is a method of addressing disagreement where no one always gets their way.[38] If those who disagree with outcomes have no reason to support them, then the referendum will have less democratic legitimacy and consequently be less successful. Further, there would be no point in having democracy if everyone agreed on all issues. One purpose of democracy is to help manage disagreement. Since this is true of democracy in general, it must be true for specific democratic processes such as elections and referendums.[39]

As with the first, this success condition has procedural and instrumental dimensions. Voters may accept the outcome because a substantively acceptable compromise has been reached, or there were meaningful opportunities for input at various stages of the referendum process, or both. It is also instrumentally valuable for decisions to command the broadest popular support. This is particularly true of the kinds of constitutive constitutional questions at issue in this book. It increases

[37] N Barber, 'Against a Written Constitution' (2008) *Public Law* 11, 17.

[38] Indeed, Seyd makes the compelling argument that some element of political disappointment is inevitable, given that different groups in democracies make conflicting demands. B Seyd, 'Exploring Political Disappointment' (2016) 69 *Parliamentary Affairs* 327, 329.

[39] Recall too that, as argued in ch 4, if it is the case that arguments for democracy slide into arguments for referendums, then arguments for referendums must slide into arguments for democracy.

the procedural value of a process for voters to see a range of views incorporated into a consultation process. One of the standard arguments against the use of referendums is that they are divisive, majoritarian, binary processes.[40] That democracy itself is not merely majoritarian, so how can it be the case that referendums are justified on majoritarian bases alone? All of these concerns are fair and important, but there is nothing necessarily divisive about referendums. Referendums, even on constitutive constitutional questions, are vulnerable to these kinds of fair criticisms. Setting a success condition for referendums as providing reasons for agreement despite disagreement helps make the case for the use of referendums stronger, not weaker. It insulates from referendums from the charge that they are processes of bare majoritarianism. The principles offered in this chapter for the use of referendums aim to make the case for using referendums stronger as well.

IV. Confronting the Case against Referendums

The aim of the principles put forward here is to make the case for the use of referendums stronger. Indeed, the principles offered here respond to arguments made against the use of referendums. There are two broad arguments against the use of referendums, and they come from two directions. These two challenges reflect different approaches to democracy. The first argument against the use of referendums is that they are what might be called *too* democratic. This first worry is that referendums undermine representative democracy because referendums are mob rule.[41] Either for institutional or epistemic reasons, representatives are better placed than voters to make decisions. The second challenge to the use of referendums comes from taking the opposite approach to democracy. This second approach argues that referendums are not democratic *enough.* On this view, voting in a referendum does not offer any meaningful connection between voters and outcomes. Elites have so much agenda-setting power in referendums that referendums do not actually offer voters any control over democratic processes.[42] Consider these two sets of concerns in turn, and why the four principles put forward above can help to address them. The concerns that referendums are too democratic, or not democratic enough, are serious, but these concerns can all be avoided by understanding referendums as exercises in representative democracy.

[40] 'In the environmental policy plebiscites we looked at, the reasoned and moderate views of the majority could not be captured with the direct democratic institution that was used, and in fact those views were not reflected in the final elections results. Similarly, in the plebiscite concerning crack and cocaine, the majority of voters, who linked the two sentencing measures, were not able to see their preferences realised. The voters in these examples, not unlike many voters in the real world, had nuanced, carefully considered views that are not easily captured by institutions of direct democracy.' J Haskell, *Direct Democracy or Representative Government? Dispelling the Populist Myth* (Perseus 2000) 154.

[41] ibid, 85.

[42] 'For Barber, who advocates strong democracy, even referendums are probably not enough. He says instead that Strong democracy requires unmediated self-government by an engaged citizenry.

A. Referendums are *too* Democratic

The view that referendums are too democratic will be considered first. Haskell thinks that referendums necessarily undermine representative institutions because of their inherently populist tendencies.[43] He argues that constitutional questions are not binary. He thinks that referendums disrupt and undermine representative institutions, which have stronger democratic credentials. Haskell is right to say that if referendums are treated as exceptional democratic processes, then they are very likely to undermine representative democracy. He is also right to say that referendums can be blunt majoritarian processes. Referendums are not, however, necessarily blunt majoritarian instruments. Particularly if voters are included in the content-creation stage of referendums, for example in the construction of peace treaties or through citizens' assemblies, they can help to establish consocational power-sharing frameworks. Haskell is right to argue that referendums can undermine representative democracy, but they can support representative democracy if the grain of the referendum runs with the broader grain of representative democracy. Referendums run with the grain of a representative democracy if the purpose of different democratic processes is to give direction to representatives. Justifying referendums normatively, and designing them practically, as devices of representative democracy, avoids the kinds of concerns Haskell raises. When referendums are integrated into institutions of representative democracy, they are not blunt, majoritarian processes of mob rule. They are just one way among many of providing direction to representatives, and a 'safety valve'[44] to make sure that representatives are acting at the voters' direction.

The kinds of concerns Haskell raises, for instance that referendums undermine representative democracy speak to the abuses of referendums by dictators. The guidelines put forward here seek to mitigate those kinds of abuses, but of course they can never be eliminated entirely. Crucially, the arguments made above that votes at most can be choices rather than decisions. This means there is always an agenda-setting role for elites and representatives. There is always the potential that referendums will be abused to bolster the personal legitimacy of representatives. Given the necessity of representatives for referendums, the potential for this abuse is inevitable, but this abuse is no more inevitable than it is for democracy in general. Referendums, like elections, are (among other things) instruments that can be used for better or worse democratic ends. Haskell's related concern that referendums are binary, majoritarian processes is surmountable by focusing on the representative quality of referendums. It should never be suggested that the question on the ballot is the beginning and the end; representative questions are

It requires institutions that will involve individuals at both the neighborhood and the national level in common talk, common decision-making and political judgement and common action.' B Barber, *Strong Democracy: Participatory Politics for a New Age* (University of California Press 1984) 251.

[43] Haskell (n 40) 176.

[44] M Qvortrup (ed), *Referendums Around the World: The Continued Growth of Direct Democracy* (Palgrave MacMillan 2014) 12.

inchoate and so representation will be necessary to give effect. The idea is not that the question or matter itself is binary, but rather that voting inevitably involves the aggregation of political will.

Using the voting stage of a referendum as a process of ratification addresses many of the concerns with referendums from those who think they are *too* democratic. The Fabians, for instance, were opposed to the use of referendums on the basis that the purpose of democracy was to give assent to results rather than projects.[45] The Fabians were right about this. It is difficult to assess and hold representatives accountable for democratic decisions and outcomes when framed *ex post* rather than *ex ante*. Part of seeing referendums as democratic decisions like any other is in holding representatives accountable for their role in referendum processes. It is not possible to maintain this accountability if referendums are used only as devices of initiation. By maximising the representativeness of referendums, however, it is possible to anticipate many of the arguments against their use from those who think referendums are *too* democratic.

B. Referendums are not Democratic *Enough*

The second type of argument against the use of referendums argues that they are not democratic enough. Referendums are not really instances of direct democracy because elites play such an influential role in referendums that referendums only offer votes superficial control over the content of referendums.[46] The arguments made in this book are entirely sympathetic to this approach. It is deeply misleading to suggest that referendums, where they are defined as votes without any involvement at the content-creation stage, offer any direct control to voters over democratic processes. This is one of many important reasons to let go of the labelling of referendums on fundamental constitutional questions as exceptional, directly democratic processes. The argument made here is not to say that deep democratic participation is unnecessary for democracy. It is to agree with those who argue that voting is itself not a method of deliberation.[47] It is therefore necessary to engage voters in other parts of the referendum process, namely the content-generation phase through consultative processes and citizens' assemblies.

To sum up: the view that referendums are either too democratic or not democratic enough are both helpful, but ultimately unpersuasive. The concerns driving both views are significant and rightly challenge the helpfulness of casting referendums on fundamental questions exceptional democratic processes. It is right to worry that referendums disrupt and undermine representative democracy. This provides a compelling reason not to treat referendums as exceptional democratic

[45] ibid 6.

[46] David Miller makes this argument, for instance, in arguing that referendums are not synonymous with self-determination. D Miller, *Is Self-Determination a Dangerous Illusion?* (Polity 2020) 64.

[47] As argued in ch 3, section V.

processes, but it is not a sufficient reason to preclude their use altogether. On the other hand, it is right to say that referendums do not offer direct control over representatives or the content of political questions. Responding to this second argument against the use of referendums requires understanding referendums as longer processes of consultation, allowing many forms of participation. None of this is to suggest that all concerns with the use of referendums can be addressed. This is not possible for any democratic process; all democratic processes are tools that may be used for better and worse ends. Indeed, one fear that unites both the arguments that referendums are too democratic and that they are not democratic enough is the worry that they can be manipulated by elites. This can never be avoided altogether. Referendums are tools like any other democratic device that can be used for better or worse ends. The aim of the methods put forward here is not to make the abuse of referendums impossible, but rather to mitigate against abuse.

C. Arguments of Practice and Principle

These two approaches – referendums are *too* democratic and not democratic *enough* – argue that referendums cannot be successful. This is either because referendums are democratic processes which undermine representative democracy or because they are not robust enough to count as democratic. The problems these traditions raise are both of practice and principle.[48] Irrespective of the quality of constitutional design, the fundamental conception of democracy that referendums offer is not democratic, either because referendums are insufficiently representative, or not representative enough. While this section has confronted the problems of design, it does so in pursuit of a normative point. The normative picture of referendums, as processes which provide direction to representatives, speaks to the normative concerns of both approaches. It recognises the necessity of representatives to democracy, as those such as Haskell argue. It also takes seriously the limits on democracy, and why alternative substantive methods of participation are required, emphasising the importance of protests and citizens' assemblies. In confronting arguments in practice against the use of referendums, it allows for the confrontation of arguments of principle.

[48] As Oliver helpfully puts this question: 'Can all referendum pathologies be cured using Stephen's prescriptions? Stephen's answer would appear to be that most (all?) objections of principle are in fact problems of process and design and therefore remedial.' Tierney replies 'I do endeavour to explore fully the three main failings from which referendums have suffered: what I call the elite control syndrome, the deliberation deficit, and the majoritarian danger. It is my view that these objections, when valid as descriptions of particular referendums, are largely problems of practice not principle, and secondly that the recent turn in deliberative democratic theory provides practical ways of overcoming these problems.' P Oliver and S Tierney, 'Book Review/Response Constitutional Referendums' *International Journal of Constitutional Law* (25 February 2014), www.iconnectblog.com/book-reviewresponse-stephen-tierney-and-peter-oliver, accessed 24 October 2023.

V. Referendums as 'Remedies'

The methods outlined above are offering an account of what it means in practice for referendums to be exercises in representative democracy. These methods are meant to help remedy the failings of referendums, but not in the way that is usually understood. Referendums are often pitched as a remedy for the failings of representative democracy.[49] It is the 'mood of the times',[50] Hollander says, that referendums are 'crisis-solving devices'.[51] Tierney argues that referendums may address democratic deficits by bringing voters closer to the decision-making process.[52] In particular, they are treated as solutions to the democratic deficits created by political parties. Political parties are thought to introduce too much mediation into democratic processes, leaving voters distant and dislocated.[53] Indeed, the idea of referendums as remedying party democracy is a longstanding idea. It is central to the justifications of referendums offered over a century ago by Schmitt[54] and Dicey.[55] Bogdanor, too, writing in the Diceyean tradition argues that referendums provide a remedy for the rigidity of the party system.[56] Referendums are also argued to have related remedial functions. Bogdanor also argues that referendums may perform an educative function by engaging voters with issues.[57] Finally, Ackerman says that constitutional moments such as referendums allow voters to set their differences aside and come together. He says that 'apathy will give way to concern, ignorance to information, selfishness to serious reflection on the country's future'.[58] On these visions of referendums as a remedy, referendums

[49] Hollander (n 5) 4.
[50] ibid.
[51] ibid.
[52] Tierney offers the most nuanced version of this view. He is clear that it is not necessarily the case that referendums can address democratic deficits, but he thinks they might. He says: 'It might well be that … the referendum can help fill the gap between the growing interest of people in politics – "cognitive mobilisation" and their aspirations for a greater role in, and heightened control over, decision-making on the one hand, and on the other hand the tapering away of traditional patterns of political participation such as party membership and voting and weakening chains of responsibility binding political actors.' Tierney (n 1) 8.
[53] P Mair, *Ruling the Void: The Hollowing of Western Democracy* (Verso Books 2013).
[54] Real business takes place, not in the open sessions of a plenum, but in committees and not even necessarily in parliamentary committees, and important decisions are taken in secret meetings of factions leaders … responsibility is transferred and even abolished, and in this way the whole parliamentary system finally becomes only a mere façade concealing the dominance of parties and economic interests.' C Schmitt, *The Crisis of Parliamentary Democracy* [1926] (Ellen Kennedy tr, MIT Press 1986) 20.
[55] The referendum's 'strongest recommendation is that it may keep in check the inordinate power now bestowed on the party machine'. AV Dicey, *Introduction to the Study of the Law of the Constitution* (RE Michener ed, 8th rev edn, Liberty Fund 1982) cix.
[56] 'The referendum, because it gives an equal value to every vote, yields due weight in deciding political issues to that important segment of political opinion which is not merely party opinion.' V Bogdanor, *The People and the Party System* (Cambridge University Press 1981) 82.
[57] 'The referendum brings the voter directly into contact with these interests; it requires him to pay attention to public issues if he is to cast his vote intelligently … The voter may ask himself … what is for the good of the country. It may, therefore, have a profoundly educative effect upon the electorate.' ibid.
[58] B Ackerman, *We the People, Volume 1: Foundations* (Belknap Press 1993) 287.

are external fixes to ordinary processes of representative democracy. This is one way to think about the remedial powers of referendums. It is not, however, the only way. It is also not the best way.

There are two ways to think about the remedial power of referendums. One as a remedy external to a representative system. On this view, referendums are exceptional processes which are brought in to solve a problem. On this view, that referendums are a categorically different type of process that may be used to address the failings of representative democracy. While it is right to say that referendums can help remedy limitations of everyday democratic processes, it is essential to recast the meaning of a remedy. An alternative meaning of remedy is: a countervailing force within a system?[59] Referendums are an internal corrective to help ensure existing representative processes. This way of thinking about remedies is like one of bicameralism, for instance. Is an upper house a cure for the failings of a lower one? Yes and no. Each legislative chamber complements the purposes of the other, and each plays a different role. That different institutions have different responsibilities does not make one a remedy to the other. Another example of countervailing correctives within the same system is the appellate court process. Sometimes, another layer of review is necessary in decision-making. It would be unhelpful and misleading, however, to suggest that the existence of an appellate court system is an external remedy to the failings of trial courts. It may be that there are issues in a case which can only be addressed, or better addressed, by appellate courts rather than trial courts. The reverse may also be true. The point is this: appellate courts and trial courts, like different bodies of a legislature, serve different purposes and are better placed to perform different roles. They are positioned differently with different virtues. These institutions can certainly help each other, and may play a corrective role, but it is misleading to treat them as external, exceptional remedies coming into 'fix' the inherent limitations of the other.

The bicameral and appellate court examples are useful because they demonstrate that the relationships between these different bodies are parts of a single system. It is not the case that these are two tracks in a democracy that are distinct from each other. These are not different orders of decision-making with different normative rationales. On the two-track view of referendums as directly democratic, referendums are special, fundamentally different kinds of processes which temporarily displace existing systems. The two-track way of thinking about referendums is not as bicameralism or appellate courts, but rather as referendums as trump cards which override decisions made by other means with weaker democratic credentials. It is not merely that referendums are reliant on representative

[59] Bogdanor himself uses the idea of referendums as a remedy in both of these senses, even though he says they rely on different arguments: 'The case for the referendum based on its educative nature and the need to encourage participation relies upon arguments of an entirely different type. For they reflect not a conservative scepticism towards representative institutions, nor a belief that the source of authority lies with government, but a view that authority derives from the electorate itself.' Bogdanor (n 56) 85.

systems, although they are, it is that they are inextricable parts of the representative processes. Treating referendums as representative processes is not without its difficulties, however. It creates new challenges. Voting is a simple way of engaging voters in processes of constitutional changes, whereas more iterative processes require much greater thought and care. These problems are planning are, however, problems worth having. The simplicity that referendums appear to offer when focused on the act of voting is illusory. While designing referendums to provide the most effective direction to representatives requires reflection, the next chapter demonstrates through case studies that using the methods outlined above leads to far better results in the long term.

VI. Conclusion

The general claim advanced in this book is that referendums should not be used *because* there are certain decisions that cannot be made by representatives. Instead, referendums are better understood as one way among many that voters provide direction to representatives. In supporting that master thesis, the purpose of this chapter was to lay out methods for maximising the quality of direction provided to representatives on this alternative rationale. The principles put forward in this chapter normalise the use of referendums with significant constitutional content. They integrate referendums into the ordinary democratic processes of representative democracy, to make the use of referendums consonant with other democratic values. These methods sought to ensure that advantages of representative democracy in general, particularly accountability, also translate into processes such as referendums.

Some applications of the use of referendums will be contingent across contexts, but there are general principles of referendums as democratic devices that cut across different jurisdictions. Four broad principles were put forward here: (i) referendums should be understood holistically as composed of a series of stages, (ii) used for a range of reasons to manage disagreement, and (iii) to the greatest extent possible, the voting stage of a referendum process should be one of ratification. Fourth and finally (iv) to better resolve disagreement, special majority requirements should be employed to maintain the equality on which representative democracy relies. While how these principles will apply, and what it means to succeed, will vary to some extent across contexts, this chapter did argue that it is possible to establish that the minimal success conditions of referendums can be defined as (i) providing clear outcomes and (ii) providing voters with reasons to support democratic decisions that they disagreed with.

Finally, the chapter demonstrated why the principles offered here for the use of referendums help to respond to arguments against the use of referendums, both in practice and in principle. Both the concerns that referendums are too democratic, and that they are not democratic enough, can be addressed by recasting referendums as representative democracy. Referendums have come to be justified as remedies to representative democracy, as ways of re-engaging voters in their democracies, and as giving them control over their constitutional settlements. This chapter argued that this cannot be the case. Referendums cannot be remedies for the failings of representative democracy. Representative democracy can, however, be a remedy for the failings of referendums.

6

Three Case Studies

I. Introduction

This chapter explores three referendums in detail. These three examples demonstrate the power of understanding referendums as exercises in providing direction to representatives, and the risks of not doing so as well. The chapter's first case study is the referendum of 2016 in the United Kingdom on withdrawal from the European Union ('Brexit'). This first referendum is a cautionary tale. It identifies the risks of treating referendums as devices to circumvent, rather than provide direction to, representatives. The second case study is often taken to be the gold standard for referendums in comparative constitutional law: the Belfast Agreement in Northern Ireland in 1998. This referendum has much to commend it, but this chapter raises doubts about it as well. The third case study is the Chilean process of constitutional reform. This reform process was sparked off by protests in 2019 but the proposed constitution was not ratified by the referendum held in 2022.

Each of these cases studies evaluates a referendum by reference to the principles identified in the last chapter for providing effective direction to representatives. These four ways of providing effective direction to representatives are: (i) framing referendums wholistically as composed of a series of stages; (ii) using referendums to address disagreement; (iii) treating the voting stage of referendums as a process of ratification, and finally (iv) using special majority requirements. This chapter also evaluates referendums against the two minimal success conditions for referendums identified in chapter five: (i) clarity of outcomes and (ii) the provision of reasons for voters to support outcomes that they disagree with.

A few notes about methodology. The three case studies in this chapter were selected because they are about different kinds of fundamental constitutional change. The subject of the first case study is European integration; the second case study is on the (proposed) creation of a new constitution; and the third case study involves the signing of a peace treaty.[1] These case studies consider different kinds of constitutional questions because this allows for a broader exploration of how

[1] Although note this arguably also was the creation of a new constitution. Lord Bingham said in *Robinson v Secretary of State for Northern Ireland* that the Belfast/Good Friday Agreement (which became the basis for the Northern Ireland Act 1998): 'The 1998 Act does not set out all the constitutional provisions applicable to Northern Ireland, but it is in effect a constitution' *Robinson v Secretary of State for Northern Ireland* [2002] UKHL 32 at para [11].

referendums have been used on these matters, and to what effect. Although these three referendums are compared, they are not being used to draw straightforward comparisons. They are different. The aim of this chapter is to draw out, rather than to minimise, this complexity. While trends are identified, each referendum is evaluated on its own terms. Each case study begins with a brief overview of the relevant referendum to place it in its legal and political context. It is with the legal and political context of Brexit that this chapter begins.

II. Brexit in 2016

A. Introduction to the Referendum Experience

The 2016 Brexit referendum was the second referendum on European integration held in the UK. The first referendum on European integration was held in 1975 to affirm the UK's membership of the then European Economic Community (EEC), which it had joined in 1973.[2] While the 1975 EEC referendum was the first UK-wide referendum, the possibility of using referendums in the UK has been debated since the Great Reform Acts.[3] The uptick in the use of referendums in the UK in the 1970s reflects a worldwide uptick in in the use of referendums that happened around that time.[4] Subsequently, referendums were used repeatedly, and principally, to establish the devolution settlement in Scotland, Wales, and Northern Ireland.[5] Each of these referendums was conducted by a different process. This is because there is no legislation in the United Kindom prescribing which questions must be put to a referendum, or how and when. Each referendum is the result of enabling legislation which is passed on an *ad hoc*[6] basis. To the extent that referendums are controlled by legislation, it is by the Political Parties, Elections, and Referendums Act 2000 (PPERA 2000).[7] This is an administrative

[2] The first UK-wide referendum in 1975 endorsed continued membership of the EEC by a considerable margin 67.2 per cent for 'yes' to 32.8 per cent for 'no' on a 64 per cent turnout. Constitution Committee, 'Referendums in the United Kingdom' (2009) 12th Report of Session 2009–10, 9.

[3] 'How were the "people" – the newly enfranchised electorate – to exercise their power: solely through representative institutions, or through the machinery of direct democracy? This was the central issue in the constitutional debates of the years between 1890 and 1912.' V Bogdanor, *The People and the Party System* (Cambridge University Press 1981) 11.

[4] S Tierney, *Constitutional Referendums: The Theory and Practice of Republican Deliberation* (Oxford University Press 2012) 1.

[5] Referendums on devolution in Scotland and Wales were held in 1979 and 1997. The devolution proposals were not approved in 1979 but were in 1997. A border poll was held in Northern Ireland in 1973, and the referendum on the Belfast Agreement will be considered in greater detail below. Constitution Committee (n 2) 9.

[6] ibid 20.

[7] Beyond the PPERA 2000, there are two other important sources of guidance with respect to the use of referendums in the UK. Some requirements for the use of referendums can be found in the Acts that make up the devolution settlement: the Scotland Act 2016, the Wales Act 2017, and the Northern

rather than substantive Act. The greatest degree of guidance comes from s 101 of the Act, which requires only that enabling legislation must be used to call referendums in the UK.[8] The PPERA 2000 is open-ended, however, as to how this enabling legislation may work. This means, in effect, that the question of when and how referendums are used is determined by the kind of legislation that the government of the day can get through Parliament.

Although deeper European integration occurred in phases, referendums were not held in the UK on other milestones such as the signing of the Maastricht[9] and Lisbon[10] Treaties. Referendums were, however, held in other countries on these treaties,[11] repeatedly resulting in changes to the treaties.[12] The inconsistent use of referendums on European integration in the UK created a longstanding problem of democratic legitimacy with the UK's membership of the European Union. Prime Minister David Cameron tried to address this democratic deficit, and the political divisions in his own party created by this deficit, by calling a referendum in 2016. The 2016 referendum was called not to ratify a new treaty on European integration, which at that point would have automatically been required by s 8 of the European Union Act 2011. It was held instead because of a manifesto commitment which had been made by the Prime Minister in an attempt to appease his backbenchers. The 2016 Brexit referendum was a tool used by the executive for party management.[13]

This 2016 referendum was a failure of constitutional process and design, but it was not a one-off failure. The circumstances in which Prime Minister David Cameron found himself were a result of a decades-long systemic failure to identify a coherent role for referendums in the UK. David Cameron was by no means the

Ireland Act 1998. The existence of the Scottish and Welsh Parliaments is not to be abolished unless with the consent of people voting in a referendum. The Northern Ireland Act is slightly different in that s 1(2) clarifies if there is a majority vote in a referendum to no longer be a part of the UK, then the Secretary of State has a duty to bring forward proposals for a change in the relationship. Finally, the European Union Act 2011 required a referendum on any future European integration; however, this has now been repealed by the European Union (Withdrawal) Act 2018.

[8] '"Referendum" means a referendum or other poll held, in pursuance of any provision made by or under an Act of Parliament, on one or more questions specified in or in accordance with any such provision.' PPERA 2000, s 101(2)(a).

[9] D Baker, B Gamble, and S Ludlam, 'The Parliamentary Siege of Maastricht 1993: Conservative Divisions and British Ratification' (1994) 47 *Parliamentary Affairs* 37, 37.

[10] Although Prime Minister Tony Blair promised one on the Lisbon Treaty and later reneged. This decision was, unsuccessfully, challenged on the grounds that voters had a legitimate expectation would have a vote in a referendum. *R (on the Application of Wheeler) v Office of the Prime Minister* [2008] EWHC 1409.

[11] SB Hobolt, *Europe in Question: Referendums on European Integration* (Oxford University Press 2009) 1.

[12] 'The no-votes in referendums in France and the Netherlands in 2005 put an end to the Constitutional Treaty, and the Irish electorate caused another political crisis in Europe by rejecting the Lisbon Treaty.' ibid.

[13] Hollander's analysis of referendums across the European Union shows that they tend to be used in exactly this way across the continent, not only in the UK, arguing that 'strategic motives are decisive' in holding referendums. S Hollander, *The Politics of Referendum Use in European Democracies* (Palgrave Macmillan 2019) 5.

first Prime Minister to use referendums in a politically convenient rather than principled way.[14] Indeed, the 1975 referendum on continued membership of what was then the EEC was also held to help address a problem within a political party, in that case the Labour Party rather than the Conservative Party.[15] This *ad hoc* use of referendums in the UK reflects an approach where referendums are used to resolve political problems in representative democracy. This is exactly the wrong approach. Referendums are more successful, this book argues, when they are integrated into existing institutions to ensure accountability and to provide direction to representatives. The following section will consider how and why referendums are used more effectively when integrated with institutions of representative democracy.

B. Understanding Referendums Wholistically

The enabling legislation for the 2016 Brexit referendum, the European Union Referendum Act 2015, did not conceive of the referendum as a series of stages. The vote was the beginning and the end of the consultation process with voters and the question on the ballot paper was framed in simple terms: either remain a member or leave the European Union. In neither the negotiation process on the withdrawal agreement nor the referendum were polls or consultations held on what voters might seek from a reformed relationship with the European Union. A citizens' assembly was eventually held to establish voters' priorities, but not until after the referendum itself had been held and not by the Government.[16] Further, the legal consequences of the referendum outcome if it resulted in a vote to leave were unclear. This could be seen in the court case *R (Miller) v Secretary of State for Exiting the European Union* [2017] UKSC 5, in which all parties agreed that the referendum result itself was insufficient to trigger a change in law.[17]

[14] Already in 2009, the Constitution Committee of the House of Lords argued: 'The balance of the evidence that we have heard leads us to the conclusion that there are significant drawbacks to the use of referendums. In particular, we regret the *ad hoc* manner in which referendums have been used, often as a tactical device, by the government of the day.' Constitution Committee (n 2) 20.

[15] R Saunders, *Yes to Europe!: The 1975 Referendum and Seventies Britain* (Cambridge University Press 2018) 57, 175.

[16] Citizens' Assembly on Brexit, 'About the Citizens' Assembly' *The Constitution Unit, UCL* (2017), citizensassembly.co.uk/wp-content/uploads/2017/12/Citizens-Assembly-on-Brexit-Report.pdf, accessed 9 August 2021.

[17] The majority say: 'Both sides of the argument proceed on the basis that the referendum on membership of the EU was held under the European Union Referendum Act 2015 ("the 2015 Act"), which resulted in a vote to leave the EU, does not provide the answer. The Secretary of State's argument proceeds on the basis that the Crown has taken the decision under Article 50(1), accepting the result of the referendum. The Miller claimants argue only that Parliament can take that decision. Both the Secretary of State and the Miller claimants proceed on the basis that the referendum result was not itself a decision by the UK to withdraw from the EU, in accordance with the UK's constitutional requirements, and that the 2015 Act did not itself authorise notification under Article 50(2). In these circumstances, there is no issue before the court as to the legal effect of the referendum result. Nor

Framing a referendum as a singular vote distinct from representative democracy, without clear legal implications, set democratic institutions against each other. The worst example of this is the infamous *Daily Mail* headline asserting that judges were 'enemies of the people' for 'obstructing' Brexit by holding that the law required a vote by Parliament before notice of withdrawal from the European Union could be given under Article 50 of the Treaty on European Union (TEU).[18] The UK Government repeatedly argued that the referendum result in itself gave it a direct mandate from the people.[19] Later, under another Prime Minister, the Government argued that democracy required the bypassing of representatives and the prorogation (ie, suspension) of Parliament, since the House of Commons had become effectively deadlocked during the process of settling the nature of the UK's future relationship with the EU.[20] This prorogation was in service of the higher democratic purpose of giving effect to Brexit. The vote-centric nature of the 2016 referendum led to the impression that representatives would not be involved in interpreting and executing the referendum's outcome. This approach was misleading. Further, the vote-centric approach to referendums taken by the enabling legislation made it difficult to address the underlying disagreement.

C. Referendums as Addressing Disagreement

The vote on 23 June 2016 was not framed as meaningfully addressing disagreement. It need not have been this way. The referendum could have been connected more closely, for example, to specific issues regarding the UK's membership of the European Union. Indeed, the 2016 referendum campaign was preceded by a process of negotiation on the terms of the UK's EU membership. While David Cameron did not achieve all his objectives in the negotiation process, he did have some limited successes.[21] This process of negotiation before the referendum was a significant similarity between the 1975 EEC referendum and the 2016 referendum.

is this an appropriate occasion on which to consider the implications for our constitutional law of the developing practice of holding referendums before embarking on major constitutional changes: a matter on which this court has heard no argument.' *R (Miller) v Secretary of State for Exiting the European Union* [2017] UKSC 5 at para [171].

[18] J Slack, 'Enemies of the People: Fury over "Out of Touch" Judges Who Have "Declared War on Democracy" by Defying 17.4m Brexit Voters and Who Could Trigger Constitutional Crisis' *Daily Mail* (4 November 2018), www.dailymail.co.uk/news/article-3903436/Enemies-people-Fury-touch-judges-defied-17-4m-Brexit-voters-trigger-constitutional-crisis.html, accessed 19 August 2021.

[19] Arguing it was her responsibility to 'implement the referendum result'. T May, 'Theresa May's Brexit Speech in Full' *The Telegraph* (17 January 2017), www.telegraph.co.uk/news/2017/01/17/theresa-mays-brexit-speech-full, accessed 21 December 2017.

[20] H White, 'Proroguing Parliament Would Be Undemocratic' *Institute for Government* (6 June 2019), www.instituteforgovernment.org.uk/blog/proroguing-parliament-would-be-undemocratic-and-probably-trigger-election, accessed 23 August 2021.

[21] Cameron arguably made some progress on his objectives on sovereignty, welfare and migrant benefits, economic governance, and competitiveness. J Smith, 'David Cameron's EU Renegotiation and Referendum Pledge: A Case of Déjà Vu?' (2016) 11 *British Politics* 324, 326.

The relationships between these two negotiation processes and their respective referendum campaigns were, however, totally different. In 1975, there was a strong – albeit not universally held – sense that a new deal was being endorsed. The changes secured in the 1974 renegotiation addressed doubts that many voters had about membership of the EEC. Harold Wilson had successfully secured reforms from the EEC on Commonwealth trade, aid and development, the Common Agricultural Policy, and the budget.[22] The approval of these reforms was central to the 'yes' vote in the 1975 referendum.[23] While, like the 2016 process, the 1975 process was not linked to a clear constitutional event such as the signing of the Maastricht or Lisbon Treaties, 1975 was different from 2016 because in 1975 there was a much deeper connection between the negotiations that preceded the voting stage and the voting stage of the referendum. The 1975 process was framed not only as about the vote, but about the substance of the negotiations that preceded it. In this way, the referendum was not about responding to or resolving disagreement. No compromises were discussed which would address different points of view. It was a bare, majoritarian process which placed the debate in stark 'yes' or 'no' terms. There is nothing inevitable about treating referendums this way, and they are used in a wide range of more constructive ways around the world. Indeed, as recently as 2011, referendums had been used in a more constructive way to address disagreement *in the UK*. The next section explains why.

D. The Voting Stage as a Process of Ratification

Voting, as argued in chapter two, is – at most – a process for ratification. Voting can only confirm or veto proposals for reform.[24] Voting is not a substantive opportunity to participate in consultations, and it should not be given the normative authority to suggest that it can. The process on 23 June 2016 was not a ratificatory referendum. This was reflected in the nature of the question on the ballot: 'Should the United Kingdom remain a member of the European Union or leave the European Union?'[25] As Walker argued in May 2016, there were innumerable possible answers to this question, and possible future relationships with the European Union.[26] A leave vote did not specify any of these possible relationships.

[22] Saunders (n 15) 90.

[23] 'As *The Economist* put it, the "concessions which Mr Harold Wilson won … are not in themselves significant. But the winning them, and the manner of winning them, were." The effect of all this was substantial. Unlike in 2016, the conclusion of the renegotiations produced a significant and enduring shift in the polls.' ibid 93.

[24] While Schmitt's theory of plebiscitary democracy is generally abhorrent, on this point he is entirely correct. C Schmitt, *Legality and Legitimacy* (Duke University Press 2004) 90.

[25] Government of the United Kingdom, 'EU Referendum' gov.uk (24 June 2016) www.gov.uk/government/topical-events/eu-referendum/about, accessed 19 August 2021.

[26] N Walker, 'The Brexit Vote: The Wrong Question for Britain and Europe' *UK Constitutional Law Association* (21 June 2016), ukconstitutionallaw.org/2016/06/21/neil-walker-the-brexit-vote-the-wrong-question-for-britain-and-europe, accessed 7 July 2016.

While the referendum outcome clearly established the need for constitutional change, the content of that constitutional change was indeterminate.

Some of the referendums held in the UK since the 1970s have had a ratificatory structure. These included the two devolution referendums of 1979[27] and especially the Alternative Vote referendum in 2011. Contrast, for instance, the enabling legislation in the Alternative Vote referendum with that of the Brexit referendum in 2015. In the Alternative Vote enabling legislation, s 8 of the Parliamentary Constituencies and Voting Act 2011 outlined two possible paths for the legislation depending on the results of the referendum.[28] If most votes in the referendum were for the proposed changes, then the Secretary of State was to introduce an order bringing the changes in legislation into force. If, on the other hand, most votes were against the changes, then the Secretary of State was to bring an order repealing the legislation. The enabling legislation for the 2016 Brexit referendum, by contrast, made no such provisions for the outcome of the vote. The Parliamentary Constituencies and Voting Act 2011 demonstrates that the question of how a referendum outcome interacts with existing law is not an unsolvable problem in the UK, but rather one that has only sometimes been answered in enabling legislation.

It is not always the case that referendums can have only a ratificatory structure. As the Independent Commission on Referendums rightly highlighted in the wake of Brexit, referendums should ideally be used post-legislatively, but this is not always possible.[29] Sometimes, the Commission concluded, multiple votes will be necessary, and in those circumstances, it is necessary to clarify up front whether a second vote may be required.[30] This possible need for multiple votes further demonstrates a point about referendums made in chapter five. In the case of an initiatory and ratificatory referendum, neither vote is sufficient to provide direction to representatives. It is these votes taken together, and the broader process of which they are a part, which is better understood as the referendum process.

[27] 'Do you want the provisions of the Scotland Act (or Wales Act) 1978 to be put into effect?' Constitution Committee (n 2) 9.

[28] '(1)The Minister must make an order bringing into force section 9, Schedule 10 and Part 1 of Schedule 12 ("the alternative vote provisions") if: (a) more votes are cast in the referendum in favour of the answer "Yes" than in favour of the answer "No", and (b) the draft of an Order in Council laid before Parliament under subsection (5A) of section 3 of the Parliamentary Constituencies Act 1986 (substituted by section 10(6) below has been submitted to Her Majesty in Council under section 4 of that Act. (2) If more votes are not cast in the referendum in favour of the answer "Yes" than in favour of the answer "No", the Minister must make an order repealing the alternative vote provisions.' Parliamentary Constituencies and Voting Act 2011, s 8.

[29] 'Wherever possible, a referendum should come at the end, not the beginning, of the decision-making process. It should be post-legislative, deciding whether legislation that has already passed through the relevant parliament or assembly should be implemented.' UCL Constitution Unit, 'Report of the Independent Commission on Referendums', 10, www.ucl.ac.uk/constitution-unit/sites/constitution-unit/files/ICR_Final_Report.pdf, accessed 30 October 2023.

[30] 'Sometimes a referendum may be needed earlier: for example, it initiate intergovernmental negotiations. In such cases, the government initiating the referendum should set out precise plans of what will be done in the event of a vote for change; the enabling legislation would set out a two-referendum process, for use in the event the settlement does not deliver what was promised.' ibid.

Indeed, more than three votes may be required for a referendum to succeed. The case study of Chile in 2020 discussed below is just one such example.

E. Special Majority Requirements

The Brexit referendum of 2016 did not employ any special majority requirements. The outcome was instead a straightforward matter of which proposition received more votes. There are at least three types of special majority requirements. The first is a threshold of either (i) numbers of voters, which there is precedent for in the UK,[31] or (ii) a supermajority of votes, which might be defensible for a process of constitutional change.[32] Additionally, (iii) special majority requirements could be geographical. These kinds of special majority requirements, for instance, require majorities in subnational units for constitutional change to occur.[33]

The lack of special majority requirements created difficult asymmetries in the Brexit referendum. This was because the impact of Brexit was more acute in Northern Ireland, the site of the UK's only land border with the European Union, as opposed to the rest of the UK. Northern Ireland was left in the position of having voted for continuing membership of the European Union, while also experiencing the greatest impact of leaving. If one of the purposes of referendums is to address disagreement, special majority requirements make it more likely that referendums can achieve that objective by ensuring that there is broad agreement from voters with the reforms. Additionally, special majority requirements are effective ways of integrating referendums into representative democracy by ensuring protections for various regions and minorities. This means that referendums are more likely to satisfy their two success conditions: providing clarity of guidance to

[31] Devolution did not proceed after the referendums in 1979 because the threshold requirement that not less than 40 per cent of the total electorate had to vote 'yes'. Although 51.6 per cent of those who voted supported devolution, this was only on a 63.6 per cent turnout. Constitution Committee (n 2). There was an analogous requirement in Wales, but the referendum failed at the earlier hurdle as only 20.3 per cent of voters supported devolution in the first place. ibid 1.

[32] Indeed, Rogoff argued that this was one of the tragedies of Brexit. 'The real lunacy of the United Kingdom's vote to leave the European Union was not that British leaders dared to ask their populace to weigh the benefits of membership against the immigration pressures it presents. Rather, it was the absurdly low bar for exit, requiring only a simple majority. Given voter turnout of 70%, this meant that the leave campaign won with only 36% of eligible voters backing it.' K Rogoff, 'Britain's Democratic Failure' *Project Syndicate* (2016), www.project-syndicate.org/commentary/brexit-democratic-failure-for-uk-by-kenneth-rogoff-2016-06, accessed 2 September 2019.

[33] As in other countries, where sometimes agreement of more than half of the states or provinces is required for constitutional changes. This is required, for instance by Article V of the American Constitution. 'The Congress, whenever two thirds of both houses shall deem it necessary, shall propose amendments to this Constitution, or, on the application of the legislatures of two thirds of several states, shall call a convention for proposing amendments, which, in either case, shall be valid to all intents and purposes, as part of this Constitution when ratified by the legislatures of three fourths of the several states, or by conventions in three fourths thereof, as the one or the other mode of ratification may be proposed by the Congress.'

representatives, and reasons for voters to support outcomes with which they disagree. These success conditions are discussed in the section following.

F. The Success Conditions of Referendums

Not all referendums are created equal. As the previous chapter argued, there are many reasons a referendum may be successful. It may affirm an effective new constitutional settlement, enable equality, or help provide responses to historic unfairness and injustices. While these instrumental and content-specific successes are important, the previous chapter identified a minimal two features of referendums which are required if they are to provide direction to representatives. These success conditions are: (i) clarity of outcomes and (ii) providing voters with reasons to support outcomes, even those they disagree with. The 2016 Brexit referendum will be evaluated against these two success conditions now.

i. Clarity of Outcomes

The outcome of the Brexit referendum was unclear. As explained above, the ballot question did not distinguish between innumerable possible relationships with the European Union.[34] This was only one of the ways, however, in which the referendum outcome was unclear. The clarity of the 2016 referendum was also undermined by the Electoral Commission's conclusion that the Leave Campaign broke campaign finance laws. As the Commission said, this breach undermined public confidence in the referendum outcome.[35] A lack of integrity in the process undermined the clarity of the outcome. Integrity of process is particularly important for referendums. The periodic nature of elections helps to ensure accountability in democratic processes, and if legislators break campaign rules, there may be consequences at the next election. Representatives may be removed, or their credibility may be undermined. In referendums, however, this is not possible. This is particularly true when referendums are seen as one-off exceptional events. This is another of the many reasons it is essential to integrate referendums into broader processes of representative democracy. This also helps ensure clarity by maintaining the integrity of the referendum process and outcome, and this in turn helps provide clarity on the outcome. Finally, this absence of clarity also had

[34] Walker (n 26).

[35] 'Vote Leave was the designated lead campaigner for the leave outcome at the referendum. We found that it broke the electoral rules set out by Parliament to ensure fairness, confidence, and legitimacy at an electoral event. Serious offences such as these undermine public confidence in our system and it is vital, therefore, that they are properly investigated and sanctioned.' Vote Leave eventually withdrew their appeal of the decisions and paid a fine of £61000. Electoral Commission, 'Media Statement: Vote Leave' *The Electoral Commission* (29 March 2019), www.electoralcommission.org.uk/media-statement-vote-leave, accessed 9 August 2021.

the insidious effect of giving those who did not support the substantive outcome of the referendum a reason to challenge it. Therefore, the 2016 Brexit referendum did not meet the first criteria for success.

ii. Reasons for Voters to Support Outcomes they Disagree with

In an election, one of the reasons for a voter to support a winner they disagree with is because if at a future date their preferred candidate eventually succeeds, they want their candidate to prevail as well.[36] These shared practices, and shared perceptions of legitimacy, help institutions, and establish shared conventions. Indeed, these shared conceptions of legitimacy help democracies to endure despite disagreement. These kinds of reasons to support outcomes hold far less power in referendums, particularly if those processes are held on a one-off exceptional basis. Further, in elections, there are a range of ways in which voters' views may be represented. This is true even if a voter's preferred outcome does not prevail. For instance, a range of political parties compose a legislature. Therefore, even if a voter's assigned representative does not reflect the voter's views, there may be others in a legislature who can still speak up for those views. Finally, legislatures provide opportunities for feedback, debate, and compromise, recognising that not everyone will be equally impacted by legislation and there will be a range of individual circumstances which may need to be considered. All these institutional actions and actors help provide voters with reasons to support outcomes they disagree with. Even if their preferred outcome does not prevail, in elections at least, this does not mean the absence of representation.

As with elections, it is possible for referendums to provide voters with reasons to support outcomes that they disagree with. Such reasons are far more likely to arise, however, when referendums are understood wholistically as a series of stages, the aim of which is to address disagreement. Processes such as polls, citizens' assemblies, and consultations can help to engage voters at both the content-setting and ratificatory stages. Particularly at the content-setting stage, taking feedback on board in proposals for reform is a way of providing voters with reasons to support outcomes they disagree with. Even if a voter's view does not prevail, a qualification or exception to a proposal recognising their specific circumstances may well provide them with a reason to support an outcome anyway. These opportunities and possibilities are central to referendums' legitimacy. None of these kinds of consultation or engagement processes happened before, during, or after the Brexit referendum. The bare majoritarian nature of the referendum did not provide those who disagreed with the referendum many

[36] For a helpful account of the shared institutional norms and legitimacy around the idea of 'loyal opposition', see G Webber, 'Loyal Opposition and Political Constitutionalism' (2016) *Oxford Journal of Legal Studies* 1, 3.

reasons to support it. Neither the process nor the outcome spoke to a range of views on European integration.

G. Conclusion

The 2016 Brexit referendum is a textbook case of how not to hold a referendum. On even most quotidian questions, the legislative process is demanding. There are opportunities for feedback, through Select Committees, white papers are published, and a range of views are expressed in Parliament through both the governing and smaller parties. No one always gets their way, but these opportunities for debate and feedback are significant. These are developed processes of providing direction to representatives. The central failing of the Brexit referendum is that it understood the role of a referendum as bypassing rather than providing direction to representatives. The referendum process treated the vote as the beginning and the end of the referendum process, rather than understanding it wholistically. It made no effort to address disagreement, or to recognise those who would be disproportionately impacted, such as in Northern Ireland. It did not provide a clear outcome, ie one which even voters who did not agree with it would have reason to support. The tactical failure of Brexit was in Prime Minister Cameron treating it as a shortcut to managing problems within his own party. One-off votes offer no direct shortcut to compromise or consensus. Referendums can play a part in addressing disagreement, but such processes are demanding and require deep engagement with representatives. The next two referendums, on the Belfast Agreement and the Chilean process of constitutional reform, demonstrate just how demanding successful referendum processes are.

III. The Belfast/Good Friday Agreement in 1998

A. Introduction to the Referendum Experience

The referendum in Northern Ireland in 1998 can only be understood in historical context. When the Irish Free State was established by the Anglo-Irish Treaty in 1921, six of the northern counties of Ireland remained part of the United Kingdom. In the decades following partition, the border between Northern Ireland and Ireland was a source of violence.[37] At least 3,600 deaths, and tens

[37] For a comprehensive account of these decades see C Townshend, *The Partition: Ireland Divided, 1888–1925* (Penguin 2021), particularly chapter 2: 'Why Politics Failed and Violence Began' and chapter 3: 'The Rationality of War: The Troubles Generation'.

of thousands of injuries, are attributable to this violence, sometimes known as 'The Troubles'.[38] Peace talks, interspersed with ceasefires, were held throughout the 1980s and 1990s. In 1998, a peace treaty was negotiated between the north and south of Ireland called the Belfast Agreement, also known as the Good Friday Agreement. Under the Belfast Agreement, the British and Irish governments each agreed to hold referendums on 22 May 1998. The referendum in Ireland would amend the Constitution of Ireland to reflect the Agreement. The referendum in Northern Ireland approved the Agreement reached in the Multi-Party talks, with the referendum question asking voters if they supported it in its totality.[39] The Northern Ireland Act 1998 of the British Parliament implemented many of the provisions of the Belfast Agreement and ended direct rule in Northern Ireland.

The referendum on the Belfast Agreement in 1998 was the second of two votes held on the relationship between Northern Ireland and the United Kingdom.[40] A referendum was also held in 1973 which asked two questions: 'Do you want Northern Ireland to remain part of the United Kingdom? or 'Do you want Northern Ireland to be joined with the Republic of Ireland outside the United Kingdom?'[41] This 1973 Border Poll was overwhelmingly boycotted by the nationalist community, with only 1.1 per cent voting in support for joining with the Republic of Ireland.[42] The boycott was a predictable failing in the structure of the referendum itself. A letter to the *Times of London* warned that without connecting the border poll to the reforms outlined in the Government's white paper, the vote would become a straightforward majoritarian headcount.[43] That is exactly what happened, and the vote did nothing to address the underlying disagreement. The referendum on the Belfast Agreement in 1998 was very different from the 1973 border poll. The Belfast Agreement was approved by 71.12 per cent of voters in Northern Ireland and 94.39 per cent in the South of Ireland.[44] Unlike in 1973, the voting stage of the 1998 referendum came at the end of a long consultative process. There were both indirect and explicit consultations.[45] The consultative process

[38] K McEvoy and J Morison, 'Beyond the "Constitutional Moment": Law, Transition, and Peacemaking in Northern Ireland' (2003) 26 *Fordham International Law Journal* 960, 962.

[39] 'Do you support the Agreement reached at the Multi-Party Talks in Northern Ireland and set out in Command Paper 3883?' Constitution Committee (n 2) 10.

[40] A referendum was, controversially, not held on Home Rule for Ireland despite strong objections from AV Dicey. For a discussion of Dicey's opposition to home rule see M Qvortrup, 'A.V. Dicey: The Referendum as the People's Veto' (1999) 20 *History of Political Thought* 531. There was also no 'plebiscite' held on the process border-drawing in the partition, although it was considered. Townshend (n 37) 140–43.

[41] Constitution Committee (n 2) 9.

[42] ibid.

[43] *The Times* (16 January 1973).

[44] Constitution Committee (n 2).

[45] 'In fact, civil society's mobilization and its efforts to influence the negotiations were such that they helped sustained the momentum in the negotiations.' J Amaral, *Making Peace with Referendums* (Syracuse University Press 2019) 93.

was composed of a series of polls,[46] and the establishment of the Civic Forum for Northern Ireland.[47]

In addition to taking a different process, the content of the Agreement in 1998 was different from 1973. The Multi-Party Agreement was a consocational peace treaty and power-sharing agreement.[48] The ballot question itself asked: 'Do you support the Agreement reached at the Multi-Party talks in Northern Ireland and set out in Command Paper 3883?'[49] This does not mean that support for the Belfast Agreement was universal. There was opposition, for example from the Democratic Unionist Party who were opposed to the release of paramilitary prisoners as part of the Agreement.[50] While support for the Belfast Agreement was by no means unanimous, and the outcome was imperfect, this referendum succeeded where many other referendums in the UK have failed. One of the reasons this referendum succeeded is because it was not a way of bypassing representatives. Unlike the Brexit referendum, the referendum in Northern Ireland in 1998 was inseparable from a much broader and deeper process of consultation and compromise. The voting stage of this referendum is best understood as a process where voters made choices about the decisions of representatives, as these next sections demonstrate.

B. Understanding Referendums Wholistically

The referendum on the Belfast Agreement is sometimes argued to be the gold standard for referendums.[51] The process is understood to have given rise to an enduring peace treaty which did succeed in addressing disagreement and creating a new framework for sharing power across religious lines. The referendum on the Belfast Agreement demonstrates that referendums can only be understood wholistically. The degree to which referendums succeed or fail is not just a result

[46] 'Eight surveys of public opinion were conducted on issues central to the Northern Ireland peace process between April 1996 and May 2000 and for seven of these polls the party negotiators were involved in drafting and agreeing the questions. This involved "in depth interviews with party negotiators, the testing of their proposals by public opinion survey and the publication of the results of these polls in the popular press," making the process transparent, engaging elites and ordinary citizens in a genuine dialog, and allowing "politicians on both sides of the conflict to map out areas of compromise and common ground without running the danger of getting to far ahead of their supporters."' Tierney (n 4) 251, citing McEvoy and Morison (n 38); C Irwin, *The People's Peace Process in Northern Ireland* (Palgrave Macmillan 2002) 1.

[47] For an excellent study of the Civic Forum for Northern Ireland see: LS Pålshaugen, *The Northern Ireland Civic Forum and a Politics of Recognition* (Institute for British-Irish Studies, University College Dublin 2004).

[48] Amaral (n 45) 89–93.

[49] Constitution Committee (n 2) 10.

[50] Hayes and McAllister also provide an excellent study of this, and how dissatisfaction with the agreement continues to undermine the executive. B Hayes and I McAllister, 'Who Voted for Peace? Public Support for the 1998 Northern Ireland Agreement' (2007) 16 *Irish Political Studies* 73.

[51] R Levy, I O'Flynn, and HL Kong, *Deliberative Peace Referendums* (Oxford University Press 2021) 98.

of the voting stage, but of the processes of consultation and inclusion that precede or follow them. Indeed, both the sceptics and supporters of the Belfast Agreement agree on this point: the success or failure of referendums can only be understood in the round, by evaluating the process wholistically as composed of a series of stages. The challenge of successful referendums is in achieving this by making the processes as broad and inclusive as possible. The shape, content, and inclusiveness of the negotiation process and opportunities for consultation matter enormously. For better or worse, the voting stage of a referendum, in successful referendums, is almost an afterthought.

Three studies of peace referendums, which employ Northern Ireland as a (relative) success story, confirm that voting was only one part of a successful process of consultation, negotiation, and reconciliation. Amaral stresses exactly this point by drawing a comparison between the referendum on the Belfast Agreement and the referendum in Cyprus about the Annan plan, which failed.[52] Amaral argues that the (again, at least relative) openness and inclusiveness of the peace process in Northern Ireland was the key to its success at the voting stage.[53] Similarly, Levy, O'Flynn, and Kong emphasise the deliberative processes surrounding the referendum. The process was so successful, they argue, because the deliberative character of the referendum bridged normative divides and establish new constitutional norms which have allowed the peace agreement to endure.[54] Finally, Tierney also emphasises the deliberative quality of the 1998 referendum. Tierney stresses that the success was the result of the 'full engagement and inclusion of both national communities in the decision-making process *prior* to the referendum'.[55]

This is not to suggest, or to say these writers suggest, that the referendum on the Belfast Agreement, or the Agreement itself, was perfect. It has many critics.[56] Cochrane is a vocal sceptic, arguing that this referendum was a result of agreement among elites, but it has never meaningfully translated to change on the ground.[57] The actual work of reconciliation in Northern Ireland, Cochrane argues,

[52] The Annan plan was led by former UN Secretary General Kofi Annan to bring about an agreement between the Greek Cypriot and Turkish Cypriot leaders. Amaral (n 45) ch 4.

[53] This idea is best captured in the epigraph to Amaral's book where she quotes American diplomat Harold H Saunders saying: 'Peace treaties do not make peace; people make peace.' ibid.

[54] Levy, O'Flynn, and Kong (n 51) 98.

[55] Tierney (n 4) 74 (emphasis in original).

[56] Amaral herself cautions against treating the referendum as an unqualified success arguing: 'unfortunately, and despite its unquestionably positive outcome, the referendum experience and the split in the vote between the two communities, along with constant implementation setbacks, have generated a general sense in Northern Ireland that the agreement has not yet delivered on its promises and might collapse at any time, a fear that continues to polarize politics'. Amaral (n 45) 103. Cochrane is even more doubtful than Amaral arguing: '[M]any people [regard] the sometimes-functioning Assembly and Executive (and by extension the GFA itself) as an expensive political decoration, rather than as a set of institutions that could provide political stability and augment the quality of their lives. Looked at from this perspective, the GFA had not stopped paramilitary violence; it had not significantly improved community relations … when the ambitious language of the GFA was set against the sectarian reality … it was found sadly wanting.' F Cochrane, *Northern Ireland: The Fragile Peace* (Yale University Press 2021) 213.

[57] Cochrane (n 56) 212.

did not happen in referendums or weighty constitutional rhetoric, but instead is happening (to the extent it is happening at all) through grassroots work.[58] It is necessary to take Cochrane's critiques seriously, but the referendum on the Belfast Agreement does have much to commend it. The vote in the referendum was the result of broad and deep cross-community consultation and engagement. Both the successes and failures of the referendum in Northern Ireland, however, can only be understood wholistically. Studying the voting stage of the referendum alone explains very little about its failures and successes in addressing disagreement, as the referendum on the Belfast Agreement demonstrates.

C. Referendums as Addressing Disagreement

One of the key reasons that the Belfast Agreement should be understood as successful was that the aim of the peace process was to address disagreement. The previous 'yes/no' Border Poll in 1973, by contrast, took a majoritarian approach to addressing disagreement. The power-sharing approach of the Belfast Agreement was entirely different. In addition to the content of the Agreement seeking to address disagreement, the process by which the referendum was reached sought to address disagreement as well. This meant the inclusion not only of the leading political parties, but of smaller political parties.[59] Elections to the Peace Forum included a broad range of representatives.[60] Indeed, the function of the Belfast Agreement is to establish a power-sharing agreement. The aim of such a consocational agreement is to *address* disagreement, rather than to tally votes and pick a side. While, as conceded above, the Agreement has its shortcomings, it was nevertheless a genuine attempt to find a compromise and bring an end to the conflict.

D. The Voting Stage as a Process of Ratification

The referendum on the Belfast Agreement was a clear instance of the voting stage of the referendum acting as a process of ratification. The question on the ballot asked whether voters 'supported' the command paper concluded by the Multi-Party talks. These talks had made tough decisions and concessions. There were innumerable possible relationships between the north and south of Ireland, and it

[58] As Cochrane puts it: '[L]ocal level co-operation had a longer-lasting impact, and relationship[s] [were] built from the ground level upwards that arguably [were] much more valuable that the rhetoric contained in the GFA about "safeguards" and "rights".' ibid 219.

[59] Even those connected to violent organisations. D Horowitz, 'Explaining the Northern Ireland Agreement: The Sources of an Unlikely Constitutional Consensus' (2002) *British Journal of Political Science* 193, 212.

[60] '[The forum] was comprised of 60 members appointed for three years to work on a voluntary basis with the support of a secretariat. The Forum was specifically designed to represent a part of society not caught up in the party political system.' Pålshaugen (n 47) 9.

is easy to imagine voters supporting peace in the abstract, or unwilling to support peace in the abstract, because of a lack of clarity about what it would entail. Unlike the Brexit referendum, there was a proposal on the table for voters to accept or reject in its entirety.

This is not to say the agreement was complete. It was long and fraught with questions, some still unresolved.[61] These limitations demonstrate that even in the most comprehensive and consultative agreements, the outcome will still be inchoate. All referendum outcomes will still require representatives to interpret and give life to them. These limitations aside, ratification remains by far the superior approach to the voting stage of a referendum. The Belfast Agreement demonstrates this, because it offered voters a set of tough choices and asked if they were prepared to make that compromise. It did not, as with the Brexit referendum in 2016, allow voters to imagine their individual ideal agreement for themselves. The limitations of the Belfast Agreement demonstrate that a proposal or piece of legislation will never exhaust the meaning of a referendum outcome, and representatives will need to take their direction from it as they execute it. This necessarily incomplete nature of referendum outcomes means it is even more important to see referendums as integrated into processes of representative democracy, the aim of which is to provide ongoing direction to representatives.

E. Special Majority Requirements

The philosophy of special majority requirements was essential to the success of the referendum on the Belfast Agreement. The entire peace process was, by necessity, consocational. It was not driven by the philosophy of simple majoritarianism. Referendums were held both in Northern Ireland, on the agreement itself, and in Ireland to amend the constitution to incorporate the Agreement. The requirement of cross-community consensus was also forward-looking. The Agreement itself holds that consent for Irish unification must be 'freely and concurrently' given by both Ireland and Northern Ireland.[62]

This philosophy of super-majoritarianism was essential to the cognate institutions of the peace process as well, such as the Civic Forum for Northern Ireland. The aim was to make sure that a broad cross section of communities and interests were reflected in the agreement. This included victims of terrorism, business leaders, faith-based bodies, industries such as agriculture, and trade unions. This recognition that the agreement would have impact on different sectors, and an

[61] For a helpful account of these see Cochrane (n 56), ch 7 –'The Incomplete Agreement: The Good Friday Compromise'.

[62] '… it is for the people of the island of Ireland alone, by agreement between the two parts respectively and without external impediment, to exercise their right of self-determination on the basis of consent freely and concurrently given, North and South, to bring about a United Ireland.' The Belfast Agreement 1998, s 1(ii).

iterative process of engaging with those sectors, is against the philosophy of referendum as bare, simple majoritarianism. This philosophy of super-majoritarianism holds that the consultation process is trying to resolve the agreement in a way that works for the widest possible range of voters.

To sum up these four sections: the referendum on the Belfast Agreement was, at least in part, successful. It demonstrates many of the principles of treating referendums as exercises in representative democracy. The voting stage of the referendum was a choice about decisions made by representatives. The peace process was designed to address disagreement across different communities. This was not a process where voters made decisions *instead* of representatives, but rather a process whereby voters were engaged in decision-making and engaged in making choices about decisions made by representatives. This engagement is the key to both the success of this referendum and understanding referendums as exercises in representative democracy. While imperfect, this process should be understood as a success, as the following sections demonstrate.

F. The Success Conditions of Referendums

The Belfast Agreement referendum process was imperfect. It did not address, and it cannot play the role of, for instance, a Truth and Reconciliation Commission. It did go a long way, however, to meeting the two minimal success conditions of referendums identified in chapter five. Recall that these minimal success conditions were argued to be (i) providing a clear outcome that (ii) even those who did not agree with the outcome had reasons to support. Consider how the referendum satisfies each of these success conditions in turn.

i. Clarity of Outcomes

While the meaning of a referendum on a large and complex treaty is necessarily inchoate, the outcome of the 1998 referendum should nevertheless be understood as clear. That is because (i) the framework in which representatives were expected to work was clear; (ii) the legitimacy of the process was clear; and (iii) the outcome was clear. All of this contributed to the success of the referendum. While there was disagreement about what the Multi-Party Agreement meant, and what the consequences of its use would be, there was no question as to whether the proposal succeeded or failed. By this measure, the 1998 Belfast referendum was successful, and a great deal more successful than the Brexit referendum discussed above.

ii. Reasons for Voters to Support Outcomes they Disagree with

The purpose of the peace process in Northern Ireland was to establish an agreement with enough support to last. This required achieving buy-in, even from those who did not support every part of the proposal. The breadth and depth of the consultation discussed above, and the consocational nature of the agreement itself, did provide those with certain misgivings reason to nevertheless support it. This can be distinguished from the Brexit referendum, which did not include this kind of broad and deep consultation. Doubtless there was disappointment, particularly around the release of prisoners, when deciding to vote for or against the agreement, but the fact that the process was consocational provided an additional reason to support the agreement. This was a reason of *form* to support the outcome irrespective of whether a voter supported the content. As a way of managing disagreement, as Wollheim rightly argues, democratic processes must provide at least some such indirect reasons to be justified.[63]

G. Conclusion

The 1998 referendum on the Belfast Agreement has much to commend it. It was a process in which the voting stage of a referendum was inseparable from the larger whole. A proposal was put to voters for approval which made real trade-offs, such as regarding the release of paramilitary prisoners, and made those difficult choices clear to voters up front. It was designed to seek agreement across communities. For all its failings, it provided a clear outcome that voters had at least some reason to support, irrespective of whether they agreed with that outcome. This referendum should not be understood as an exercise in direct democracy because it was not a process of bypassing representatives or making decisions *instead* of representatives. It was a clear case of voters making a *choice* about a decision, ie the Multi-Party Agreement, which had been made by representatives.

IV. Chile in 2019

A. Introduction to the Referendum Experience

The process of Chilean constitutional reform was sparked in 2019 by protests over metro fares in particular,[64] but also by deep inequality and demands for the expansion of social and political rights.[65] In response to these protests, 10 leading

[63] Wollheim argues these reasons are necessary because one will never support all the specific substantive outcomes in democracy, but nevertheless need a reason to support democracy as a whole. R Wollheim, 'A Paradox in the Theory of Democracy' in D Weiss, P Laslett, and WG Runciman (eds), *Philosophy, Politics and Society* (Blackwell 1962).

[64] 'Chile Protests: Unrest in Santiago over Metro Fare Increase' *BBC News* (19 October 2019), www.bbc.co.uk/news/world-latin-america-50106743, accessed 9 August 2021.

[65] C Sabatini and L Jefferson, 'The Truth Is, Chile Is Unequal: What's Behind Chile's Protests' *Chatham House* (18 December 2019), www.chathamhouse.org/2019/12/truth-chile-unequal-whats-behind-chiles-protests, accessed 9 August 2021.

political parties came to an agreement to begin the process of establishing a new constitution through a referendum.[66] This roadmap was subsequently formalised into a series of constitutional amendments.[67] The process of constitutional reform was divided into three stages. First, an 'entry' vote on whether voters wanted a new constitution.[68] Second, if the first vote 'approved' a new constitution, the question of who should compose the convention to draft the new constitution.[69] Members of the convention had nine months, which could be extended once for an extra three months, to draft a new constitution, which was to be approved or rejected in a third ratificatory vote to be held on 4 September 2022.[70] In the first 'entry' vote in October 2020, 80 per cent of Chileans approved of initiating a constitution-making process through a Constitutional Convention. Voters also determined that the Constitutional Convention should be composed of popularly elected members rather than existing representatives.[71] An election was held to elect those members in 2021. This Constitutional Convention was the first such institution in the world to have complete gender parity by design: 155 members, 78 men and 77 women. It reserved 17 seats for indigenous people who were elected in a separate, parallel ballot. There were at least six members from the LGBTI community, and the average age was 45.[72]

While this first phase in the Chilean process of constitutional reform clearly had much to commend it in terms of its broad representative credentials, it had serious flaws as well. Voter turnout dropped sharply when electing delegates to the Constitutional Convention, which may be attributed in part to general scepticism about democracy in Chile, particularly in the urban and youth populations.[73] The challenges facing the first Convention were so enormous that expectations were

[66] 'Acuerdo Por La Paz Social y La Nueva Constitución (Agreement for Social Peace and the New Constitution)' (11/19), obtienearchivo.bcn.cl/obtienearchivo?id=documentos/10221.1/76280/1/Acuerdo_por_la_Paz.pdf, accessed 9 August 2021.

[67] P Rodrigo and G Correa, 'Symposium on Chilean Referendum Part I: Drafting a Constitution on a Clean Slate' *International Constitutional Law Blog* (1 November 2020), www.iconnectblog.com/symposium-on-chilean-referendum-part-i-drafting-a-constitution-on-a-clean-slate, accessed 31 October 2023.

[68] 'The first question was: "*Do you want a New Constitution?*" which must be answered by "Approve" or "Reject" – a simple "yes" or "no" was considered too politically charged by the 1988 Referendum held under Pinochet.' ibid.

[69] 'The question was: '*What kind of body should draft the new Constitution? A Mixed Constitutional Convention of popularly elected members and incumbent members of Congress in equal parts?* [,] *Or a Constitutional Convention of exclusively popularly elected members?*' ibid.

[70] 'Finally, a confirmatory referendum will *Approve* or *Reject* the proposed text. If the new constitution is approved, it would be sworn and proclaimed and enter into force upon its official publication. At the same time, the current Constitution would be automatically repealed.' ibid (emphasis in original).

[71] '78% of those who voted supported a new constitutional text through a 100% elected body.' M Ríos Tobar, 'Chile's Constitutional Convention: A Triumph of Inclusion' *UNDP in Latin America and the Caribbean* (3 June 2021), www.latinamerica.undp.org/content/rblac/en/home/blog/2021/chile-s-constitutional-convention--a-triumph-of-inclusion.html, accessed 24 August 2021.

[72] ibid.

[73] 'Participation [is] well below the world average of 64,5%, particularly among the urban poor and youth.' Ríos Tobar (n 71).

overwhelmingly high.[74] Indeed, the first proposed constitution was decisively rejected by voters with 61.89 per cent voting against the proposal.[75] There are a range of potential reasons why the first proposed constitution may have been rejected, including its comprehensive and controversial content with an expansive conception of social and political rights. Further factors may be lies told by individual delegates to the Convention, online disinformation, and divisions within political parties about whether to support the reforms.[76] The failure to ratify the constitution does not mean, however, that the process was without virtue. Features of the Chilean experience demonstrate the power and potential of understanding referendums as processes which provide direction to representatives.[77] This need for an iterative relationship between voters and representatives is even clearer in the subsequent approach to constitutional reform.

At the time of writing, a further process of constitutional reform is underway in Chile. The principal difference between the current process and the last is the establishment of three different bodies with distinct mandates and memberships, rather than a single Constitutional Convention. This time, there will be an Expert Commission of professionals and academics with 24 experts (12 appointed by each house of Congress). This expert body will propose a new constitution to the second body: the Constitutional Council. The new Constitutional Council, made up of 50 directly elected delegates, has responsibility for debating and approving the new draft constitution proposed to them by the experts. The third body is the Technical Admissibility Committee, also elected by Congress, with responsibility for determining whether any provision of the proposed constitution violates any of part of the cross-party 'Agreement for Chile' which established this process of constitutional reform in the first place.

In the current process of constitutional reform, concerns have been raised about the representatives serving in the three constitutional bodies. While delegates to the first Constitutional Convention were criticised for being too far to the left of voters, the current concern is that the process has shifted too far to

[74] 'Yet the realization of the full democratic potential of this constitutional change depends on the still uncertain ability of constitution makers to compromise on a text that is not only seen as legitimate among ordinary citizens but also promotes coherent goals, effective institutions, and good governance.' G Negretto, 'Deepening Democracy? Promises and Challenges of Chile's Road to a New Constitution' (2021) *Hague Journal on the Rule of Law* 335, 335.

[75] G Pino and others, 'Third Time's a Charm? Chile Embarks on a New Constitution-Making Process' *Constitutionnet* (3 February 2023), constitutionnet.org/news/third-times-charm-chile-embarks-new-constitution-making-process, accessed 24 October 2023.

[76] A range of incidental reasons of this kind is considered in M Carrasco, 'Why we failed to approve the new Chilean constitution: the need for a cultural transformation' *LSE* (15 September 2022), blogs.lse.ac.uk/latamcaribbean/2022/09/15/why-we-failed-to-approve-the-new-chilean-constitution, accessed 26 August 2023.

[77] While some it is sometimes argued that the Chilean process is a moment of constituent power or constitutional moment, Verdugo and Prieto rightly offer a contrasting view arguing that this is a form of negative or 'aversive' constitutionalism in the same manner advocated here. A discussion of both approaches is found in: S Verdugo and M Prieto, 'The Dual Aversion of Chile's Constitution-Making Process' (2021) 19 *International Journal of Constitutional Law* 149.

the right.[78] There is a concern too that while the first process of constitutional reform may have been too participatory, the current process is not participatory enough.[79] What these debates about politicisation, and the strengths and weaknesses of both processes demonstrate, is the inseparability of representatives from processes of constitutional change. Neither process of constitutional reform in Chile can be understood as process of direct democracy. In both processes, there is an iterative relationship between representatives and voters, with each shaping the actions of the other. Confronting this reality of the depth of the interplay between voters and representatives in Chile is essential to understanding the ways in which the processes have succeeded and failed.

B. Understanding Referendums Wholistically

The process of constitutional reform in Chile is demanding. It has been the result of, *inter alia*, a vote to begin a process of constitutional change, a vote to reject the proposed change, and two votes to elect delegates to two different constitutional conventions. Such a thorough process is demanding, and this demandingness comes with risks. Voter fatigue may be reflected in turnout dropping off in the elections for members of the Convention,[80] although by some metrics support for constitutional reform remains high. While demandingness does create risks,[81] in the Chilean process it is clear what is being asked at each stage and what the role of the vote is at each of these stages. These different votes establish a framework in which representatives in the Constitutional Convention can act on voters' behalf. There is no way to understand this process except in the round. Each of the four votes is inseparable from the larger whole.

This wholistic approach to the referendum process affords voters far more control over the outcome. While the concerns over the capture of representatives are justified, these different votes offer multiple opportunities for voters to weigh in both on which representatives are acting on their behalf and what they want those representatives to do. Further, even if a voter disagrees at one stage in the

[78] Pino and others (n 75) and C Schneider and S Williamson-García, 'Chile's New Constitutional Process Shifts Right' *Nacla* (15 February 2023), nacla.org/chiles-new-constitutional-process-shifts-right, accessed 26 August 2023, who flag that 'Hernán Larraín, whose extended family became one of the wealthiest clans in Chile largely due to its close relationship to former dictator Augusto Pinochet, will preside over the Council'.

[79] ibid.

[80] 'In the election held on 15 and 16 May, 6,458,760 persons voted, for a total of 14,900, 190 persons registered, which is to say, 43.4 per cent. This figure represents a drop in voter turnout as compared to the plebiscite (50.9 per cent) and the 2017 elections … but an increase compared to the previous 2016 local elections when 35 per cent of registered voters went to the polls.' D Zovatto and M Jaraquemada, 'Analysis of the Elections in Chile' *International Institute for Democracy and Electoral Assistance* (25 May 2021), www.idea.int/news-media/news/analysis-elections-chile, accessed 2 June 2022.

[81] A helpful discussion of voter fatigue in the context of constitutional referendums is found in Tierney (n 4) 295.

process, there are still opportunities and reasons for that voter to participate at subsequent stages. The process has been designed as a back-and-forth conversation between voters and representatives, and that conversation only makes sense in its totality.

Breaking the constitutional reform process down into a series of clearly defined, distinct stages brings other advantages as well. It clearly identifies the roles for voters, as well as what kinds of representatives are acting in what capacity. Unambiguous direction is provided to representatives about the decisions that are reached. On this wholistic picture, it is very difficult to pick out any single moment as more constitutionally significant than others. There are many possible moments which might be described as constitutionally fundamental, including the initial protests in October 2019, the agreement by the political parties to hold the first Convention, as well the final ratification whenever that may be. Nothing is to be gained by trying to define one single constitutional moment – the parts of the process cannot be separated from the whole, and the process is better for being broadly understood.

C. Referendums as Addressing Disagreement

The Convention on the Chilean constitution sought to address disagreement. It did this by incorporating many kinds of representation into its membership. The law was changed to require gender parity[82] and, as discussed above, a separate, parallel process was established to ensure the participation of indigenous people elected by other indigenous people. This effort to make sure the Convention was representative in several ways speaks to the effort to ensure the new constitution speaks to a range of different experiences to address disagreement. The very creation of a Constitutional Convention, and then a Constitutional Council, was an attempt to find a new way forward for Chile which commanded broad public support.

D. The Voting Stage as a Process of Ratification

In addition to there being four different voting stages of the Chilean process of constitutional reform, the purpose of each of these votes is also clear. This can be

[82] 'Following the March 4th gender parity vote, Chile will be the first country in the world with the possibility of building a new constitution in a constitutional convention with gender parity. Without a doubt, this would deepen gendered perspectives of institutional change. Additionally, introducing a gender perspective to the Constitutional Convention process would allow Chile to re-build institutions and create new social agreements based on feminist institutional frameworks.' J Arce-Riffo, 'Gender Parity in the Chilean Constitutional Convention: What Does It Mean for Chilean Democracy?' Oxford Human Rights Hub (4 April 2020), ohrh.law.ox.ac.uk/gender-parity-in-the-chilean-constitutional-convention-what-does-it-mean-for-chilean-democracy, accessed 2 June 2022.

seen in that the votes are each usefully framed, either as elections, or as processes of 'approval' and 'rejection'. This process demonstrates as well that while it may be true that a vote is required to initiate a process of constitutional reform, this by no means exhausts the votes that may be required to provide direction to representatives. While this process may seem onerous, the process of Brexit discussed in section II above took longer than the design of the Chilean Constitutional Convention, and the challenges of Brexit – particularly with respect to Northern Ireland – remain ongoing in 2023.

E. Special Majority Requirements

The approach to addressing disagreement in the Chilean process of constitutional reform was not majoritarian. The first Convention was generally free to choose its own rules with the exception that it could not change the necessary two-thirds majority required for 'the norms of the new constitution'.[83] While the criticisms of the second Constitutional Council are important, there were still efforts to try to address disagreement and achieve a widespread consensus. Voting for the Constitutional Council was compulsory, to ensure wide participation.[84] The Constitutional Council will still have an equal number of men and women. The second Constitutional Council was explicitly bound by 12 constitutional principles from the Agreement for Chile which established the process of constitutional change. The aim of neither the Convention nor the Council was to propose a new constitution that would achieve 50 per cent + 1 support; rather, it was to be responsive to the concerns of Chileans of many backgrounds, within a broader framework guided by the principles of representative democracy.

F. The Success Conditions of Referendums

The passing of a proposed constitution should not be the only arbiter of whether the process has been success. Indigenous people have 'already won', argued indigenous activists in Chile, insofar as they have achieved a new level of constitutional recognition.[85] After the first failed constitution, there was a clear model for reform on the table which could be debated. The proposed alternative was

[83] Rodrigo and Correa (n 67).

[84] Voting was also compulsory on the previous draft constitution, but not for previous delegates to the Constitutional Convention.

[85] '"Whether this constitution is rejected or approved [by the plebiscite], I believe that Chile's Indigenous people have already won" said Rosa Catrileo, who represents the Mapuche, the country's largest Indigenous group. "We have made our demands visible on a national level, and so never again will be excluded from the conversation."' J Bartlett, 'Chile Finalises New Draft Constitution to Replace Pinochet-Era Document' *The Guardian* (16 May 2022), www.theguardian.com/world/2022/may/16/chile-constitution-new-draft-pinochet, accessed 3 June 2022.

substantively ambitious in ensuring gender parity, reducing inequality, and making the Government responsible for combating and mitigating the impacts of climate change.[86] Doubtless there are concerns with the ongoing process, and many of those concerns are justified, but the current process of constitutional change in Chile demonstrates how demanding it is to create the texts of new constitutions, and that success does not require the absence of disagreement.

i. Clarity of Outcomes

The draft constitution arising from the first Convention would have been the longest in the world.[87] Indeed, a sub-committee has been set up to streamline it.[88] This length is excessive, but regardless of whether voters agree with it, there is no doubt what model of constitution they would be asked to adopt or reject. This clarity alone does not mean a constitutional project is a success, but it does mean that a success condition of a referendum has been met. Whatever the limitations of the Chilean process, it is clear *who* is voting for *what* at *what point*. That must mark the process out as (at least a limited) success.

ii. Reasons for Voters to Support Outcomes They Disagree With

The Chilean process of constitutional reform offers voters three reasons to support outcomes that they disagree with. The first is the broad representative quality of both the Convention and the Council, the second is the super majoritarian aims of the Conventions, and the third is the consultative nature of the process. That is not to say any of these reasons are dispositive, but that the proposed constitution was not accepted does not necessarily mean the process is a failure. It means instead that the process of comprehensive constitutional reform was even more demanding and took even longer than initially planned. Indeed, it successfully established a model that Chilean voters did not accept. That is not terribly surprising given the scale of the undertaking in creating a new constitutional text. Whatever comes next, the Chilean process of constitutional reform from 2019 to 2022 raises the bar for the role of referendums in the process of constitutional change. Voters still have good reasons to be engaged in a democratic process even after four years of work and so, even if there are tragedies within this larger constitutional story, there are success stories as well.

[86] 'Among the long list of rights and freedoms the draft enshrines, the new constitution makes higher education free, ensures gender parity across government and makes the state responsible for preventing, adapting to and mitigating climate change.' ibid.

[87] 'With 499 articles, Chile's new constitution would be the world's longest, prompting some concern over the "maximalist" approach taken by the delegates.' J Bartlett, 'In Chile, Constitutional Convention Announces Full Draft of New Constitution' *Constitutionnet* (17 February 2022), constitutionnet.org/news/chile-constitutional-convention-announces-full-draft-new-constitution, accessed 3 June 2022.

[88] ibid.

G. Conclusion

The process of constitutional reform in Chile has been a long and complex one. It demonstrates how difficult it is to create new constitutional texts, and how demanding the process of constitutional change can be. There are both tragedies and success stories within this larger narrative, and neither the successes nor the tragedies mitigate the importance of the other. This section has argued that both the tragedies and the successes of the Chilean experience demonstrate the need for understanding referendums as processes of representative democracy, deeply integrated into broader processes of representative democracy. Without keeping the representativeness of referendums front and centre, it is not possible to understand where the process has succeeded and where it has failed. The process failed insofar as the first proposed constitution failed to reflect and command the support of Chileans, but knowing for certain that a draft constitution does not represent voters' views is a democratic success story as well.

V. Conclusion

These three referendums, either through the power of their example or counterexample, demonstrate what it means for referendums to be exercises in representative democracy. As referendums become more representative, they become more institutionalised. This happens in three ways. First, they become more deeply integrated with other institutions of representative democracy. That is to say: it is clear how their outcomes and processes interact with existing institutions. Second, they introduce additional representative processes such as civic forums and citizens' assemblies. Third, they give effect to the same principles and values as ordinary representative democracy such as accountability and rights for minorities through processes such as special majority requirements.[89]

One striking feature of these examples is how demanding referendum processes can be. Indeed, it might be argued that these processes are unreasonably demanding. This is a feature, not a bug, of successful referendums. What these three referendums all demonstrate, albeit in very different ways, is how difficult it is to meaningfully address deep disagreement. The Brexit referendum especially demonstrates that there are no shortcuts to deep agreement on issues that are fundamentally contested. The issues that tend to be put to a referendum are difficult for a reason and require real compromise and sacrifice to address. There is nothing direct about successful representative processes, and they are not bound by the voting processes. They are much longer processes of negotiation and contestation involving at least one, and potentially many, choices about decisions made by representatives.

[89] These three types of institutionalisation are discussed in ch 4.

7

Conclusion

This chapter offers the book's conclusion. First, it recapitulates the purpose of the book, underlining its key messages in section I. Section II traces the arguments made in the book and connects the chapters of the book to these key messages. Sections III and IV demonstrate how understanding referendums as representative democracy helps move past the debates about whether they are liberal or populist democratic processes. Finally, section V demonstrates that the arguments here make a difference in constitutional law and practice by changing *how*, *when*, and *why* referendums are used. The book concludes by emphasising the need for change in the way referendums are understood all over the world, and the emancipatory potential of understanding referendums as exercises in representative democracy.

I. Purpose and Message of the Book

In making his case for the distinction between *pouvoir constituant* and *pouvoir constitute*, ie constitutive and constituted powers, Sieyès was arguing from a commitment to liberty and individual agency.[1] From the commitment that voters were free and equal, the argument that some fundamental constitutional decisions must be made by voters rather than representatives was thought to follow naturally. Locke, is of course, makes similar argumentative moves. He famously said that 'MEN being, as has been said, by nature, all free, equal and independent, no one can be put of this estate, and subjected to the political power of another, without his own consent'.[2] Drawing on Locke, Madison argues that the right to create constitutions follows from the inalienable rights of people born as free and equal.[3] What unites these, and the many theorists who draw a distinction between constitutive and constituted powers, is a commitment to the idea that people are born

[1] L Rubinelli, *Constituent Power: A History* (Cambridge University Press 2020) 50–52.

[2] Locke, of course, goes on to say that '[t]he only way whereby any one divests himself of his natural liberty, and puts on the *bonds of civil society*, is by agreeing with other men to join and unite into a community'. J Locke, *The Second Treatise of Government* [1689] (Hackett 1980) 95 (capitalisation in original).

[3] 'The transcendent and precious right of the people to "abolish or alter their government as to them shall seem most likely to effect their safety and happiness."' A Hamilton, J Madison, and J Jay, *The Federalist Papers* [1788] (Penguin Classics 1987) No 40, 257, 258.

free and equal, and the view that this commitment entails that voters must be the ultimate source of authority in a democracy.[4]

The commitment to the freedom and equality of people is a terrific and terrifically important historical development. It is one of the triumphs of the enlightenment. This book has argued, however, that it does not follow from the maxim that all people are born free and equal that they must author the texts of their constitutions through processes such as referendums. The book is not by any means the only work to argue this. Verdugo helpfully demonstrates the wide range of concerns with this way of thinking. He rightly argues that a tipping point may have now been reached where it is time to let go of the idea of constituent power, and therefore the distinction between constitutive and constituted powers.[5] Verdugo is responding to the fact that the distinction between constitutive and constituted powers creates a paradox of constitutionalism. Loughlin and Walker helpfully explain this paradox when they say that 'constitutionalism is underpinned by two fundamental though antagonistic imperatives: that governmental power ultimately is generated from "the consent of the people" and that, to be sustained and effective, such power must be divided, constrained, and exercised through distinctive institutional forms'.[6] This paradox, as Loughlin and Walker persuasively show, is at the heart of contemporary constitutional law and theory.[7] Verdugo rightly argues that the challenges of grappling with this paradox mean it has now outlived its usefulness.[8] This book is part of the literature trying to imagine what a future for constitutional law may look like post-paradox. The work of Goldoni and Wilkinson on the pre-eminence of the material constitution,[9] and Arato's model of post-sovereign constitution-making are two important contributions to the work of finding a new way forward. Although, to be clear about the contribution this book is making, the view expressed here is very different than Arato's. Arato does not advocate for abandoning the idea of constituent power – he thinks it still survives in a post-sovereign way.[10]

[4] Different versions of this distinction are discussed at ch 1, section II.

[5] Verdugo offers a helpful survey of those challenging the helpfulness of this distinction including Kelsen, Arendt, Dyzenhaus, Jackson, Vinx, Comella, Landau, Hasebe, and Duke. S Verdugo, 'Is it Time to Abandon the Theory of Constituent Power?' (2003) 21 *International Journal of Constitutional Law* 14, 18.

[6] M Loughlin and N Walker, *The Paradox of Constitutionalism* (Oxford University Press 2007) 1.

[7] ibid.

[8] 'In contrast to the wide use of the constituent power theory, and against its defenders and redeemers, I argue that the attempts to recover the theory are problematic, and that the claim to abandon the theory should be seriously discussed. From a descriptive point of view, those attempts are not able to present an accurate picture of how constitution-making processes operate, unless they present a minimal definition of constituent power in terms of the power to create a constitution – but then, the main features of the theory and its normative appeal get lost.' Verdugo (n 5) 20.

[9] Discussed particularly in ch 2, section VI.

[10] Arato's model is a 'post sovereign, post-revolutionary, round-table-led and multi-stage paradigm of constitution making'. Arato's approach is in support of Michelman's ideas, which are challenged in ch 2, section V. A Arato, *Post Sovereign Constitution Making: Learning and Legitimacy* (Oxford University Press 2016) 10. J Colón-Ríos, *Constituent Power and the Law* (Oxford University Press 2020) 305.

But it remains very hard to move forward. It is so difficult to let go of the appeal of distinguishing between constituent and constituted powers.[11] This is because the idea of two-track democracy is thought to be conceptually required for democracy. Colón-Ríos helpfully captures the moves in the argument for two-track democracy, and the power of this argument, when he says it is the 'sovereign people, and not its representatives who must determine the content of the fundamental law. If those limits are not respected, the constitution-making body, would as Napoleon, be crowning itself the true sovereign.'[12] This book has sought to show that this approach, accepted by Colón-Ríos and shared by so many others[13] is not misguided, but it is misleading. Representatives are not crowning themselves sovereign if they determine or shape the text of constitutions. This is because the deeper material authority to create constitutions is never something that can be limited or given away. The legitimacy of a constitution always remains a question for voters to answer, irrespective of how their representatives act.

Indeed, Colón-Ríos's own work comes within a whisker of taking this approach and explicitly moving past the paradox of the constitutionalism. By emphasising the distinction between sovereignty and constituent power, Colón-Ríos puts forward an account of constituent power as a juridical concept where, in Michelman's terms, constituent power is 'always under law'. Nevertheless, Colón-Ríos remains committed to the core argumentative moves challenged in this book. Colón-Ríos still thinks he can and must save the distinction between constitutive powers, 'understanding constituent power as a juridical concept capable of placing limits on the constituent authorities opens the way for radical forms of political participation: if there are things that the ordinary institutions of government, even meeting special thresholds, cannot do, then it will be necessary to channel the exercise of constituent power through participatory mechanisms of constitutional change.' So, like Arato, Colón-Ríos thinks the distinction between constituent and constituted powers should be maintained, despite its limitations in order to preserve the emancipatory and revolutionary power of democracy.

This book has not sought to challenge or limit the emancipatory or revolutionary power of democracy. It has, however, argued that a revolutionary or emancipatory power of democracy does not require two tracks of decision-making for people and politicians. Referendums help to explain and demonstrate why these two decision-making tracks are unnecessary, and the explanatory power of referendums in this context runs two ways. Referendums both demonstrate the limitations of understanding democracy in this two-track way and offer a vision of how voters can exercise their ultimate authority together with representatives. This alternative conception of referendums works because voters do not literally

[11] 'Verdugo captures how hard it is to move forward when he says: 'How would anyone dare to challenge the view that the people have – and should have – the exclusive and absolute power to shape the constitutional order?' Verdugo (n 5) 16.

[12] Colón-Ríos (n 10) 305.

[13] As discussed in ch 1, section II.

or metaphorically delegate their authority to representatives on a limited basis. The constitution of legitimate authority is better understood as a practice and a dialogue between representatives and voters. Representatives can be a legitimate source of authority in a democracy, and their actions help to construct the actions of voters as the ultimate source of authority.

This picture of representatives as one legitimate source of authority might seem radically undemocratic. The enlightenment view of constitutions as authored came about in tandem with the enlightenment idea that life was self-authored. This idea that both life and constitutions can be self-authored is 'unrelinquishable'.[14] Although appealing, this view is not correct. People do not need to be complete control of their lives to be autonomous. From the claim that voters are the *ultimate* source of authority in a democracy, it does not follow that voters are the *only* source of authority. Additionally, a picture where voters directly control their constitutions is neither possible nor desirable. Democracy is not about the direct control or authoring of anything by anybody. Indeed, chapter three argued that the proposition that anything in a democracy, including a constitution, can be directly controlled or authored is profoundly undemocratic. The idea of directness undermines the messy mediation which is essential for democratic decision-making.

This is all to say: the purpose of this book was to show that it does not follow from the inalienability of individual freedom and equality that democratic constitutions either can or must be controlled through processes such as referendums or citizens' assemblies where voters make decisions instead of representatives. Constitutions, constitutional law, and constitutional theory should be more modest than this. There are limits to the degree of popular control that voters can exercise over constitutions through processes such as referendums and citizens' assemblies. On the other hand, however, this book has argued that constitutions, constitutional law, and constitutional theory should also be more ambitious than to accept two-track democracy as a given. There are all kinds of ways voters exercise control over constitutions, and referendums and citizens' assemblies are only a few significant processes among many. Processes such as protests may be constitutionally ambiguous expressions of voters' agency but, as chapter two argued, such protests over *inter alia* economic hardship are what has tended to prompt constitutional change.[15] The ambiguity of legitimate authority as a practice, rather than a discrete act through an act like a referendum, should not detract from its significance. The ultimate message of this book is that voters can shape their constitutions through referendums, but not only referendums. Further, the power voters have to exercise their ultimate authority through referendums is only one part of their broader ability to construct their constitutions everyday through the material practice of the constitution.

[14] F Michelman, 'Constitutional Authorship by the People' (1999) 74 *Notre Dame Law Review* 1605, 1606.

[15] As argued in ch 2, section V about protests in America, France, and Chile.

II. Overview of the Book's Arguments

This book challenged a way of thinking about referendums in the process of constitutional change. It sought to normalise referendums on constitutive constitutional issues. It argued that – even when asking the most fundamental questions – referendums are not exercises in higher-order law-making. Referendums are better understood, it argued, as processes of representative democracy. In making a case for this approach to referendums, this book fell into two broad parts: one negative, one positive. The first part explained and interrogated the picture of referendums on fundamental constitutional issues as processes of higher-order law-making. Chapter two introduced and challenged the idea of high-order law-making, and chapter three challenged the idea that referendums could be exercises in higher-order law-making. The second part of the book put forward the alternative of referendums as representative democracy and explained why this alternative makes a difference in practice.

Chapter two introduced the first idea challenged in this book: the claim that democratic constitutions require some decisions to be made by voters rather than by representatives. Chapter two raises three concerns with this idea. The chapter began, however, by explaining why, and how, so many constitutions and constitutional theorists distinguish between decisions that must be made by the people and those that can be made by politicians. The argument for this distinction is simple and persuasive: democracy means rule by the people, and rule by the people requires the people to be in control of the ultimate conditions of authority in a democracy. Without that control – without voters making fundamental constitutional decisions – systems cease to be democratic. While the argument clearly has persuasive power, chapter two nevertheless argued that this conclusion does not follow.

Chapter two challenged this understanding of authority. It argued that legitimate democratic authority does not require voters, either conceptually or practically, to make decisions about fundamental constitutional choices instead of representatives. Conceptually, it is not necessarily the case, because voters do not delegate their power to representatives on a limited basis. Therefore, neither *ultra vires* arguments nor conflict-of-interest arguments for limited powers of representatives can succeed. That is to say: it is within representatives' power in a democracy, at least conceptually, to make decisions on fundamental constitutional issues. This is *not* to say that it is ideal for representatives to make decisions on fundamental constitutional issues without additional input from voters. There are all kinds of good reasons for voters to weigh on these questions. Outcomes of fundamental constitutional processes are often irreversible, and their consequences are deeply entrenched. The subject matter of such processes may be particularly divisive, or disproportionately impact minorities. These are all very good reasons to hold referendums on fundamental constitutional changes. The point of the chapter was only that there is nothing *conceptually* necessary in a democracy requiring fundamental constitutional issues to be made by representatives. Authority is not established in a singular, static way. It is an ongoing relationship of legitimacy that depends on the actions of both the governors and the governed. Further, representatives are themselves a legitimate source of authority which inevitably shape the actions of voters in expressing their ultimate authority. There is nothing undemocratic about this because authority cannot be fixed, allocated, or transferred, still less – as chapter three argues – by referendums.

Chapter three introduced the second idea challenged in this book, which builds on the first. The second idea is this: referendums are a way that voters can make decisions instead of decisions being made by representatives. This chapter dissected every part of this claim that referendums are ways that the *people*, come *together*, to make *decisions*, *instead* of representatives making decisions. It raises four challenges to this second idea. The chapter began by arguing that the people are not the sort of group that can decide – at least not together. Whatever the people do together, it is not deciding, and such an outcome is certainly not a decision taken by the people instead of representatives. Each of these claims is independent of each other and can succeed even if the others fail. The chapter concluded by introducing an alternative conception of referendums. It argued instead that referendums are ways that *voters* make *choices* about decisions made by *representatives*. The second part of the book develops this alternative in detail.

Chapter four shifted the focus of the book toward an alternative understanding of the role for referendums on fundamental constitutional questions. In making a case for this alternative, this chapter had five sections. The first section explained this alternative account of referendums as providing direction to representatives. This alternative account is defined in the following four sections by four commitments: (a) referendums are negotiation processes; (b) referendums cannot be distinguished from elections; (c) referendums are not bare votes; and (d) referendums on constitutional issues are not 'overriding' in any way. Referendums should be understood as representative both because this offers them a stronger normative justification, and because it better descriptively captures how referendums work in practice.

Chapter four argued that, like democracy itself, referendums require both instrumental and procedural justifications and may be valuable for both instrumental and procedural reasons. Indeed, referendums have multiple rationales, and these rationales may conflict with each other. Referendums are best understood as having piecemeal sources of legitimacy, rather than being justified narrowly by the basis of the social contract. On the exceptionalist, two-track view of democracy, referendums are required on fundamental constitutional issues because there are some decisions that cannot be made by representatives. This chapter argued instead that there are all kinds of normative reasons to hold referendums, even on fundamental constitutional issues, and those reasons will vary from case to case. Referendums should particularly be used when decisions will be deeply entrenched, or where there is a gap between the views of voters and representatives (or as between representatives), or where referendums can help to address deep disagreement. This pluralistic approach to justifying referendums means there are all kinds of reasons to use them, and that makes the case for their use more nuanced and compelling.

Chapter five put forward principles for putting this vision of referendums into practice. It argued that (i) referendums should be understood holistically as composed of a series of stages; (ii) referendums should be used for a range of reasons to manage disagreement; and (iii) to the greatest extent possible, the voting stage of a referendum process should be one of ratification. Fourth and finally, (iv) to better resolve disagreement, special majority requirements should be employed to maintain the equality on which representative democracy relies. While how these principles will apply, and what it means to succeed, will vary to some extent across contexts, this chapter argued that it is possible to establish that the minimal success conditions of referendums can be defined as (i) providing clear outcomes and (ii) providing voters with reasons to support democratic decisions that they disagreed with.

Finally, chapter five demonstrated why the principles offered here for the use of referendums help when responding to arguments against the use of referendums, both in practice and in principle. Both the concerns that referendums are too democratic, and that they are not democratic enough, can be addressed by recasting referendums as representative democracy. Referendums have come to be justified as remedies to representative democracy, and as ways of re-engaging voters in their democracies and giving them control over their constitutional settlements. This chapter argued that this cannot be the case. A referendum cannot be a remedy for the failings of representative democracy. Representative democracy can, however, be a remedy for the failings of referendums.

Finally, chapter six put the principles of referendums as representative democracy into action. It considered three case studies where referendums had taken place – the United Kingdom in 2016, Northern Ireland in 1998, and Chile from 2019 onwards. Each of these cases studies evaluated a referendum by reference to the principles identified in chapter five of providing effective direction to representatives. These four ways of providing effective direction to representatives are: (i) framing referendums wholistically as composed of a series of stages; (ii) using referendums to address disagreement; (iii) treating the voting stage of a referendum as a process of ratification; and finally (iv) using special majority requirements. This chapter also evaluates referendums against the two minimal success conditions for referendums identified in chapter six: (i) clarity of outcomes and (ii) the provision of reasons for voters to support outcomes that they disagree with. These three referendums, either through the power of their example or counterexample, demonstrate what it means for referendums to be exercises in representative democracy.

III. The Future of Referendums in Representative Democracy: The False Choice of Liberalism and Populism

Debates about the use of referendums in representative democracies are not new. They arise at moments of democratic transition and crisis. They were explored along with the expansion of universal suffrage. As Bogdanor says in the United Kingdom, for instance:

> How were the 'people' – the newly enfranchised electorate – to exercise their power: solely through representative institutions, or through the machinery of direct democracy? This was a central issue in the constitutional debates of the years between 1890 and 1912.[16]

Despite these debates in the nineteenth century, it was not until the 1970s, there was a marked, sharp increase in the use of referendums.[17] As Altman says: 'Referendums are used twice as frequently today compared with fifty years ago and almost four times more than at the turn of the twentieth century.'[18] Several trends are responsible for this. Referendums have become inextricably connected to process of European integration,[19] self-determination,[20] and Soviet and Russian contraction[21] and expansion.[22]

In addition to their roles in these specific political projects, a general rationale for referendums has also emerged: that they have a role to play remedying democratic deficits. The idea that referendums are a remedy for fixing crises of party democracy remains influential today. Indeed, Hollander argues: 'This crisis discourse has, in fact, become the *raison d'être* of a "renaissance" of referendum literature in recent decades.'[23] A democratic deficit often associated with referendums is declining membership in political parties.[24] Again, however, the claim that referendums are responses to the crises of party democracy goes back at least

[16] V Bogdanor, *The People and the Party System* (Cambridge University Press 1981) 11.

[17] 'The use of referendums around the world has proliferated remarkably in the past 30 years. It has been estimated that of the 58 functioning electoral democracies of more than three million, 39 had conducted at least one national referendum between 1975 and 2000.' S Tierney, *Constitutional Referendums: The Theory and Practice of Republican Deliberation* (Oxford University Press 2012) 1.

[18] D Altman, *Direct Democracy Worldwide* (Cambridge University Press 2011) 10–11.

[19] S Hollander, *The Politics of Referendum Use in European Democracies* (Palgrave Macmillan 2019) 1.

[20] A Cassese, 'Self-Determination of Peoples: A Legal Reappraisal' (21st Century Trust Conference – Ethnic Conflict in the Wider Europe: Causes, Prevention and Cures, June 1997), www.21stCenturyTrust.org/1997.html, accessed 15 September 2020.

[21] S White and RJ Hill, 'Russia, the Former Soviet Union and Eastern Europe: The Referendum as a Flexible Political Instrument' in M Gallagher and PV Uleri (eds), *The Referendum Experience in Europe* (Palgrave 1996) 153.

[22] Referendums were used to consolidate Russian power in Crimea in 2014. 'Crimea Referendum: Voters "Back Russia Union"' *BBC News* (16 March 2014), www.bbc.co.uk/news/world-europe-26606097, accessed 7 October 2020.

[23] Hollander (n 19) 4.

[24] M Qvortrup (ed), *Referendums Around the World: The Continued Growth of Direct Democracy* (Palgrave MacMillan 2014) 5.

100 years. The theories of referendums put forward by Schmitt and Dicey are both motivated by the idea that referendums can fix problems of party democracy created by political parties. Writing about the Weimar Republic in 1923, Schmitt says:

> Small and exclusive committees of parties or of party coalitions make their decisions behind closed doors, and what representatives of the big capitalist interest groups agree to in the smallest committees is more important for the fate of millions of people, perhaps than any political decision.[25]

Similarly, writing about the United Kingdom in 1885, Dicey says that both in the United Kingdom and around the world '[t]rust in elected legislative bodies is … dying out under every form of popular government. The party machine is regarded with suspicion, and often with detestation, by public-spirited citizens.'[26] Schmitt advocates instead for a plebiscitary theory of democracy where voters acclaim a 'government or some other authoritarian organ'.[27] In contrast to Schmitt's approach to referendums as positively acclaiming the executive, Dicey seeks to use referendums as devices to limit them. For Dicey, the referendum is 'the people's veto'[28] and a 'negative and conservative' democratic device, seeking to constrain the actions of a party majority in Parliament.[29] Despite disagreeing on the ends of their proposed reforms, Schmitt and Dicey agree on the means: referendums have the potential to address what ails representative, party democracy.[30]

The passages could have been written today. These concerns are a helpful reminder that, as Runciman rightly says, democracy is perpetually in crisis.[31] The particular version of this 'crisis' at issue today is the supposed conflict between liberalism and populism.[32] The question of whether liberal, representative democracy is dying, and if it is, what the role of referendums as populous and precipitating that decline or offering an alternative way to enliven institutions.[33]

The dichotomy between liberalism and populism is a false choice in thinking about referendums. Referendums have the potential to be both liberal and populist democratic processes, and they have both tendencies within them. They are democratic tools like any other. Elections can also be used in despotic ways to consolidate power; the same is true of referendums. Because of the necessary

[25] C Schmitt, *The Crisis of Parliamentary Democracy* (Ellen Kennedy tr, MIT Press 1986) 49–50.

[26] AV Dicey, *Introduction to the Study of the Law of the Constitution* (Roger E Michener ed, 8th rev edn, Liberty Fund Inc 1982) cxv.

[27] C Schmitt, *Legality and Legitimacy* (Duke University Press 2004) 90.

[28] Dicey (n 26) cix.

[29] ibid cxiv.

[30] Qvortrup and I develop and defend the interconnectedness of the arguments Schmitt and Dicey make about referendums: M Qvortrup and L Trueblood, 'Schmitt, Dicey, and the Power and Limits of Referendums in the United Kingdom' (2022) 42 *Legal Studies* 396.

[31] Runciman argues that the success democracy has had recovering from crises has bread complacency and the view that democracies can muddle through anything. D Runciman, *The Confidence Trap* (Princeton University Press 2014) 29.

[32] JW Müller, *What is Populism?* (University of Pennsylvania Press 2016) 2.

[33] ibid 102.

agenda-setting role of representatives in determining the content of representatives, there is always the potential that representatives will abuse them towards their ends. There is always that potential for elite manipulation. The indispensable role of representatives in referendums requires confronting this possibility in questions of constitutional design. Referendums are not necessarily liberal or populist democratic processes; they are just ways of referring questions back to voters.

IV. Moving Past Liberalism and Populism

Further, treating referendums as instances of representative democracy is about integrating the strengths of both liberalism and populism. It integrates these two forces by putting forward a theory of referendums that takes both the majoritarian and counter-majoritarian parts of democracy seriously. The argument is made across the book, rather than any single chapter, so it is worth restating its commitments up front before retracing them. The moves are this: (i) democracy cannot be understood as only a procedural ideal because substantive limitations – protections on equality, for instance – must be in place to protect the very possibility of majoritarianism. Therefore, (ii) these substantive requirements to protect democracy must involve more than rule by the majority. Unusually, the third claim says, (iii) unlike arguments for democracy in general, referendums are often justified on a purely majoritarian basis. Fourth and finally, (iv) the principles of democracy in general should apply to referendums in particular. Democracy, to work properly, has both majoritarian and counter-majoritarian elements. For referendums to work well, they also must have both majoritarian and counter-majoritarian elements.

Both majoritarianism and counter-majoritarianism raises risks in the context of referendums. While Tierney acknowledges the risks of majority decision-making, he nevertheless cautions against abandoning the idea. He says:

> While the danger to minorities in majority decision-making can be very real, we should also be alive to the opposite concern. To grant minority vetoes can be to replace the tyranny of the majority with the hegemony of the minority.[34]

Tierney is right that neither the majority nor the minority ought not to have a privileged position in a democracy. Tierney is also right to suggest that representative democracy itself relies on the logic of majority decision-making in many cases. The point, however, is that the tyranny of the majority and minority are separable from each other. They are not separable because, as Beitz argues in response to the question of whether a good procedure can ever justify an undemocratic outcome:

> If one wishes to maintain a procedural view, this question must be answered by showing that the favoured procedures have a value whose value is both overriding and

[34] Tierney (n 17) 41.

> independent of considerations about the political result that the normal operation of these procedures would produce.[35]

Beitz must be right about this. The value of democratic decisions cannot be just that they are made by the majority. That a majority voted for a proposition well be important and valuable, but it is neither a necessary nor sufficient condition for a good democratic decision. Otherwise, Beitz is saying, the tyranny of the majority could collapse into the tyranny of the majority. The conception of equality on which majoritarianism relies could be undermined without substantive limits to majoritarianism. As Dworkin says, it must be a substantive not merely a procedural ideal for the outcomes of democratic decisions not to undermine their constituent processes.

> The majoritarian conception of democracy is defective because it cannot explain, on its own, what is good about democracy. Mere weight of numbers, on its own, contributes nothing of value to a political decision. We need a deeper and more elaborate account that tells us what conditions must be met and protected in a political community before majority rule is appropriate for that community.[36]

Dworkin is right about this. There is no *prima facie* reason to think that a policy outcome is justified because the majority prefers it?[37] Equally, however, Tierney was right to stress the risks and dangers of the tyranny of the majority as well. The point of understanding referendums as representative democracy was to put forward a conception of referendums that took both these impulses – the populist tendency towards majoritarianism, and the liberal tendency towards, counter-majoritarianism – seriously. This section, and this book, have sought to show that democracy requires both majoritarianism and counter-majoritarianism to be taken seriously, and that any theory of referendums needs to take both the majoritarian and counter-majoritarian parts of democracy seriously as well.

V. Practical Implications

The arguments made in this book have a practical impact in three ways. First, they impact *how* referendums are used. Second, they shape *what* kinds of questions are put to a referendum. Third, they change the reasons *why* referendums are held. This third consequence is the most important. There are many good reasons to hold referendums on fundamental constitutional questions. This book just makes one kind of claim about the reason to hold one kind of referendum: the idea that fundamental constitutional decisions cannot be made by representatives is not a

[35] C Beitz, *Political Equality* (Princeton University Press 1989) 95.

[36] ibid 70.

[37] R Dworkin, *Is Democracy Possible Here?: Principles for a New Political Debate* (Princeton University Press 2008) 70.

good reason to hold a referendum. The section concludes by underlining the high stakes in understanding referendums as exercises in representative democracy.

A. How Referendums are Used

The claim that referendums are exercises in representative democracy changes how they are used in practice.[38] Referendums then cease to be used in an *ad hoc* way to remedy representative democracy, or bypass representatives, and instead start to be deeply integrated into exercises of representative democracy. The principles identified in chapter five offer a picture of how referendums can work in this way. Constitutions must clarify a consistent role for referendums. Referendums should, wherever possible, be used post-legislatively or after the development of a proposal for reform. If referendums cannot be used post-legislatively, or post-proposal, they should be bookended with a second vote as part of the referendum. Voters must be involved in the decision-making stage through consultations and citizens' assemblies.

B. What Questions are Put to a Referendum

Referendums have been used to consider a whole variety of questions, both constitutional and non-constitutional. They have been used to ask the public scientific,[39] practical,[40] and moral[41] questions. This book argued that the question of whether an issue should be put to a referendum is not only about its content, but also about its form and the type of disagreement that it addresses. Referendums should be held, and constitutions should require referendums to be held, when this would help provide better direction to representatives. The point of this book was to argue that there are all kinds of reasons it may be helpful to provide additional direction to representatives beyond elections. This book argued that these reasons may apply in the same way to both constitutional and policy issues. The next and final section explains what some of the right reasons to hold a referendum may be.

C. Why Hold Referendums?

There are all kinds of reasons that it could be beneficial to provide further direction to representatives, and so to hold a referendum. For example, a question

[38] A longer account of the principles which guide the use of referendums as representative democracy is the subject of ch 4.

[39] Referendums on nuclear power, for example, have been held in Austria, Bulgaria, Italy, Lithuania, Sweden, and Taiwan.

[40] As in Sweden on which side of the road to drive on in 1955.

[41] As with issues of same-sex marriage, for instance, as held in Australia and in Ireland.

could be particularly significant, but if it has emerged since the last election manifesto was drawn up it might be unclear how voters expect their representatives to act. There may be benefits to providing further direction to representatives because an outcome will be deeply entrenched, or there is a particularly large gap between what representatives and voters think. Constitutions could have fallen out of step with social norms and require reform. There can also be countervailing reasons *not* to hold referendums, reasons of timing, issues, or circumstances. The purpose of this book was not to exhaustively catalogue the reasons referendums may justifiably be held. It was to widen the range of relevant reasons, and to decouple democracy from the argument that certain fundamental questions need to be put to a referendum because they cannot be made by representatives.

D. The Stakes of Getting Referendums Wrong

The questions raised by referendums have high stakes. Referendums force conversations about the meaning of abstract ideas self-determination, voting, and equality, as well as the possibility of nationhood. Demands for referendums have high stakes too. Calls for referendums on constitutive constitutional questions often arise from experiences of war, division, corruption, incompetence, tyranny, and oppression. Appeals for referendums are driven by people's search for control over their constitutions and, fundamentally, the project of self-government. Referendums are sought in these circumstances because the standard picture of referendums on fundamental constitutional questions has enormous emancipatory power.

This picture of referendums is by no means a misguided one, but it is a misleading one. This two-track picture of democracy where referendums are exceptional sets referendums a task they cannot possibly achieve. Referendums, particularly the voting stage of referendums, do not bring peace, create nations, or address disagreement. Referendums do not bridge divisions or find compromises. Voting is not the same as changing or creating constitutions. On its own, voting is neither a necessary nor a sufficient condition for self-determination and self-government. There are serious risks to democracy from thinking that voting in a referendum is a solution to a political problem, a war, or on its own enough to establish a constitution. Voting cannot address democratic deficits or offer control over constitutions, and there are serious risks to democracy from thinking about referendums this way. Fundamentally, referendums are not remedies to the problems and perils of representative democracy. They never remove the need for representatives, with all the mediation, compromise, and messiness that representation entails. When referendums are treated as remedies to representative democracy, they undermine the representative institutions on which they rely both conceptually and practically.

VI. Concluding Thought: The Need for Change

As with most questions in life and in theory, whether a referendum is a good idea depends on the context. The main reason referendums are valuable is that democracy is not a seminar in legal and political theory. At some point decisions must be made. There is a need for groups to come to clear conclusions that voters have reason to support irrespective of whether they agree with them. This is what democracies are for, and sometimes referendums are well placed to be a part of that process. Above all, however, the message of this book is that referendums should not be used because certain kinds of fundamental decisions cannot be made by representatives. This is the wrong kind of reason for their use. Democratic constitutions do not require fundamental decisions to be made by voters but, even if they did, referendums could not play that role. Referendums should instead be used to help provide direction to representatives, even on the most fundamental issues. This book both shows why this is normatively necessary and how this is descriptively possible.

Constitutions are not just constituted in moments, and they are not just constituted in texts. They are ongoing processes of constitution and re-constitution; they are continually in flux. Constitutions are processes of negotiation between authorities and the public. Referendums are more useful when they are seen as part of this ongoing process of negotiation, rather than as one-off moments on a higher democratic plane. It is tempting in constitutions, as it is in life, to think we alone are the authors of the story, and that there is a clear, direct connection between our actions and the results of those actions. This temptation should be resisted. Constitutions are not authored singularly, still less by referendums. Referendums cannot offer the kind of agency that is necessary for collective constitutional authorship. The fact that they cannot play this role demonstrates that the search for singular, collective constitutional authorship is a hopeless business. Referendums are just one of many, ordinary, ways that direction is provided to representatives.

The idea of democracy, and representative democracy, is an evolving one: 'rule by the many' has meant different things throughout history.[42] Referendums are institutions. Institutions can change. This book has argued that the use of referendums should change. It has been assumed for too long that referendums are instances of direct democracy, ie ways to bypass representatives, particularly on fundamental constitutional questions. The purpose of referendums is not to offer voters a way to bypass representatives and make decisions directly, but rather to provide direction to representatives. This is particularly important when decisions are irreversible, going to be heavily entrenched, or there is a significant gap between what voters and representatives think. While referendums are not usually

[42] 'The history of democracy is often confusing, partly because this is still very much an *active* history.' D Held, *Models of Democracy* (Polity 2006) 3 (emphasis in original).

understood to be providing direction to representatives, one of the great merits of referendums is that they are flexible processes. How they are used can, and should, change. Voters always have the power to change their constitutions. It is that possibility, and not the periodic potential of referendums, that gives voters and democracy their emancipatory power.

BIBLIOGRAPHY

Ackerman, B, *We the People, Volume 1: Foundations* (Belknap Press 1993).

Ackerman, B, *We the People, Volume 2: Transformations* (Belknap Press 1998).

Albert, R, *Constitutional Amendments: Making, Breaking, and Changing Constitutions* (Oxford University Press 2019).

Altman, D, *Direct Democracy Worldwide* (Cambridge University Press 2011).

Altman, D, *Citizenship and Contemporary Direct Democracy* (Cambridge University Press 2018).

Amaral, J, *Making Peace with Referendums* (Syracuse University Press 2019).

Arato, A, *Post Sovereign Constitution Making: Learning and Legitimacy* (Oxford University Press 2016).

Arce-Riffo, J, 'Gender Parity in the Chilean Constitutional Convention: What Does It Mean for Chilean Democracy?' *Oxford Human Rights Hub* (4 April 2020).

Arpaly, N and Schroeder, T, 'Deliberating and Acting for Reasons' (2012) 121 Philosophical Review.

Baker, D, Gamble, B, and Ludlam, S, 'The Parliamentary Siege of Maastricht 1993: Conservative Divisions and British Ratification' (1994) 47 *Parliamentary Affairs* 37.

Barber, B, *Strong Democracy: Participatory Politics for a New Age* (University of California 1984).

Barber, N, 'Against a Written Constitution' (2008) *Public Law* 11.

Barreyro, M, '"Direct Democratic Institutions": Direct and Democratic' (2019) 10 *Jurisprudence* 313.

Bartlett, J, 'In Chile, Constitutional Convention Announces Full Draft of New Constitution' *Constitutionnet* (17 February 2022).

Bartlett, J, 'Chile Finalises New Draft Constitution to Replace Pinochet-Era Document' *The Guardian* (16 May 2022).

BBC News, 'Crimea Referendum: Voters "Back Russia Union"' *BBC News* (16 March 2014).

BBC News, 'Matteo Renzi's Referendum Defeat Risks Italy Political Crisis' *BBC News* (5 December 2016).

BBC News, 'Chile Protests: Unrest in Santiago over Metro Fare Increase' *BBC News* (19 October 2019).

Beitz, C, *Political Equality* (Princeton University Press 1989).

Blessett, B, 'Disenfranchisement: Historical Underpinnings and Contemporary Manifestations' (2015) 39 *Public Administration Quarterly* 3.

Blount, J, 'Participation in Constitutional Design' in T Ginsburg and R Dixon (eds), *Comparative Constitutional Law* (Edward Elgar 2011).

Bogdanor, V, *The People and the Party System* (Cambridge University Press 1981).

Bora, B, 'Turkey's Constitutional Reform' *Aljazeera* (17 January 2017).

Bowler, S and Glazer, A (eds), *Direct Democracy's Impact on American Political Institutions* (Palgrave 2008).

Bratton, M and van de Walle, N, 'Popular Protest and Political Reform in Africa' (1992) 24 *Comparative Politics* 419.

Canovan, M, 'The People' in J Dryzek, B Honig, and A Phillips (eds), *Oxford Handbook of Political Theory* (Oxford University Press 2008).

Carrasco, M, 'Why we failed to approve the new Chilean constitution: the need for a cultural transformation' *LSE* (15 September 2022).

Cassese, A, 'Self-Determination of Peoples: A Legal Reappraisal' (21st Century Trust Conference – Ethnic Conflict in the Wider Europe: Causes, Prevention and Cures, June 1997).

Chambers, S, 'Constitutional Referendums and Democratic Deliberation' in M Mendelsohn and A Parkin (eds), *Referendum Democracy: Citizens, Elites, and Deliberation in Referendum Campaigns* (Palgrave 2001).

Christiano, T, *The Rule of the Many* (Westview Press 1996).
Christiano, T, 'The Authority of Democracy*' (2004) 12 *Journal of Political Philosophy* 266.
Citizens' Assembly on Brexit, 'About the Citizens' Assembly' *The Constitution Unit, UCL* (2017).
Clarke, H, and others, 'Why Britain Voted for Brexit: An Individual-Level Analysis of the 2016 Referendum Vote' (2017) 70 Parliamentary Affairs 439.
Cochrane, F, *Northern Ireland: The Fragile Peace* (Yale University Press 2021).
Colón-Ríos, J, *Constituent Power and the Law* (Oxford University Press 2020).
Dicey, AV, *Introduction to the Study of the Law of the Constitution* [1915] (Roger E Michener ed, 8th rev edn, Liberty Fund 1982).
Dworkin, R, 'Hart's Postscript and the Character of Political Philosophy' (2004) 24 *Oxford Journal of Legal Studies* 1.
Dworkin, R, *Is Democracy Possible Here?: Principles for a New Political Debate* (Princeton University Press 2008).
Dyzenhaus, D, 'The Politics of the Question of Constituent Power' in M Loughlin and N Walker (eds), *The Paradox of Constitutionalism* (Oxford University Press 2007).
Electoral Commission, 'Media Statement: Vote Leave' *The Electoral Commission* (29 March 2019).
el-Wakil, A, and McKay, S, 'Disentangling Referendums and Direct Democracy: A Defence of the Systemic Approach to Popular Vote Processes' (2020) 56 *Representation* 449.
Elkins, Z, and Hudson, A, 'The Constitutional Referendum in Historical Perspective' in D Landau and H Lerner (eds), *Comparative Constitution Making* (Elgar 2019).
Erb, K, 'On July 4, How Taxes, Tariffs, and Tea Led to American Independence' (Forbes 2018).
Espejo, P, *The Time of Popular Sovereignty: Process and the Democratic State* (Pennsylvania State University Press 2011).
'Extraordinary Majority Requirements and the Equal Protection Clause' (1970) 70 *Columbia Law Review* 486.
Evans, J, *Voters & Voting: An Introduction* (Sage 2004).
Fisher, S, and Renwick, A, 'Do People Tend to Vote against Change in Referendums?' *The Constitution Unit* (22 June 2016).
Gallagher, M, and Uleri, P (eds), *The Referendum Experience in Europe* (Macmillan 1996).
Galligan, B, 'Amending Constitutions through the Referendum Device' in M Mendelsohn and A Parkin (eds), *Referendum Democracy: Citizens, Elites, and Deliberation in Referendum Campaigns* (Palgrave 2001).
Gamble, B, 'Putting Civil Rights to Popular Vote' (1997) 41 *American Journal of Political Science* 245.
Gardner, J, 'Reasons for Teamwork' (2002) 8 *Legal Theory* 495.
Gelman, A, and King, G, 'Estimating Incumbency Advantage without Bias' (1990) 34 *American Journal of Political Science* 1142.
Goldford, DJ, *The American Constitution and the Debate over Originalism* (Cambridge University Press 2005).
Green, L, *The Authority of the State* (Oxford University Press 1990).
Guerrero, A, 'The Paradox of Voting and the Ethics of Political Representation' (2010) 38 *Philosophy and Public Affairs* 272.
Griffith, JAG, 'The Political Constitution*' (1979) 42 *Modern Law Review* 1.
Hamilton, A, Madison, J, and Jay, J, *The Federalist Papers* [1788] (Penguin Classics 1987).
Haskell, J, *Direct Democracy or Representative Government? Dispelling the Populist Myth* (Perseus 2000).
Hayes, B, and McAllister, I, 'Who Voted for Peace? Public Support for the 1998 Northern Ireland Agreement' (2007) 16 *Irish Political Studies* 73.
Held, D, *Models of Democracy* (Polity 2006).
Hershovitz, S, 'Legitimacy, Democracy, and Razian Authority' (2003) 9 *Legal Theory* 201.
Hobolt, SB, *Europe in Question: Referendums on European Integration* (Oxford University Press 2009).
Hollander, S, *The Politics of Referendum Use in European Democracies* (Palgrave Macmillan 2019).
Horowitz, D, 'Explaining the Northern Ireland Agreement: The Sources of an Unlikely Constitutional Consensus' (2002) *British Journal of Political Science* 193.

Hume, D, *Essays, Moral, Political, and Literary* (EF Miller ed, Liberty 1777).
Irwin, C, 'The People's Peace Process: Northern Ireland and the Role of Public Opinion Polls in Political Negotiations' (1999) 30 *Security Dialogue* 305.
Irwin, C, *The People's Peace Process in Northern Ireland* (Palgrave Macmillan 2002).
Kalyvas, A, 'Popular Sovereignty, Democracy, and the Constituent Power' (2005) 12 *Constellations* 223.
Kahn, PW, 'Political Time: Sovereignty and the Transtemporal Community' (2006) 28 *Cardozo Law Review* 259.
Kelsen, H, *General Theory of Law and State* (Harvard University Press 1949).
King, J, 'The Democratic Case for a Written Constitution' (2019) 72 *Current Legal Problems* 1.
Kleinig, J, 'The Nature of Consent' in F Miller and A Wertheimer (eds), *The Ethics of Consent: Theory and Practice* (Oxford University Press 2009).
Klosko, G, *Political Obligations* (Oxford University Press 2008).
Kobach, K, *The Referendum: Direct Democracy in Switzerland* (Dartmouth Publishing Company 1993).
Kuo, M, 'Cutting the Gordian Knot of Legitimacy Theory? An Anatomy of Frank Michelman's Presentist Critique of Constitutional Authorship' (2009) 7 *International Journal of Constitutional Law* 683.
Kutz, C, 'The Collective Work of Citizenship' (2002) 8 *Legal Theory* 471.
Landemore, H, 'When Public Participation Matters: The 2010–2013 Icelandic Constitutional Process' (2020) 18 *International Journal of Constitutional Law* 179.
Lane, M, 'Popular Sovereignty as Control of Office-Holders: Aristotle on Greek Democracy' in R Bourke and Q Skinner (eds), *Popular Sovereignty in Historical Perspective* (Cambridge University Press 2016).
Lawson, G, *Politica sacra et civilis* [1660] (C Condren ed, Cambridge University Press 1992).
Lee, D, *Popular Sovereignty in Early Modern Constitutional Thought* (Oxford University Press 2016).
Lenowitz, J, '"A Trust That Cannot Be Delegated:" The Invention of Ratification Referenda' (2015) 109 *American Political Science Review* 803.
Lenowitz, J, *Constitutional Ratification Without Reason* (Oxford University Press 2022).
Lessnoff, M, *Social Contract Theory* (Blackwell 1990).
Levy, R, O'Flynn, I, and Kong, HL, *Deliberative Peace Referendums* (Oxford University Press 2021).
Leyland, P, *The Constitution of the United Kingdom: A Contextual Analysis* (4th edn Hart 2021).
Lijphart, A, *Patterns of Democracy: Government Forms and Performance in Thirty-Six Countries* (Yale University Press 1984).
Locke, J, *The Second Treatise of Government* [1689] (Hackett 1980).
Loughlin, M, *The Foundations of Public Law* (Oxford University Press 2010).
Loughlin, M, 'On Constituent Power' in M Dowdle and M Wilkinson (eds), *Constitutionalism Beyond Liberalism* (Cambridge University Press 2017).
Loughlin, M and Walker, N, *The Paradox of Constitutionalism: Constituent Power and Constitutional Form* (Oxford University Press 2007).
Mackie, G, 'Deliberation and Voting Entwined' in A Bächtiger and others (eds), *The Oxford Handbook of Deliberative Democracy* (Oxford University Press 2018).
Mair, P, *Ruling the Void: The Hollowing of Western Democracy* (Verso Books 2013).
May, T, 'Theresa May's Brexit Speech in Full' *The Telegraph* (17 January 2017).
McCormick, J, 'Identifying or Exploiting the Paradoxes of Constitutional Democracy? An Introduction to Carl Schmitt's Legality and Legitimacy', *Legality and Legitimacy* (Duke University Press 2004).
McEvoy, K, and Morison, J, 'Beyond the "Constitutional Moment": Law, Transition, and Peacemaking in Northern Ireland' (2003) 26 *Fordham International Law Journal* 960.
Mendelsohn, M, and Parkin, A, 'Introduction', *Referendum Democracy: Citizens, Elites and Deliberation in Referendum Campaigns* (Palgrave Macmillan 2001).
Michelman, F, 'Always under Law' (1995) 345 *Constitutional Commentary* 227.
Michelman, F, 'Constitutional Authorship by the People' (1999) 74 *Notre Dame Law Review* 1605.
Michelman, F, 'Ida's Way: Constructing the Respect-Worthy Governmental System' (2003) 72 *Fordam Law Review* 345.
Miller, D, *Is Self-Determination a Dangerous Illusion?* (Polity 2020).

Miller, R, 'Self-Determination in International Law and the Demise of Democracy' (2003) 41 *Columbia Journal of Transnational Law* 601.

Millette, D, Lambert, M-E and Gall, GL, 'Quebec Referendum of 1995' (*Encyclopedia Britannica*).

Müller, JW, *What Is Populism?* (University of Pennsylvania Press 2016).

Neely, S, *A Concise History of the French Revolution* (Rowman and Littlefield 2007).

Negretto, G, 'Deepening Democracy? Promises and Challenges of Chile's Road to a New Constitution' (2021) *Hague Journal on the Rule of Law* 335.

Niesen, P, 'Extinguishing the Burning Embers: Rubinelli on Sieyès' *Verfassungsblog* (19 December 2020).Nowell-Smith, PH, 'Choosing, Deciding and Doing' (1958) 18 *Analysis* 63.

Oldenquist A, 'Choosing, Deciding, and Doing' in P Edwards (ed), *The Encyclopaedia of Philosophy* (Collier-MacMillan 1967).

Oliver, P, and Tierney, S, 'Book Review/Response Constitutional Referendums' (*International Journal of Constitutional Law*, 25 February 2014).

Orgad, L, 'The Preamble in Constitutional Interpretation' (2010) 8 *International Journal of Constitutional Law* 714.

Pålshaugen, LS, *The Northern Ireland Civic Forum and a Politics of Recognition* (Institute for British-Irish Studies, University College Dublin 2004).

Patberg, M, *Constituent Power in the European Union* (Oxford University Press 2020).

Piris, C, *The Lisbon Treaty: A Legal and Political Analysis* (Cambridge University Press 2010).

Pitkin, H, *The Concept of Representation* (University of California 1967).

Pino, G, and others, 'Third Time's a Charm? Chile Embarks on a New Constitution-Making Process' *Constitutionnet* (3 February 2023).

Plamenatz, J, *Consent, Freedom and Political Obligation* (2nd edn, Oxford University Press 1968).

Plotke, D, 'Representation Is Democracy' (1997) 4 *Constellations* 19.

Qvortrup, M, 'A.V. Dicey: The Referendum as the People's Veto' (1999) 20 *History of Political Thought* 531.

Qvortrup, M (ed), *Referendums Around the World: The Continued Growth of Direct Democracy* (Palgrave 2014).

Qvortrup, M, *The Referendum and Other Essays on Constitutional Politics* (Hart 2019).

Qvortrup, M, 'Schmitt, Dicey, and the Power and Limits of Referendums in the United Kingdom' (2022) 42 *Legal Studies* 3.

Qvortrup, M, and Trueblood, L, 'The Case for Supermajority Requirements in Referendums' (2023) 21 *International Journal of Constitutional Law* 187.

Raz, J, 'Reasons for Action, Decisions and Norms' (1975) 84 *Mind* 481.

Riker, W, *Liberalism Against Populism* (Freeman and Company 1982).

Ríos Tobar, M, 'Chile's Constitutional Convention: A Triumph of Inclusion' *UNDP in Latin America and the Caribbean* (3 June 2021).

Rodrigo, P, and Correa, C, 'Symposium on Chilean Referendum Part I: Drafting a Constitution on a Clean Slate' *International Constitutional Law Blog* (1 November 2020).

Rogoff, K, 'Britain's Democratic Failure' *Project Syndicate* (2016).

Rousseau, JJ, *Of the Social Contract and Other Political Writings* [1762] (Penguin 2012).

Rubinelli, L, *Constituent Power: A History* (Cambridge University Press 2020).

Runciman, D, *The Confidence Trap* (Princeton University Press 2014).

Sabatini, C, and Jefferson, L, 'The Truth Is, Chile Is Unequal: What's Behind Chile's Protests' *Chatham House* (18 December 2019).

Saunders, R, *Yes to Europe!: The 1975 Referendum and Seventies Britain* (Cambridge University Press 2018).

Schiller, T, and Setälä, M, *Referendums and Representative Democracy: Responsiveness, Accountability, and Deliberation* (Routledge 2009).

Schmitt, C, *Constitutional Theory* [1928] (J Seitzer trs, Duke University Press 2008).

Schmitt, C, *Verfassungslehre* (Duncker and Humblot 1928).

Schmitt, C, *The Crisis of Parliamentary Democracy* [1926] (Ellen Kennedy tr, MIT Press 1986).

Schmitt, C, *Legality and Legitimacy* [1932] (J Seitzer trs, Duke University Press 2004).
Schneider, C, and Williamson-García, S, 'Chile's New Constitutional Process Shifts Right' *Nacla* (15 February 2023).
Schrag, P, *Paradise Lost: California's Experience, America's Future* (University of California Press 2004).
Schumpeter, J, *Capitalism, Socialism, and Democracy* (George Allen & Unwin Ltd 1943).
Setälä, M, *Referendums and Democratic Government* (Macmillan 1999).
Seyd, B, 'Exploring Political Disappointment' (2016) 69 *Parliamentary Affairs* 327.
Shapiro, S, 'Massively Shared Agency' in M Vargas and G Yaffe (eds), *Rational and Social Agency: The Philosophy of Michael Bratman* (Oxford University Press 2014).
Sieyès, E, *Political Writings: Including the Debate between Sieyès and Tom Paine in 1791* (M Sonenscher ed, Hackett 2003).
Simmons, AJ, *Moral Principles and Political Obligations* (Princeton University Press 1979).
Sinnott, R, and Elkink, JA, 'Attitudes and Behaviour in the Referendum on the Treaty of Lisbon: Report prepared for the Department of Foreign Affairs' (6 March 2009).
Slack, J, 'Enemies of the People: Fury over "out of Touch" Judges Who Have "Declared War on Democracy" by Defying 17.4m Brexit Voters and Who Could Trigger Constitutional Crisis' *Daily Mail* (4 November 2018).
Smith, G, 'The Functional Properties of the Referendum' (1976) 4 *European Journal of Political Research* 1.
Smith, J, 'David Cameron's EU Renegotiation and Referendum Pledge: A Case of Déjà Vu?' (2016) 11 *British Politics* 324.
Somek, A, and Wilkinson, M, 'Unpopular Sovereignty' (2020) 83 *Modern Law Review* 955.
Steinberger, PJ, *The Idea of the State* (Cambridge University Press 2004).
Strachey, L, *Queen Victoria* (Harcourt, Bruce and Company 1921).
Suksi, M, *Bringing in the People: A Comparison of Constitutional Forms and Practices of the Referendum* (Cambridge University Press 1993).
Thatcher, M, EC Membership (Referendum) (Hansard, 11 March 1975).
Thomas, WI, and Thomas, DS, *The Child in America: Behavior Problems and Programs* (AA Knopf 1928).
Tierney, S, 'Constitutional Referendums: A Theoretical Enquiry' (2009) 72 *Modern Law Review* 360.
Tierney, S, *Constitutional Referendums: The Theory and Practice of Republican Deliberation* (Oxford University Press 2012).
Tierney, S, '"And the Winner Is … the Referendum": Scottish Independence and the Deliberative Participation of Citizens' *Centre on Constitutional Change* (29 September 2014).
Townshend, C, *The Partition: Ireland Divided, 1888–1925* (Penguin 2021).
Tuck, R, 'Democratic Sovereignty and Democratic Government' in R Bourke and Q Skinner (eds), *Popular Sovereignty in Historical Perspective* (Cambridge University Press 2016).
Urbinati, N, 'Representation as Advocacy: A Study of Democratic Deliberation' (2000) 28 *Political Theory* 758.
Van Crombrugge, R, 'Are Referendums Necessarily Populist? Countering the Populist Interpretation of Referendums through Institutional Design' (2020) 56 *Representation* 109.
Venice Commission, 'Referendums in Europe – An Analysis of the Legal Rules in European States' (2005) 287/2004.
Verdugo, S, 'Is it Time to Abandon the Theory of Constituent Power?' (2003) 21 *International Journal of Constitutional Law* 14.
Verdugo, S, and Prieto, M, 'The Dual Aversion of Chile's Constitution-Making Process' (2021) 19 *International Journal of Constitutional Law* 149.
Waldron, J, *Law and Disagreement* (Oxford University Press 1992).
Waldron, J, 'The Core of the Case Against Judicial Review' (2006) 115 *Yale Law Journal* 1346.
Walker, M, *The Strategic Use of Referendums: Power, Legitimacy, and Democracy* (Springer 2003).
Walker, N, 'The Brexit Vote: The Wrong Question for Britain and Europe' *UK Constitutional Law Association* (21 June 2016).

Weale, A, *The Will of the People: A Modern Myth* (Polity 2018).
Weale, A, 'Three Types of Majority Rule' (2019) 90 *Political Quarterly* 62.
Weale, A, *Modern Social Contract Theory* (Oxford University Press 2020).
Weatherford, R, 'Choosing and Deciding' in T Honderich (ed), *The Oxford Companion to Philosophy* (2nd edn, Oxford University Press 2005).
Webber, G, 'Loyal Opposition and Political Constitutionalism' (2016) *Oxford Journal of Legal Studies* 1.
Webber, J, *The Constitution of Canada: A Contextual Analysis* (Hart 2021).
Whelan, F, 'Prologue: Democratic Theory and the Boundary Problem' (1983) 25 *Nomos* 13.
White, H, 'Proroguing Parliament Would Be Undemocratic' *Institute for Government* (6 June 2019).
White, S, and Hill, RJ, 'Russia, the Former Soviet Union and Eastern Europe: The Referendum as a Flexible Political Instrument' in M Gallagher and P Uleri (eds), *The Referendum Experience in Europe* (Palgrave 1996).
Wolff, J, 'Political Obligation: A Pluralistic Approach' in M Baghramian and A Ingram (eds), *Pluralism: The Philosophy of Politics and Diversity* (Routledge 2000).
Wollheim, R, 'A Paradox in the Theory of Democracy' in D Weiss, P Laslett, and WG Runciman (eds), *Philosophy, Politics, and Society* (Blackwell 1962).
Wollstonecraft, M, *An Historical and Moral View of the Origin and Progress of the French Revolution and the Effect It Has Produced In Europe* (London 1794).
Young, IM, 'Deferring Group Representation' (1997) 39 *Nomos* 349.
Zovatto, D, and Jaraquemada, M, 'Analysis of the Elections in Chile' *International Institute for Democracy and Electoral Assistance* (25 May 2021).

INDEX

www.ingramcontent.com/pod-product-compliance
Ingram Content Group UK Ltd.
Pitfield, Milton Keynes, MK11 3LW, UK
UKHW020821290926
15470UKWH00003B/1292

9 781509 940806